*Changing Lives*

# *Series in Critical Narrative*

Donaldo Macedo, Series Editor
*University of Massachusetts Boston*

Now in Print

*The Hegemony of English*
by Donaldo Macedo, Bessie Dendrinos, and Panayota Gounari (2003)
*Letters from Lexington: Reflections on Propaganda*
New Updated Edition
by Noam Chomsky (2004)
*Pedagogy of Indignation*
by Paulo Freire (2004)
*Howard Zinn on Democratic Education*
by Howard Zinn, with Donaldo Macedo (2005)
*How Children Learn: Getting Beyond the Deficit Myth*
by Terese Fayden (2005)
*The Globalization of Racism*
edited by Donaldo Macedo and Panayota Gounari (2006)
*Daring to Dream: Toward a Pedagogy of the Unfinished*
by Paulo Freire (2007)
*Class in Culture*
by Teresa L. Ebert and Mas'ud Zavarzadeh (2008)
*Dear Paulo: Letters from Those Who Dare Teach*
by Sonia Nieto (2008)
*Uncommon Sense from the Writings of Howard Zinn* (2008)
*Paulo Freire and the Curriculum*
by Georgios Grollios (2009)
*Freedom at Work: Language, Professional, and Intellectual Development in Schools*
by María E. Torres-Guzmán with Ruth Swinney (2009)
*The Latinization of U.S. Schools: Successful Teaching and Learning in Shifting Cultural Contexts*
by Jason G. Irizarry (2011)
*Culture and Power in the Classroom: Educational Foundations for the Schooling of Bicultural Students*
by Antonia Darder (2011)
*Changing Lives: Working with Literature in an Alternative Sentencing Program*
by Taylor Stoehr (2013)

# *Changing Lives*

## *Working with Literature in an Alternative Sentencing Program*

Taylor Stoehr

Routledge
Taylor & Francis Group
LONDON AND NEW YORK

First published 2013 by Paradigm Publishers

Published 2016 by Routledge
2 Park Square, Milton Park, Abingdon, Oxon OX14 4RN
711 Third Avenue, New York, NY 10017, USA

*Routledge is an imprint of the Taylor & Francis Group, an informa business*



Library of Congress Cataloging-in-Publication Data
Stoehr, Taylor, 1931–
Changing lives : working with literature in an alternative sentencing program / Taylor Stoehr.
p. cm.
ISBN 978-1-59451-863-8 (hardcover : alk. paper)
1. Ex-convicts—Education—Massachusetts—Case studies. 2. Ex-convicts—Books and reading—Massachusetts—Case studies. 3. Literature—Study and teaching—Massachusetts—Case studies. 4. Sentences (Criminal procedure)—Massachusetts—Case studies. 5. Probation—Massachusetts—Case studies. I. Title.
HV8883.S76 2012
365'.66609744—dc23
2012027722

ISBN 13 : 978-1-59451-863-8 (hbk)
ISBN 13 : 978-1-59451-864-5 (pbk)

Typeset by Chris Davis, Mulberry Tree Enterprises.

*To John Christopher*

*The love of our neighbor, in all its fullness, simply means being able to say to him, "What are you going through?" It is a recognition that the sufferer exists, not only as a unit in a collection or a specimen from the social category labeled "unfortunate," but as a man, exactly like us, who was one day stamped with a special mark of affliction.*

—Simone Weil

# *Contents*

# Foreword

Teaching and learning from humans caught in the carceral matrix bring most of our common notions about citizenship, crime and punishment, justice and discrimination, education and rehabilitation, and familial and social health into question and into focus.

Important social and personal questions are highlighted by the life stories and reflections of those on probation and seeking to not reenter prison, or return as wards of the state subject to all of its disciplinary and punitive powers. We do not always as a society attempt to answer pressing questions. Still, our struggles to address these queries that reflect upon the character of our democracy cast important illumination.

Even when we cannot coherently answer—or respond without the reflex bias of our privilege and security—we must ask key queries raised by Taylor Stoehr's *Changing Lives: Working with Literature in an Alternative Sentencing Program.* What are healthy families and compassionate parenting? What is the nature of individual and communal forgiveness? How does a society stratified by class, race, and privilege shape its penal system to reproduce captivity rather than citizenship?

And, finally, there is the self-interrogation: Who are we to ask these questions—the "free," the academic teacher among the "unfree," largely black and Latino men (unfortunately our discussions of women and incarceration still remain somewhat sidelined) attempting to escape recidivism and poverty.

*Changing Lives* acknowledges the importance of these questions for a democracy historically built upon racial captivity. This alternative sentencing program uses literature rooted in black experiences of struggle. Stoehr's primary texts, and tests of a social and communal literacy, are familiar: Frederick Douglass's slave narrative, Malcolm X's autobiography, Richard Wright's novel *Black Boy.*

The questions that he and his colleagues, which include students, pose and live in relation to these texts evoke life lessons that we rarely master given the denial about the pressing demands on our intellects and our souls: How should "the weak defend themselves against the strong"? When should we resist or retreat in the face of oppression? How is "manliness related to violence"? When you "hit bottom" how do you feel while in "despair" and somehow learn "to seek or grant forgiveness"?

What we learn from self-inflicted and social- and state-produced trauma will change our lives. One of the best ways to walk a path of (self-)transformation is for individuals and society to learn more about the lives of those most intimate with the stigma, shame, regulation, and disenfranchisement based in incarceration.

The United States has the highest incarceration rate in the world, with over two million people imprisoned, most largely for nonviolent drug offense. With racial disparities in policing, arrests, and sentencing, and expanding numbers of women and children in state custody and legal captivity, the life of our democratic culture is changing. Creating alternative sentencing programs is not only compassionate and caring. It is also urgently needed to promote a just society, one in which democracy is not so fused to captivity that we become a nation of illiterates concerning freedom.

—Joy James
Presidential Professor of the Humanities
Williams College

# *Acknowledgments*

My gratitude to those who read drafts and earlier versions of the manuscript: John Christopher, Robert Couture, John and Prue Dings, Susan Jenkins, Hon. Robert Kane, Hon. Thomas May, Tam Linn Neville, Herbert Stern, Theresa Torchia, Sondra Upham, Robert Waxler, and Gordon Wheeler. Their counsel has been invaluable.

A version of Chapter 7, "Street Smarts," first appeared in the *Massachusetts Review.*

# *Introduction*

Working with "ex-offenders"—men[1] on probation—it has been important to me not to know their offenses, so that I can side with them and not against them. By the time we meet they have already undergone whatever penalty was imposed, almost certainly with side effects not officially part of their sentence. Having "paid their debt," they are now asked to "prove" themselves (the root meaning of "probation")—that is, prove themselves fit to return to society and make a fresh start. As nationwide recidivism rates suggest, their situation is precarious, for they typically lack both material resources and social networks to help them reestablish themselves in a world that has never welcomed them with open arms, while the ordeal of shame and punishment has undermined their confidence and self-esteem, crucial factors in starting a new life. Nor are they really allowed "a fresh start" so long as they carry their felony records with them, making it hard to find a decent job, get public housing, or even (in some states) exercise the right to vote. They may have served their sentences, but most of them will be paying interest on their debt to society for a long time to come.

Terms of probation often require men to attend regular sessions in "anger management," "substance abuse," and similar treatment programs as part of their reentry process, most of these tending to emphasize their weaknesses and the need for correction. However appropriate to the causes for their incarceration, participants can experience these mandated programs as being condemned and punished all over again, understandably enough since what they need most is something that might enrich their lives and encourage the belief that there is a place for them in the social order after all—job training, for instance, or, better yet, job placement, even if it is only part-time work in some voluntary public service that could foster a positive feeling about themselves. Somebody has got to believe in them, if they are to believe in themselves.

A probationer wants to know: Are you for me or against me? How we answer that question may influence his attitude in every new encounter outside prison walls. If our reply is distrustful or punitive, the reaction is likely to be belligerent or evasive. Even though most offenders do recognize and accept their own guilt, they are convinced that the authorities have always been their enemies. The raised fist and wagging finger are very familiar to these men, most of whom have faced it all their lives—from parents, in school, in the streets, in the courts, and in prison. They are expecting more of the same, and they have learned to imitate it in self-defense.

Current popular feeling about "criminals" has been shaped by sensationalizing images in the media and cheap rhetoric in the mouths of demagogues playing to our anxieties. Actual contact with men who have been in trouble with the law often tells a different story, as I try to demonstrate in this book. I invite my readers to meet these men on the most basic ground, our common humanity. It is not enough to assume a "neutral" position, a wait-and-see attitude demanding that a man prove himself worthy of his freedom. To the probationer, this is likely to seem sham neutrality, coming from representatives of a society still ranged against him. Let us begin instead by identifying with him in his immediate plight. What must it be like to come out of jail—a horrific experience for anyone—and try to build a life out of the wreckage?

No matter how central and traumatic their encounter with the criminal justice system, the men in our classes rarely view themselves as criminals. A person who sees himself that way is probably unreachable. They *do* feel the humiliation and constraints of being probationers, so it's not surprising that they join our program primarily to get six months' probation time remitted. I should point out, however, that men are offered this opportunity because their probation officers believe they can profit in much more substantial ways—that they may be ready for a major life change. And it seems to be so. By the end of our ten weeks together almost everyone feels that the shared experience of the classroom, at first dreaded as another indignity to be undergone, has served as a rite of passage leading to self-renewal and unexpected faith in themselves.

Much depends, then, on treating these men as worthy and hopeful. At least for the present, they tend to live up to whatever expectations we have for them, good or bad, so that it makes practical sense to look for the best. Practicality and results are not the only criteria, of course; I trust that our common human nature goes deeper than that. The best and the worst are not so far apart in any of us.

When I walked into my first session in 1994, I assumed that Changing Lives Through Literature aimed at something like this self-discovery and reorientation, but I saw it then only in vague outline, as yet another "remedial" course, designed to foster new interest in books and ideas, which might then serve as a stepping-stone to further education for some men, perhaps a college degree, and through that a "changed life." I assumed that past failures in the educational system could be remedied, if the pedagogy were more finely tuned to the students, or if they could be brought to apply themselves with more discipline and earnestness.

With thirty years of college teaching already behind me, I knew well enough that higher education is no yellow brick road. Although for some individuals a degree might be the gateway to social and economic mobility, for the average student it's just another tollbooth on a route paved according to status and condition. The price of passing includes not only tuition and fees but also compliance with authority—a willingness to be shepherded if not herded—that both school and prison exist to promote.

Had I lacked faith in teaching, I would not have spent so many years in classrooms, yet I was well aware of the way that "grubbing for grades" can undermine genuine learning and distract students from noticing any deeper relevance of their studies to their lives. And the by-products of coerced schooling at an early age can include mindless obedience, cutting corners, inability to concentrate, and a scorn for books. Even college students, no longer forced to attend, may bear such scars imperfectly healed.

For Changing Lives participants, most of whom had dropped out of school before either the best or the worst of such consequences had befallen them, I wanted to open up the broader vision of the world that institutions of learning ideally represent—joyful curiosity, respect for difference, and a passion for truth and justice. Moreover, since I believe in humanistic values and the life of the mind, I wanted to encourage anyone with a bent in that direction to follow it at the university—one of the few places in society where there is still a home for such pursuits.

By doing away with tests and grades, I hoped to stimulate the literary imagination without putting students through the usual drill in self-discipline. The aim was not to make things "easy," for there is a lot to be said for hard work and the pride that comes from completing a long and arduous task. But if literature were presented as yet another hurdle to be jumped, then like as not the majority would balk. Even more important, because the educational sorting and labeling system had been responsible for branding most of them as "failures," I felt the first principle of Changing Lives should be to avoid setting them up for another failure experience. Nothing could be worse.

If you ask these men, they'll tell you that more and better schooling for ethnic minorities and the poor is the only viable path to social and economic justice. Although many of them are in favor of catch-up policies like affirmative action, what they ultimately insist on is simple fairness and equal funding. At the same time, almost all of them believe it is too late to benefit from any such changes themselves. Their faith in education is almost entirely for their children.

By and large I agree with this realistic assessment of their own situation, though I'm less confident about the chances for their children. Nonetheless, because their past failures typically began or were driven home in school, where conformity to the social order was enforced in ways they learned only to dodge or defy, I believed these men could profit by working through a new set of attitudes toward education. The reward lies not in catching up with former classmates who mastered "the three Rs" but in coming to terms with the anger, humiliation, and self-pity that have been the chief results of their schooling. This reliving and unlearning can occur in what I call a "safe emergency situation."

The idea behind a "safe emergency situation" on which our program came to be based was to reconstitute enough of the school system to call forth memories of how things originally went wrong, while at the same time altering the demands and changing the stakes, so that students could discover that their ordinary intelligence and good sense were adequate to the challenge of learning anything they really want to know.

For the first few weeks of Changing Lives Through Literature, most students don't really feel safe when they walk through the door. Some of those most fearful, or most defiant, may come empty-handed, pleading that they are slow readers, have no quiet place to study, or find the authors too difficult. These obstacles are real enough, familiar fault lines in compulsory education imposed on a nation of mixed cultures and economic classes, where teachers have always met with resistance to homework. The usual problem and the usual solution have long since fused into the hard core of modern curriculum and pedagogy, in which rituals of enforcement determine most of the assignment package, putting the cart before the horse. What pupils are asked to do at home thus serves as pretext for disciplinary routines that structure the school day—book reports, exams, and recitation. Evidence that homework was done or not done, well or badly, then eventuates in grades, report cards, tracking, and various sanctions guaranteeing that most students will be judged less than fully competent.

In the Changing Lives classroom we frequently see the extreme cases, those who hit bottom so hard in their early years of schooling that they stopped trying altogether—thinking of it as their own failure, though of course they hate the regime that put them to the test. This history of intimidation is written on their faces when we announce the first assignment. A few pages of reading and writing can stir deep feelings of inadequacy and reactivate the old dilemma: defiance or submission. To assign homework is like putting them back in third grade again, their knees too big for the desks.

At first we thought it would be possible to avoid the worst of these consequences simply by choosing texts that students would find appealing and relevant to their lives, while doing away with the goad of tests or recitation. But reaching students in our program has less to do with choosing the right text or subject matter than it does with renegotiating the kind of investment they are asked to make in preparing for class, the grounds of acquiescence in our mutual undertaking. Once students find that they are not required to swallow their daily plateful from the steam table, only in order to regurgitate it on demand, tension diminishes. There comes a moment when a man realizes that everyone in the room, whether standing up front or sitting next to him, is *actually interested* in how he sees the world. At that point he can begin to focus on what he has to say for himself rather than how to protect his dignity.

During the early semesters of the program we relied on Frederick Douglass's *Narrative of the Life of an American Slave*, Richard Wright's *Black Boy*, and *The Autobiography of Malcolm X* for our texts. As we read these books by famous black writers of long ago, probationers were surprised to encounter so many problems they were facing in their own lives—not just racism, but issues of literacy and self-respect, justice and injustice, bondage, rebirth, and reentry into civil society. Everyone saw the connection between Douglass's resolve to read and write his way out of slavery and the determination of Malcolm X to master the dictionary, penmanship, and the prison library before he left Norfolk State Prison. Indeed, a few probationers had used their own prison time like Malcolm, to educate themselves. If a man had already read Malcolm's *Autobiography,* the likelihood was that he had done so in jail, possibly in the very same prison library Malcolm frequented half a century earlier.

In any case, we too were on a quest for literacy that might prove as liberating here and now as it once had been for those legendary figures. Fortunately, the path we walked would not be so lonely as theirs had been, for we were reading these stories together, sharing our reactions every week in earnest conversation. Good literature presents a disembodied voice speaking to us so directly that it's natural to want to continue the dialogue once we have closed the book. Bringing others into this dialogue allows us to air our private thoughts publicly, and to explore their implications in today's world. Every serious author hopes for such a hearing and response.

In typical classroom circumstances the chances for a genuine interchange of this sort are minimal. Many students have had experiences like that of Richard Wright on his very first day in school, so frozen with fear that he could not write his name on the blackboard. Years later, grown men come to our program terrified of being called on to write or speak in class. It's humiliating at any age to be singled out and questioned in front of an audience. Why shouldn't the pupil play dumb when the teacher obviously knows the right answer and is just snapping the whip? But in a "safe emergency situation" it could be transformative to revisit that scene of tongue-tied anguish, so long as the result was not to reconfirm the teacher's power to intimidate, and the students' recourse to passive resistance.

At first our liveliest conversations often took place before and after class—on safe ground like a schoolyard at recess time. If things went right we might slide into full-scale discussion without formal notice that class had begun, a wonderful session with many speakers eager to talk, and a feeling of exhilaration afterward. Other nights it was like middle school, all the students silently waiting for the teacher to tell them what to think.

As for the reading itself, similar mixed results could be seen. Some students were completely caught up in it, eager to talk about the homework each week. "I used to never like to read," one man told us, "because it was hard for me to read something and remember it. But now my mind is like glue—everything sticks." For other students homework and conversation did not come easily. Even if it bears directly on one's own plight, a book you are *forced* to read is likely to seem merely admonitory, leaving you all the more closed off from other possibilities, behind an invisible wall of foregone conclusions. The danger of all vicarious experience is that it can leave you pretty much where it finds you.

I don't mean to suggest that the early years of the program were utterly bogged down in the ruts of past schooling. We had our revelatory moments—flash points when a couple of students began arguing with each other and forgot to address their remarks to the instructor. For a few minutes the spirit of shared inquiry into truth would light up the room, then die back down to a dull glow.

During those early years of experimentation we gradually realized that we could not depend on simply choosing "relevant" books. We needed to organize our readings so that they would shape a sequenced structure of feeling over the semester, each week a little more conscious and grounded in a growing awareness of common concerns. The goal was to use the historical past for new insights into personal experience in the present. To do this we needed to frame "literature" differently, against the backdrop of our own lives—our own mistakes and our true worth.

We pricked up our ears when certain passages in Douglass, Wright, and Malcolm X seemed to resonate with our immediate concerns more simply and directly than anything else we were reading. For instance, all of us had something to say about the growth of moral awareness in these authors, based on our own discovery in childhood of the difference between right and wrong. Or, another time, anecdotes from several texts reminded us of what it means to stand before an older generation—parents, teachers, masters—trying to teach us respect, self-discipline, or obedience, in ways that can be problematic. With such examples in front of us, a series of contested questions ultimately led us step by step into the issues we needed to talk about and try to resolve together.

We began with practical dilemmas of child-rearing that confront parents, whether viewed from the child's or the adult's perspective, highlighting their implications for institutions like church and school—with reverberations in law enforcement and the prison system echoing in the background: how children learn what they must know in order to survive; where they get their courage, self-esteem, and sense of righteousness; the nature of punishment and its effects on the young; and the relative power of family, school, economic status, and peer pressure on the developing social awareness and conscience.

Working through open-ended questions like these, with autobiographies and memoirs furnishing test cases and with our own experience to rely on, we could build a group consensus each semester on some basic issues of ethics, and this in turn prepared the way for conversations about still more conflicted challenges of adult life:

> *How can the weak defend themselves against the strong?*
>
> *When is it necessary to resist oppression, and when is it better to retreat?*
>
> *How is manliness related to violence?*
>
> *What do we learn from facing crisis?*
>
> *How does it feel to hit bottom, confront despair, and then to seek or grant forgiveness?*

Of course, we didn't arrive at this precise sequence overnight. Each stage of inquiry grew out of experiment, and every semester we dropped some texts and tried out new ones, poking in corners that often became doorways. It was important for us to see the larger picture, but not at the expense of self-scrutiny or our emerging awareness that everyone in the room—teachers and court officials as well as probationers—shared the same human frailty and longings. None of us had suffered the misery of slavery or genocide, and of course not all of us knew the burdens of poverty or racism firsthand. Yet, we did have in common the confusions and frustrations all people encounter while growing up and finding a place in the adult world.

Our experiments finally resulted in paring down our reading assignments to a single core author, Frederick Douglass, adding brief excerpts from others to match weekly episodes from his *Narrative*. Short responses to these readings, written at home and again at the beginning of each class, served as openings for conversations. To take full advantage of these preparations, we adopted a new classroom format that guaranteed a chance for everyone present to voice his opinion and hear a response to it from others. We divided our classes into four or five small discussion groups, with at least one staff member sitting in each. It could be noisy in a small room, but that wasn't a bad sign. Mutual trust grew from these conversations, energized by the fact that everyone cared about the issues raised, and every voice would be heard whether or not it fit the developing group consensus.

This approach takes for granted that probationers have arrived at a crisis in their lives, an emergency situation for which no solution has yet emerged. The opportunity to talk about their concerns in a safe circle of others who have also reached a crossroads in life promotes an atmosphere of high seriousness, and can give rise to surprising openness in men not ordinarily comfortable revealing their thoughts and feelings. The most reticent and inarticulate students sometimes blossomed into astonishing eloquence in these face-to-face settings. Such moments might result in major breakthroughs for a few individuals, but we counted more on modest and gradual changes in the overall conversational tone—deepening earnestness and mutual respect. If the movement is in the right direction, inching forward like this is much better than a risky leap people are not really ready for, even if there is a safety net.

I hardly need point out the implications of fishing in these deep waters. But we found that we could move through powerful emotional undercurrents without prying or therapizing, so long as we asked questions implicitly in touch with the readings and formulated on a level of ethical concern that put personal problems in wider human perspective. Here our safety net consisted of the universality of struggle and suffering, anchored in the books we were reading. These conversations and the larger discussions we later convened involving the entire class might lead anywhere, since they were not formatted or harnessed to any agenda. Both small and large group dynamics seemed to sharpen our awareness of historical pressures and social contexts without loosening the grip of personal drama in our own lives. What does it mean to grow up in a racist society? To lose your parents? To be denied the ability to read and write? To be beaten routinely and coerced to obedience? To live while plotting disobedience and secret resistance? To be caught in acts punishable by hard labor and chains? To give up in despair, hit bottom, and rise again?

This provocative scenario comes to the surface as we watch Frederick Douglass discover his own powers and claim his freedom. And because we gradually get to "know" him as a human being, his experience can be absorbed as more than a set of caveats and maxims. Identifying with his fate as it unfolds is still another way that probationers can enter a safe emergency situation, for they too struggle in desperate times, their manhood sorely tested, the outcome still uncertain. For many of these newborn readers the imaginative encounter with Douglass's *Narrative* seems a revelation—not only a heroic story they can take to heart but, even more important, a way to reconsider their own choices and consequences with open eyes and unclenched fists.

## NOTE

1. In the Dorchester District Court version of Changing Lives Through Literature, there have been men's and women's programs since our beginning in 1994. Because I have worked only with the men, I will refer to them in what follows, though much of their experience would apply to women on probation as well.

# Part One
## *Getting Started*

# Chapter 1

# *Masks*

On the first night it's always the same. When my friend Bert and I arrive at the classroom around 7:20 p.m., a few of our new students have gotten there before us, anxious not to miss their chance to cut six months off their probation time. Sometimes they'll be in little groups of two or three, but more often they'll be sitting alone, usually in the back of the room, where years of schooling have taught them to hide from the teacher's eye. At 7:30 the probation officers arrive, right on time. By a quarter to eight there are at least fifteen of us in the room—two teachers, two probation officers, and, depending on our luck in recruitment, a dozen or so men on probation from the Dorchester District Court, Boston's most active criminal court.

Except for Bert and me, most of the faces in the room will be black, though in some years almost half have been white, and there are usually a couple of light brown guys from Caribbean or Cape Verdean backgrounds, who may speak without an accent but whose names are Marcel or Mario, and whose sport is soccer. Once, there was an Asian man. The group ranges in age all the way up to seventy, but most are at the lower end, some as young as eighteen.

Whatever color or age or accent, everyone comes that first night wearing a mask. Most of them acquired this blank and impenetrable gaze very early in life, when they were told, *Big boys don't cry*, or maybe just, *Shut up! Don't bother me!* By the time they get to us, the blank look has become habitual, and seems sullen and defiant—not quite a "thuggish" look, but on the verge of it. This is the armor that life on the street requires men to wear. You can imagine it on a mug shot, with a number below.

And why not? Some of these men have done hard time in state prison, where hooded eyes and an unsmiling mouth can be a matter of survival. One and all they've been dealt the slap in the face that our justice system administers to criminal offenders—arrest, trial, punishment. Now on probation and nearing the end of the gauntlet, these men have no reason to expect anything but another humiliating experience, one last finger-wagging admonition before being flushed out on the streets again.

The situation is loaded with ambiguity as well as indignity. Is this part of their punishment, disguised as rehabilitation? Is there any chance to get something more than six months' remission of probation time? What would it be? The course is billed as "college-level," and they've come, many for the first time, to an ordinary campus classroom. But unlike students in prison-based courses, almost no one here has come into the program to further his education, though its title is Changing Lives Through Literature. For men who may not have finished high school, and who haven't read a book in years, if ever, the prospect of ten weeks of "literature" is daunting. As for the "Changing Lives" part, the main challenge they see is just to get through ten weeks without giving up any more of their autonomy than absolutely necessary. The perceived intent of every school they've ever known has been to break their spirit.

Quite a few of them are proud of their "street smarts" and can hold their own in any contest that depends on a quick mind and glib tongue. Some will have finished high school, perhaps even completed a year or two in a community college, or job training in the army—for not all our students are dropouts. But whatever their skills and resources, the entering attitude of most probationers is defensive, braced for the same old effort to convince their teachers that they are doing the assignments. For many, this is the way most of life has gone for them—dodging and bluffing, evasiveness alternating with bravado. Even for those who have avoided the streets, who have decent jobs and family responsibilities, there is a deep-seated distrust of strangers, especially people in authority, who always want something from you and must be outwitted.

But now conditions have changed: What is there to hide, after you've been caught and convicted? Having hit bottom, there may be some relief in no longer pretending you're anyone but who you are.

On the first night every student gets a copy of Frederick Douglass's *Narrative of the Life of an American Slave* in a slim one-dollar edition. The first assignment is to read a couple of chapters, just ten or twelve pages. In addition, a small packet is passed around, containing excerpts from other writers that parallel the opening passages in Douglass's story. All in all, each week's reading comes to thirty or forty pages, and there is a single question to be answered, related to the reading. Everyone gets a bluebook to write his answer in.

As I look around the room at their faces, it's easy to imagine a grueling semester trying to get them to take an interest in these readings, even though the authors have been carefully chosen to speak to their condition, starting with three whose names are familiar to most of them: Frederick Douglass, the slave who made a man of himself; Malcolm X, the hoodlum who found religion in prison, took a new name and mission, and ultimately became a public icon; and Bill Russell, the tall youngster from the Deep South who ended up a famous basketball player and coach for the all-time champions, our local Boston team. We start with these, hoping such exemplary lives may strike the right note, but it's not guaranteed. After all, Frederick Douglass, Malcolm X, and Bill Russell are faded celebrities, and being asked to read about them can seem like just another history lesson—or worse, an obvious ploy, condescending to race and predicament. Some of the white and Hispanic students may resent the bias toward black authors, but even the African American members of the class are not necessarily happy with the prospect of "studying" heroes of their culture as far away and one-dimensional as Abraham Lincoln, John Lennon, or Bill Bradley would seem to a white probationer.

As I pass out books and assignment sheets, I can see people weighing them against the six months' probation. Thirty pages seems overwhelming to some students, though the slimness of the Douglass volume is reassuring. I take time to praise Douglass, trying to make my own admiration for him apparent. He was "younger than any of you" when he escaped, I tell them, and only in his mid-twenties when he wrote this best-selling story of life in slavery. His passion for freedom made him the most important black man in America, going from total illiteracy as a slave to worldwide fame as a writer and orator, ultimately the US Consul to Haiti. I always end by advising them to skip the prefaces by the white preacher abolitionists Garrison and Phillips, whose stiff and formal prose doesn't hold a candle to Douglass's forthright idiom. By this time, they're interested. Some have already opened their books.

As students raise their hands to ask questions, I make a point of getting each man's name, trying to memorize as many as I can: Dave, Willy, Albert, José, Anthony, Trevor.

Dave, the man with a long ugly scar across his shaved skull, wants to know who takes attendance. Willy asks who will sign the papers at the end of the semester, when six months' credit will get him off probation. Albert, who looks as scruffy as a panhandler come in from the cold, wonders whether the course counts toward college credit. I tell him no, asking myself what I will say if it turns out he wants to go back to school. He's sitting right up front, where the good boys sit. José wants to keep his cell phone turned on, against our rules, because his girlfriend is pregnant and about to give birth. Anthony asks why we're reading Frederick Douglass, hinting that he knows who *that* is. And Trevor—handsome as the devil—wants to know how to find the men's room.

Here they are then, ten "black" students, three of whom might check "Hispanic" on the census, and two "white" students, Italian and Irish. Handsome, scruffy, scarred, poker-faced. One of the white guys and two or three of the others will disappear after tonight, but next week there will be some late arrivals to make up for them. An average class.

The two probation officers are black, but we've had white POs too over the years. As for the instructors, we're both white, and we're also a good deal older than anyone else in the room. Bert and I are long past retirement age—he's actually retired and working a new job as an editor, whereas I still teach at the university. Once, at a graduation ceremony for the probationers, Bert began his speech by saying that between us we had taught an entire century. For good or ill, we've been part of the educational system that has failed many of its students, people we now confront once again, trying to repair the damage.

Of course, a bad education can't be directly blamed for the offenses that have brought our students here. Very few of the probationers we meet ever protest their innocence, and even those few admit that they are guilty of *some* crime, if not the one they were accused of. Guilty or not, worthless schooling is one of the big factors in bringing them here—along with poverty, broken families, substance abuse, miserable health care, lousy jobs, and public indifference—all of which coalesce in a self-perpetuating culture of despair at the heart of the problem. "The list is endless," as one of our probation officers puts it,

> starting with prenatal care, where insurance companies and hospitals will provide better care for white females than for blacks. In the hospital white nurses treat black children differently. School teachers being made to use substandard materials to teach, coupled with improper training, treat black children differently. Police—racial profiling? Politicians using blacks to gain political advantages for their own kind. Real estate, banks, on and on.

Obviously, we are not going to reverse the effects of these chronic disorders in ten weeks of reading and writing, and yet some such desire, for each of our probationers, is the reason Bert and I keep coming out to the campus Tuesday nights.

A few of the most articulate in our groups—always black men—insist vigorously that only they themselves, working in their community, can solve these problems, by refusing roles and patterns pushed on them, by convincing their own neighborhoods to organize for the common good. Whatever else needs changing, they're probably right about this. Not many of them have a very clear notion of how to do it, but the impulse to make a difference is very strong in some of them and is often part of a more personal ambition to change their own lives. Our course may serve as a practical step in this direction, since it gives them a platform from which to practice persuading others to their views—though not, of course, on opening night when everyone is still playing his cards very close to his chest. I leave it to the reader to decide, after finishing this book, what our program has done for its graduates.

The faces fracture a bit when I announce that we are *now* going to write and begin handing out pencils and paper. A few people don't need pencils, the ones who immediately begin reading the question sheet I've given them. But the majority have worried brows and tight mouths as they look around to see what others are doing. "Write your name on the front of the bluebook," I say, to let them know that these will be collected at the end of class.

Despite their anxiety, even they are soon writing—including the probation officers and Bert. I'm the only one who doesn't have his nose in a bluebook. For the next twenty minutes I just study the faces, trying to fix them in memory. One of the POs has given me a class roster so I can try to match names to the beards and bandannas, and sad eyes.

It's Charles who has the sad eyes. He is sitting as close to the hallway door as possible, head bent down to his bluebook and face hidden by the bill of a baseball cap that I never saw him take off, though he's a man in his fifties. His pencil moves very slowly across the page. He raises his head to see whether it's time to stop, and it's then I glimpse his tired, cloudy eyes—cataracts forming there. He's got a pair of glasses tucked into the collar of his pullover, but he doesn't put them on.

We have asked everyone to answer one question:

*What are the most important things a child needs in order to grow up "normal"—a healthy, happy, worthy person?*

Charles makes a list of four that circles back on itself:

A child needs good parents
Self-respect and respect for others
A good home
Education
Parents to look after him or her
A home to comfort
Education for support
Respect for fellow men and women

That's as far as he gets.

Meanwhile, I too am watching to see who has finished writing. Charles is not the only one who works with his head bowed almost to the paper, as if their mouths had to be near their pencils, whispering words out onto the page. For them writing is a kind of talk, something they must sound in their throats before transcribing it. But in the back of the room there's a bright-faced fellow in his early twenties with bushy eyebrows, who sits straight in his chair and is writing fast, with evident ease. Luis will turn out to be the only confident writer in our class this semester. Indeed, one night he will tell Bert he'd like to *become* a writer. Whether or not he has the necessary obstinacy for such a calling, he stands out in this group of men whose hands are obviously not used to holding pencils.

The fellow with gold-rimmed glasses sitting next to Luis is José, the one whose girlfriend is pregnant. They were the first people in the room tonight, talking quietly together when we came in. I introduced myself, asked them their names and whether they knew each other. In fact they did, having met in another program administered by the courts to which they both had been sent.

"Anger management?" "Substance abuse?" "Fatherhood?" I never inquire. In general, I don't want to know why our students are in trouble with the law, how much time they've served in prison, or what the court has identified as their problem. Some of them are actually eager to tell, others embarrassed and ashamed, but it's not really helpful information for us. What I wonder about is to what degree their self-image is clouded or distorted by some label they've accepted or refused—"addict," "batterer," "drunk." The truth is that in most respects they are all quite ordinary human beings, coming out of a nightmare, trying to get their bearings again but still very much in the dark. One of the biggest problems they have now is the way they've been defined by their crime, their "record," the label society has pinned on their backs, which makes it hard for them to get a decent job or a place to live, or a life. But here in this room they're welcome regardless of their past. Whatever they need to tell, or to hide, is okay with us. To this day I don't know how Luis and José got into trouble, or what program they were ordered to attend. What I do know is that Luis once saved someone's life, and that José must have a child of school-age by now.

The first one to finish writing—to run out of things to say—is not Charles after all, but Trevor, and my initial intuition about him is already beginning to be confirmed. He doesn't want to be here, and he will do what he can to demonstrate it. When he comes back from the men's room, he sits in the far corner near Luis and José, who are still writing. His handsome face has a guarded look, and his posture—a loose, baggy slouch—is meant to communicate indifference. Looking at Trevor's writing later, I find he can string sentences together with ease, but he puts all his effort into keeping what really matters to him from coming to the surface. The result is like his demeanor, bored and boring. He's just waiting it out.

Although it proved difficult, we would be able to get behind this façade at times. With the right provocation, Trevor could break into a marvelous grin and blurt out some blunt truth about himself: "People all tellin' me I'm selfish," he laughed one night—"Well, I am!"

It was hard not to like Trevor, but we worried about whether he would be able to finish the semester, and even more, what would happen to him once he did. He looked like a repeat offender to us.

Soon others have laid down their pencils, but we make a point of waiting for the slower ones. It gives people a chance to think about where they are, what they've written, and how they feel about it.

Although I have guessed wrong about the first one to quit, I'm right about who will still be writing after everyone else is done. This was easy to predict because one member of the class is already known to us, as a painfully slow but indefatigable storyteller. Randy, the only white student who will stay all semester, was in the program last fall too, and liked it so much he has come back, even though his probation time will be over before the course ends. Because we've seen so much of him, we've heard a lot of his story. He's one of those who wants to tell it, and in his case it seems to be how he wants to be viewed too, as the man who has gone through all this.

Before he got arrested five or six years ago, Randy was a junkie. Now in his late forties, he has a quarter-century of street life behind him, though he managed to steer clear of the law for most of those years. But he's had enough of the junkie's narrow world. "Rehabilitated" to a methadone regimen, he first appeared in our class in the late 1990s, was off probation for a few years, but showed up again last fall, back in the system after stealing something and then turning himself in. An addict struggling to escape a whirlpool of self-destructive habits, he now seems to be "hooked" on reading, of all things! He's joined our class for a third time, even though he knows that most of the texts will be the same ones he read last fall. To him, that's not a drawback.

Randy has a burnt-out, expressionless face and deep-set, inward-looking eyes. His speech comes slowly and with effort, yet he can be quite articulate. He remembers every single event in the plots of our stories and is happy repeating them exhaustively. Once there was a passing reference to Joseph and his brothers in our reading, and when Randy summarized for a classmate who hadn't done his homework, he inserted a little synopsis of the Bible tale too!

Randy lives with his mother, explaining that she has put up with him so long he owes her a lot of caretaking in her old age. Clearly, she is at the center of his life. In telling stories, real or fictional, Randy sometimes loses the thread, wandering off into subplots—especially his obsession with an older brother he feels has treated their mother badly. What story will he find for himself, I wonder, when she dies? Will her death be the end or the beginning?

Our first meeting has already accomplished a lot, simply by getting a pencil in everyone's hand. By this time there are only fifteen or twenty minutes of class time left. Once Randy has finished, we ask people to mark the most important items in their lists of what it takes to grow up "normal." Here's the result I typed up when I got home, and passed around at the next class.

Dave

Family—parent or guardian, for support, discipline, nurturing, finance, guidance, love. Education—finish school, maybe more schooling.

Bert

Adults who love them and give them respect. Experiences that lead them into the world with curiosity and expectation of good results.

Luis

Love. The most important thing a child needs to grow up healthy is love. Without love a child does not feel that he's cared for or even noticed, but love can be shown in many different ways, like having little "silly sessions" as I call it.

Support. When your child is asking for *help*, give it with no hesitation. It's not you helping them cheat on a test or anything in that manner. A child needs to know you've got his or her back.

Eddie

Firstly, I would imagine as prerequisites: love, support, and nurturing all be provided on an active balanced level. Actions speaking far louder than mere words. It's ironic that as simple as this exercise initially appears, it has not taken long for numerous complexities to manifest themselves. [Eddie will drop out next class.]

Bobby, *probation officer*

Love/caring. Mentors/teachers, instructors, coaches.

Deighton

A child needs proper nutrition in order to grow up normal. A child needs proper medical care including all vaccination at different ages.

Harry

School education (being able to hold what he or she needs). Healthy home (not seeing the use of drugs etc.).

Charles

A child needs good parents. Self-respect and respect for others.

John, *probation officer*

Parents, guardians, caretakers. Loving, supportive adults who direct/steer the child—someone the child can depend on and who is loyal to the child. Self-respect, respect for others.

Randy

Loving and caring parents. A good education.

Ross

Family—father, mother, brother, sister. Love—understanding of self-worth, and loving others.

Willy

Both parents. You probably would need mother and father to be there for the child. Watching the right things. If the parents are not there for the child, then the child becomes lost.

Albert

Love. A child needs love to help him or her to grow. For when a child has love, he or she does better in everything they do. A healthy diet, because when he or she has a healthy diet, that child tends to do better in school.

Anthony

I don't think it's what a child needs; I think it's what a child needs to *learn.* They need to learn how to project themselves into the future. That's when you can tell when they're growing up.

Love, parental guidance, schooling, health—these are conventional answers. I think the need for respect and self-respect is something special to our times, but a factor that black and Hispanic men insist on much more passionately than the average white probationer does, for obvious reasons. Although we discussed all these answers in the short time remaining, we made no effort to scrutinize the rationale behind these views of childhood needs. We merely took note of our consensus on typical American values. The most probing answers were Anthony's and Eddie's, both of whom raise questions about the inquiry itself—*What's really at issue here?* But Eddie was gone by our second meeting, so his skeptical habit of mind never really had an airing, and Anthony, the youngest person in the room, turned out to be too shy or diffident to speak his mind in front of strangers, especially teachers and probation officers. Once he had identified the safe boundaries of opinion in the class, he rarely ventured beyond them, whatever his private attitude.

The truth is that our program doesn't depend on the sort of self-conscious questioning Eddie and Anthony were ready to begin. The crisis of arrest and trial, shame and punishment, leaves a probationer with plenty of questions to brood on, but for these men self-examination can only be pursued in an atmosphere of relative security—exactly the mix of love, nurturance, institutional support, and respect that they affirm as the basis for normality.

Some men find this safety zone in their families, and a few have other supportive frameworks to rely on—jobs, perhaps some programs mandated by the court. After ten weeks in the Changing Lives class, they will have created one more such haven for each other. You can see the possibility emerging the first night, in their lists of what it takes to make a normal child—a class consensus that affirms who they are, and who they want to be, in a mutually validating assent to traditional attitudes. This is a matter of identifying with group values more than personal testimony or soul-searching. Anthony's impulse to find the limits and stay within them was much stronger than his desire to shine in the classroom. Whatever new insights individuals may be capable of, the most important thing for all of them is going to be their shared perspective.

While everyone else was writing, I was learning names and deciding how to divide the class into small discussion groups, three students and one probation officer or instructor for each corner of the room, groups small enough so that each man can talk about what he's written. This helps us calm anxiety over being "quizzed," afraid the teacher is going to tell you what a fool you are. Once we get settled in our small groups, it's as if everyone has been holding his breath and can now begin to breathe again. Back in grade school this moment of relief used to come at recess. With us it happens when we start genuine conversations in which everyone can take part. Instead of worrying about what the teacher might require, each probationer now has three faces to pay attention to, all three mirroring back the look on his own face that asks, *Who are you?*

The lists we've made of what children need are helpful, first, because they confirm the basic humanity we have in common, and second, because they provide an opening for serious conversation. To begin letting go of the anger, shame, and resentment life has dealt them, these men need to talk seriously to someone outside their immediate families. In many cases they no longer trust their friends, or they take a stiff posture with them in order to hold onto their pride. But here is a room full of strangers who already know them better, at some level, than any of their friends do. These are their comrades-in-arms, with more or less the same harrowing experience behind them, no matter how different the roads that led to it. Knowing that truth, no one has to pretend he is better than he is. No one needs to brag about his close calls, or display his scars. We all know they're there, just under the surface of what each man chooses to say.

Once they begin using each other as listeners and witnesses, our students will explore just how much of their painful experience they are able to talk about outside the family, and by listening to others who are in the same boat they will clarify how they feel about themselves. Not every man will discover all of this in small group discussions, and certainly not on opening night, but the basis of such possibilities is established here, in our very first conversation about what children need.

Let me put it another way. Except for our classroom, these men have almost no place in their lives where they can join a public gathering to talk seriously about values, assessing them in the light of common experience, and working toward a more viable ethics, shared with peers and founded on something like community feeling. Such public discourse is missing in contemporary society, and not just among the men whose lives on the street have led them to the courthouse or jailhouse.

Lack of practice in direct and earnest public speech cannot permanently stifle so fundamental a human impulse. Even on this first night, full of anxiety and distrust, all that is necessary to get it going is the common plight, the well-lit boundaries, a brief period of quiet meditation, and the small circle of other faces. All around the room the voices rise and fall, and people begin looking each other in the eye.

At nine o'clock the attendance sheet is passed from one small group to another—that's the signal that class is over—but in at least half of the room conversations continue for a few more minutes. I ask for all the pencils and bluebooks and hand out next week's assignment. As they leave, several come up front to shake my hand. This always happens on opening night. Sometimes there's such a line, you'd think it was at the church door! As I say goodnight, calling each by his name, their faces are sober and serious. The masks they wore when they first arrived have softened or vanished.

# Chapter 2

# *Who Are These People?*

If a dozen men come to the first meeting, it's likely that three or four of them will drop out before the semester is half over, but on the second night there will be just as many new faces in the room, men who missed the opening class for one reason or another, at least one who spent an hour sitting in an empty classroom in the wrong building.

Sometimes my memory fails me and I'm not sure whether I've seen the face before, but I can usually go by expressions—the new people come with the guarded and apprehensive look that almost everyone wore that first night, whereas the others have begun to drop their masks.

It's useful to have a few newcomers, and a chance to explain our rules and procedures once again. We ask the rest of the class to describe the reading and writing to the new men, proving that the homework isn't too hard—look! they've done it! Often one of the younger probationers will say he's amazed by the life Frederick Douglass led. This time it's Anthony. Still in his teens himself, he's never thought about what slavery must have been like for a child growing up.

As they talk, a welcoming mood develops in the classroom, which probably does as much for the welcomer's sense of belonging as for the newcomer's reassurance. New bonds are forming, probably not perceptible to a casual observer, but revealed by where the men sit and how they look at each other. It's not just that Luis and José are quietly talking in the back corner, already their turf. Others much less gregarious are also getting comfortable, finding their own places and clearing their throats—even Randy, who sits in the very center of the room, speaking to no one. His face has that ashen methadone look, but there's a faint, enigmatic smile on his lips. He's glad to be here. By the second night he is the only white student left, but that's not why he stands out, once I've introduced him to everyone as a veteran of the course who can tell them what to expect. Here's a man who's looking forward to another round of Frederick Douglass and Malcolm X! People look him over, wondering what makes him tick, perhaps thinking, *Hey, if he can do it, so can I.*

In short, the men are sizing each other up, initially as self-defense, but also to assess how much of themselves it's safe to reveal. At the second meeting there will often be some new person whose entrance makes a dramatic impression, holding up a mirror to the class that says, as Randy's presence does, *Maybe this is who you are.* Tonight it's Neville, a rotund young man who comes huffing and puffing into the room just as we're about to start. In one respect he's the opposite of Randy, though both are cursed with addictive personalities. Randy is a loner, lost in fantasies much of the time; Neville lives in a thickly populated world, with lots of friends. In fact, he's brought one of them along with him tonight, apparently for moral support. Many of the younger men have friends on probation, and sometimes they try to hook them up with our program. Since Neville's friend is not from Dorchester, we tell him whom to contact in the Roxbury Court, give him a bluebook, and invite him to stay for tonight's session. All this negotiating takes place up in front while people are waiting for class to begin, so Neville and his friend are on stage—and it's Neville people are looking at.

Neville is so enormously overweight that he can't fit into an ordinary schoolroom chair but must find one without a desktop. Despite his bulk he's a handsome fellow, round-faced with a good grin. Already it's evident why he has lots of friends. But the more we learn about Neville, the more lonely and despairing he will seem to us. That friendly smile rarely lights up, for his life is hell.

Every probationer must live with the threat of being sent back to jail for any minor misdemeanor. This probably won't happen to Neville, for he remembers his incarceration with such loathing that he now lives very circumspectly, his vices narrowed to those that are strictly legal and in fact encouraged by society—junk food and cigarettes and late-night television. Neville hasn't always been so fat; his eating disorder began in prison, and now he carries all that weight as a constant reminder of what it was like to be caged. But now he's also plagued with asthma and insomnia, side effects of his obesity. Awake half the night alone and brooding, he smokes and eats to ease his mind, as if back in his cell again.

Most of all, Neville suffers from shame—which is surely why he tries to be invisible in our class, always tardy, never volunteering a remark, rarely handing in homework. But instead of avoiding notice, Neville fills the eye. Every Tuesday night while the seats near the door fill up, his desk-less chair waits for him on the far side of the room. He must parade in front of us all when he shows up ten minutes late.

With grotesque literalness, Neville embodies the humiliations that weigh us all down: weakness of the flesh, spiritual sloth, the intransigence of circumstance. The indignity of it strikes a chord to which each man's secret vibrates. Even Deighton, the most easygoing person in the room, whose quiet voice and gracious manners soothe the soul, has his unspoken woes. So too does Trevor, handsome and bored; so does sad-faced Charles, scruffy Albert, and even Anthony, still wet behind the ears. Most of all, Randy, the ex-junkie, has his eye on Neville from the moment he arrives.

In an ordinary college classroom Neville would draw a few embarrassed stares, and these other unhappy men might well go unnoticed. Every one of them does everything he can to stay out of my line of vision—Trevor in the back corner, Charles making himself small near the door, even Randy, who always sits in the exact center of the room, silent and motionless as a Buddha. Only Albert calls attention to himself with his faltering speeches, his own way of trying to blend in. Despite all such efforts to hide, their wounds are as palpable as Neville's shame.

Certain people in every new class—often just three or four—determine the character and direction of the whole, and this semester it will be the defeated ones, the failures and losers, starting with Neville but also including these others I'm already worrying about. Classroom chemistry is never predictable, but with probationers the catalyst of accusation and punishment is sure to precipitate a powerful reaction. Stirred deeply, stripped and bereft, these men are in crisis, some of them teetering on the brink of a conversion experience. Although there is no telling how it will play out, we can be certain that profound change is in the offing. Before the semester is over, there will be personal epiphanies and communal revelations. Whatever its character, the emerging group spirit will be the key to everything else, defining the problems faced and shaping attitudes toward them. For Neville's class, the touchstone was to be found in their sense of inward crisis—each man's battered self-esteem and irreparable losses, what it means to hit bottom.

Of course, much traditional literature is founded on such themes, and our curriculum invites each student to think about how his personal crisis is part of the universal human condition. In subsequent chapters I will recount in more detail how Neville and Albert and others were able to use the stories of Frederick Douglass and Malcolm X to think about turning points in their own lives and lift themselves out of despair, looking to the future rather than brooding on the past.

But the group spirit can develop in a much less self-examining manner. Our classes always attract some probationers whose orientation is more combative than reflective or acquiescent, who meet adversity with resistance and loud demands for a better fate. Some people automatically turn inward when they feel themselves exploited or victimized, often falling into substance abuse and addiction; others react to hardship with anger and may retaliate with violence.

Obviously there are no pure examples of these types I'm describing. Every semester we begin with a different mix of personalities, variously absorbed with themselves and the demands of society, and we gradually develop a "group attitude" that each man helps to create, through reading, writing, and talking together about the ethical dimensions of life, as exemplified in public figures like Frederick Douglass or Malcolm X.

The gradual discovery of the power of historical consciousness is one of the fundamental themes in the Changing Lives program—how one's personal plight has roots in larger public issues, opening up the possibility of new roles to play in society, and a new sense of responsible citizenship. Consider, for instance, what one student wrote about Douglass and Malcolm during the semester just before Neville's class:

> I feel that these black men show the meaning of courage because of the way they lived their everyday lives. Knowing that what they say and do can change their lives in a split second. Not only their lives. But the people in their own time. It was a movement for years and generations to come.

The probationer who came to these conclusions was a stolid fellow of twenty-five, built like a tank, a family man whose multiple arrests on minor drug charges had kept his youth in turmoil, but who was beginning to pull himself together by the time he came to us. I'll call him Donny here. His real name was equally "American" and his accent "East Boston," though Donny was Hispanic, with Mayan cheekbones and physique. He worked as an auto mechanic, drank beer, went to the movies, read the sports page, smoked weed. From outward signs, he was not someone you would expect to possess much historical imagination. In fact, Donny was not given to reflection of any kind. He was just an average guy, responding to our readings with surprise and admiration.

The core of Donny's insight was his own sudden awareness that for him and others in his class, "what [we] say and do can change [our] lives in a split second." Although he himself was as shy and reluctant to speak as anyone in Neville's semester, Donny's classmates were great believers in the power of public discourse. They were inveterate speechmakers, men who loved to argue and debate, often so long and so loud that the professor across the hall would come over and ask us to quiet down. What Donny saw as a single moment of crisis in the stories we were reading, his classmates understood as an ongoing challenge to define themselves and change the world, like Douglass or Malcolm, through ideas and speech. They realized—in classroom dynamics more than any conscious formulation growing out of our texts—how self-knowledge and historical insight can combine with eloquence and courage to give a man the power and resolve to steer his own course or to lead others against the tide.

What better models for this classroom full of street-corner orators could be found than Frederick Douglass and Malcolm X, each of whom trained himself rigorously as a platform speaker, not only to change his own life, but also to command public opinion and influence social policy?

In this book I have chosen to emphasize how one particular group, a dozen men in a single semester, wrestled with spiritual crisis—the personal stories of Albert and Neville and their classmates—but there are many variants of the collective "personality" I've been describing. Our program is framed around a polarity that allows each class to find its own balance between inner- and outer-directed attitudes toward the same problems.

To emphasize how the balance can swing in either direction, let me remind the reader that one man was a member of both classes, Randy having signed up for a second round even though it would not subtract any more time from his sentence. An addictive type, he could not resist another fix of Frederick Douglass. Of course, Randy was not a different person in these back-to-back semesters. He sat in the same place, read the same texts, and even wrote more or less the same responses to our questions. Yet all around him were different people, interacting in ways that eventually created a unique sense of community. In Donny's class, Randy was one of three whites, along with two Hispanic and five black students. Classroom dynamics certainly changed the following semester when Randy's was the only white face, but I don't think this made the crucial difference. Individual style and force of character counted for more.

In Randy's first semester with us, there were also four masters of street-corner rhetoric who were ripe for the lesson their less voluble classmate Donny found in Frederick Douglass—that history changes lives, and that exemplary lives can change history. Studying Douglass and Malcolm X helped them see that literacy and eloquence were not enough in themselves but could be used to shape ideas that might indeed influence events and change behavior. And although they rarely talked about the relevance of this lesson for their own chances in life, they understood more and more acutely as the semester went on that people will always be victims of history unless they can find ways of entering it themselves, as self-conscious agents.

I'm not saying that these men wanted to be activists in some new movement, just thoughtful and responsible citizens in their own communities. They encouraged one another to see this as a possibility, and their anger and dissatisfaction seemed to acquire a new gravity as we talked about Douglass's revelations of the slave system, Dostoyevsky's account of how punishment in his Siberian prison camp brutalized both the beater and the beaten, Tolstoy's nonviolent vision of what the weak and oppressed can do to transform their powerlessness, and, most important, Malcolm X's call for social justice "by any means necessary."

Comparing the trajectories of two such different groups, the moody types in Neville's class with the brash bunch just described, it becomes clear that there is no "right way," no guaranteed approach to the problems that probationers bring us. Even the polarity I've suggested here of inner- and outer-directed personalities actually caricatures our students, just as it would be misleading to type them as more or less violent, more or less addictive, more or less sociopathic. For the sake of their vivid examples, I have compared these two strikingly different classes that met back to back, but every semester has been a surprise, and furthermore, within each group we always see a few men utterly unlike the rest. I'll never forget the white-haired, pink-cheeked businessman who turned up once, on probation for drunk driving, third offense. Except for substance abuse he was as far as one could imagine from the men sitting around him—in ethnicity, politics, class, education, manners, and expectations. He *typed* his homework. Yet by the end of the semester, he was ready to sum up his experience in these words:

> Initially, I thought that this course would be nothing more than a means of reducing my probation. However, in the long run I feel that the class has been both rewarding and fulfilling. The small group discussions were most important to me. They were enjoyable and educational. These meetings opened my eyes to many things, and the camaraderie and stories were wonderful. For me, the groups were the life-blood of the program.

Where did this man fit on the spectrum of inner- and outer-directed? He was off the charts.

Rather than merging their identities at one or another rallying point, our probationers grow in awareness of their singularity, at the same time that they are finding how many thoughts and feelings they share. On occasion, toward the end of the semester, we have proposed a writing assignment with the title "Who Am I, Really?" This topic is guaranteed to stimulate self-assertions such as the following:

> I'm a good person and I have good intentions, but the lifestyle I've led wasn't always open to good intentions. I am a leader now. I no longer follow just cuz. I evaluate and try my best to make beneficial decisions. I'm sick and tired of beating myself up, so I accept responsibility today. It took many bad situations to make me even think about my self worth, so today my answer of who am I would have to be an individual with conscience. I'm no longer walking in circles with no hope in the dark.

Sometimes, too, a man will write a series of vivid recollections that begin to cohere as memoirs, and once grew into full-fledged autobiography. But whether or not they are inclined to self-reflection, the coming together of a dozen or more strangers week after week pushes people to say who they are, and then to think about it freshly. In our circumstances, habits of reticence or boldness are highlighted by the simple fact of public conversation; and whether he is more focused on himself or on others, each person finds a place in the circle.

Indeed, the crucial change of the Changing Lives program comes when a man breaks free of stereotypes that merely classify him as one sort of outcast or another—failure, addict, hoodlum, felon—and reenters the social world as one of the assembled peers whose personal presence establishes the body politic and legitimates the ethic by which all must live. It's one of the paradoxes of democratic culture that individual character can blossom here, despite egalitarian pressures to merge with the anonymous mass. The call to assess the moral dimension of personal and public life can bring the whole person into play, just as consensus-building and decision-making reaffirm community bonds when the stakes are high and the outcome immediate for those who have the choice to make.

# Chapter 3

# *A Typical Class*

Our readings are centered on a single life story, Frederick Douglass's *Narrative of the Life of an American Slave.* The early chapters of Douglass's *Narrative* deal with his recollections of childhood—the outward condition and inner feelings of a boy growing up in a brood of plantation chattel, fed like a barnyard animal, clothed in a shirt, sleeping on rags, with no memories of his mother except at night, when she walked a dozen miles to spend a few hours with him. Until the age of six he ran loose with his playmates, and no one but his grandmother paid him any heed. After that, he was brought to the main plantation—"the Great House"—where he glimpsed his fate when he witnessed cruel beatings of older slaves who fell afoul of their master's ill-tempered discipline.

Frederick Douglass is an excellent model for historical awareness of how one's personal plight has roots in larger public issues, opening up the possibility of new roles to play in society, and a new sense of responsible citizenship. For example, when Douglass taught himself to read and write, starting as a boy of nine, it was because he realized even then that literacy was the key to personhood, and to his vision of freedom. "If you teach that nigger how to read," he overheard his master warning his wife, "it would forever unfit him to be a slave." He did learn to read, and it did inoculate him against the slave mentality. This was his first step in understanding his condition and thereby taking a hand in his own fate.

Later, when a white farmer, Edward Covey, determined to break Douglass's spirit in order to fit him for field labor, Douglass fought back because at age sixteen he again understood what was at stake—not simply another beating but a defining moment, aimed at making him "a slave for life," as he had now learned to phrase it. "This battle with Mr. Covey was the turning-point in my career as a slave. . . . My long-crushed spirit rose, cowardice departed, bold defiance took its place; and I now resolved that, however long I might remain a slave in form, the day had passed forever when I could be a slave in fact."

Finally, after his escape four years later, Douglass devoted himself to the abolitionist movement, telling these stories over and over, because he understood that his own destiny had depended on seeing beyond personal suffering to its significance as part of the slave system.

We read a few chapters from Douglass each week, ten or twelve sobering pages, along with similar selections from other life stories—especially the *Autobiography of Malcolm X*, published after Malcolm's death by his collaborator, Alex Haley; *Second Wind*, a thoughtful memoir by basketball celebrity Bill Russell, with the assistance of Taylor Branch (later the biographer of Martin Luther King Jr.); and *Black Boy*, Richard Wright's account of childhood and youth in the Deep South. Some semesters we have added passages from still another slave narrative, Booker T. Washington's *Up from Slavery*, but the typical pattern for the first three weeks has been to look only at Douglass, Malcolm X, Russell, and Wright—vivid impressions of childhood that seem, in hindsight, to have set the terms and challenges of their future lives. From earliest childhood, all four saw looming around them the racism that throws its shadow over everything in American life, requiring every black man to find his manhood in response to injustice based on skin color.

Douglass never knew for sure who his father was. His mother labored as a field hand, so that it fell to his grandmother till age six, and then to a series of masters—one of them perhaps his father—to provide training in "the slave mentality." Malcolm X lost his father, also at age six, before he was old enough to understand why Earl Little, a lay preacher and militant Garveyite, was hated, some say murdered, by their white townsfolk. He was still just a schoolboy when his mother was sent to a madhouse, and he and his siblings were parceled out to foster homes, where Malcolm learned "his place." Richard Wright's father abandoned the family when the boy was six—the same as Douglass's age when he was separated from his grandmother and Malcolm's age when his father was killed—and Richard too was taught by threats and blows "to get out of white people's way." Of the four men we first read about, only Bill Russell had two strong parents through most of his childhood, as well as a network of other family stalwarts, none of whom allowed their dignity to be insulted. Russell was only twelve when he too lost his mother, but not before she had taught him to believe in himself, a lesson Douglass and Malcolm and Wright had to learn on their own, and at a much greater price.

All these accounts of parental presence and absence have a somewhat legendary quality, partly a result of the distance that memory interposes, and partly because subsequent events gave their lives such epic proportions. In earlier times stories like these, told and retold, would serve as cultural touchstones, setting standards and confirming community bonds. Our students sense this exemplary power even on first acquaintance; certainly no one dismisses our texts as "just stories." On the contrary, we are often asked why these authors were not taught to them in high school. But our aim in Changing Lives is not so much to find models as it is to stir interest in one's own life. We want to take ourselves as seriously as Frederick Douglass and Malcolm X took themselves.

The reader may notice here how my "we" has become more and more inclusive, from "our students" to "ourselves." We all have things to learn in this class, and among the most important is simply that we are doing it together. The point is not to remind a probationer of his failings or misfortunes, which he knows well enough, but to make our situation—his, yours, mine—seem less personal and less lonely, and to take courage from the fact that others go through even worse periods of failure and suffering, and bounce back.

> *Is it necessary to have a father, a mother, to grow up normal? What happens when a child lacks parental love and guidance?*
>
> *How do people learn to face the things that life will demand? Where do people get their courage, self-esteem, righteousness?*

These are serious questions for any man, double-edged for those in the class who are fathers too, and weighted by examples like those of Douglass and Malcolm, whose extraordinary achievements students frequently cite as they formulate answers from their own experience. Even for those students who shirk the reading—there are always a few who do—the background impression of heroic characters and events adds gravity to the issues we discuss.

We stay focused on childhood for the first four weeks, coming back to the same basic concerns in every homework assignment, and then again—insistently!—in the writing exercises that begin each class. Of course, the probationers realize that they are being asked the same questions over and over, but a different phrasing gives a different emphasis, and usually elicits a deeper response. Students who may never have thought about childhood are surprised to discover how much they have to say, even when they have already written a page or two about it before coming to class. Here, for example, is an opening exercise we use with the homework assignment just quoted:

> *What should a parent's role be in teaching children to face hardship and temptation?*
>
> *When is the use of force necessary to teach the difference between right and wrong? Can a genuine desire to be "good" be encouraged through force?*
>
> *What part does wealth or poverty play in a child's acquisition of courage, self-esteem, and righteousness?*
>
> *Which is most important?—*
> *parental guidance*
> *institutions like church and school*
> *peer pressure*
> *home environment (poverty/wealth)*

Obviously, questions like these are not aimed at testing or even teaching a class. They are posed to help us pull our thoughts together in silent meditation, pencils in hand, in order to prepare us for serious conversation with one another.

Just like everyone else, instructors and probation officers do the reading and writing, to claim our stake in the group discussion and allow us to take a role that's not merely "facilitative." Each of us is ready to tell his story and hear what others think, to fit his piece into the larger picture. This investment is crucial for classroom dynamics. You could say that reading and writing are the kindling and spark for conversation "around the campfire" on Tuesday nights. Because we take our places with something personal to offer, rather than standing up in front calling on people to recite, it is possible to trust the conversation to find its own way, without trying to keep it on track or press a meaning out of it. When things go right, everyone in the circle takes responsibility for the common inquiry, and a feeling of membership can develop in which the personal merges with the public.

Handled with respect for each person's dignity, this group dynamic helps us steer clear of the confessional approach typical of therapy programs—which no doubt has its uses but is not part of our method. To be sure, the face-to-face situation encourages us to address our true concerns in a forthright manner, and people naturally speak from personal experience when they are asked for their views of life and society. But there's no breast-beating or soul-baring, and we avoid putting individuals on the spot, relying instead on the give-and-take of consensus-building to foster mutual trust and shared ethics, the preconditions of belonging to a public world.

Probationers come to their second class having read thirty pages from the childhood memories of Douglass, Malcolm X, and Russell. (We add Richard Wright in the fourth week.) Except for a few delinquents like Neville and Trevor, they bring along some written response to the first of the double-barreled set of questions reproduced above. To illustrate their responses, I will quote from the work of Luis and Harry, probably the most alert and thoughtful members of our class this spring.

I can quote them in full because we transcribe what our students write each week on a word processor. Copies are returned at the following meeting, along with brief replies from Bert or myself, to help probationers see their writing as others see it. Our aim is not to teach conventional "writing skills," and therefore our comments simply open a dialogue on paper with the authors. We respond directly to their ideas, not with praise or advice, but just chiming in, perhaps asking about ramifications and consequences, to make it clear that we are paying attention and interested in their opinions.

In the same spirit that we type up their handwriting to make it as readable as possible, we also silently correct slips of the pen, spelling errors, and confusing syntax. Our primary aim is to punctuate rhythms as they would naturally rise and fall in speech, hoping to encourage authors to hear themselves as storytellers. Idiosyncrasies of diction or phrasing are treated as essential qualities of the student's voice. Our editorial touch is thus much lighter than the "as told to" practice of Alex Haley or Taylor Branch, but now and then we shuffle whole paragraphs around to make a more coherent argument, or simply to bring together fragments produced over a period of several weeks, and we regularly conflate homework passages and opening exercises written impromptu in class. They mesh seamlessly, as the work of Luis and Harry will illustrate.

Luis

People learn to face the things that life will demand by elder family members who have experienced things in that field and have encountered such matters. Malcolm X's mother was being harassed by the state to let the children go in foster care, and then his mom was hospitalized. Malcolm said he did not want to see her no more, cause it would have made him vicious—so some people's lives will make them stronger, though smarter. Like Bill's father Mister Charlie at a gas station: a man had disrespected him in front of his family, and Mister Charlie approached the man with a tire-iron, about to do something he would soon regret; but the man fled and the family rejoiced; but pops said, hush up. Now they moved, and now Bill was happy that his father didn't get checked—but also learned that some things are better left alone and overlooked or ignored.

Most people get their courage from their fathers. I know I have. Or moms, for conquering obstacles that come her way. Most of us have the strongest parents, but some don't have parents to guide them. But self-esteem is usually within oneself to acquire. Friends build self-esteem too.

In school I had this reading teacher, in her 30s, well-pampered and taken care of. She was the nicest, easiest person to understand and get along with. I get all my righteousness from her. She made me feel good about being good. There's always someone who inspires you, other than your parents. You can meet someone who can either put you in jail or can put you on your way to that yellow brick road to celebrity-ville.

The role as a parent I would portray would be a person who can teach, be a friend, someone children can relate to, cause grandpa only has so much to say.

You can say "you're going to burn your hand if you put it in hot water" so many times. Sometimes you just have to let them learn on their own, so now they know next time what will happen. Force is only necessary if it is necessary, like if they have a stealing problem, or they fight a lot. But other than the role of a priest, you should not be so hard, because how many of the strippers, prostitutes, and bank robbers had parents that were too hard, or they wanted to keep them locked up, and now, when you let them out, they don't know how to act. You can create an animal.

Wealth or poverty help, but you cannot spoil children too much. That's like borrowing your friend's, relative's car every other day, you get so used to using it every other day that you start to depend on it, and guess what happens when you don't let one use it that other day?

To me the most important is: *parental* guidance. You got to have some kind of parent figure, of some sort. Church and school are cool, but what happens after church and school? Peer pressure is really not important, because peer pressure leads to low self-esteem, and guess what else it leads to? You can live in a mansion, and be the biggest stuck-up son of a bitch. Money is not everything, because, say, this Beverly Hills spoiled brat got stuck in the ghetto—could they relate to people without them beating them down, or could they fit in, or can they even get along with anyone? It is good to be stable, but I seen most take it for granted.

A good parent figure will do just right.

Harry

*Hardship*—The reward of working hard pays off.

*Temptation*—Teach your family that things get better every day. No rush.

*The use of force*—My own personal force is never the key. Being stern is the way, talking and teaching the right way. Kids are like empty Microsoft hardware. You store the memory on disc.

*Wealth or poverty*—Don't really matter if it is where your heart is, and how hard you work for it.

*Parental guidance* is very important—Not being a parent but a friend, you can get more out of your (family) kids.

*Peer pressure*—See above answer. Let your kids know how important it is to talk when there is an issue. Make it so your kids are open to you. It doesn't matter if you're poor or rich, show your kids the meaning of life as a whole.

*Church and school*—Church and school start at home. Can't depend on others for the upbringing of your family. Everything starts at home.

Let me draw attention to the very different attitudes toward authorship exemplified by Luis and Harry, each of whom has his own distinctive manner. Luis uses writing to try things out, pouring forth thoughts as people will do in conversation, without questioning how they will dovetail and not worrying about consistency. Only now and then does he touch down to more deeply held opinions, such as "some things are better left alone," or "there's always someone who inspires you." If our goal were to prepare students for college work, the next step would be revision, lots of practice identifying fundamental beliefs and consolidating recurrent lines of thought, but in our class a less academic approach makes more sense. Our version of finding a "thesis" or formulating a "topic sentence" is to help a writer like Luis recognize when his heart is really in what he's saying, and when it isn't. Here, for instance, is what I said to him about his writings that week:

> Luis—I like the way you use your imagination to think of examples for the opinions you want to stress. You use two kinds of examples: some of them are "made up" out of general experience (like the "Beverly Hills" spoiled brat—someone you've never actually known, although you've probably known situations that help you imagine it); others are actual people and events from your own life, like the teacher who made such an impression on you, and gave you lessons in "righteousness." Of the two kinds of examples, the ones that have the most power to convince others are always the actual people and events. There's something about a true story that grabs the attention and makes a reader trust your ideas.

And here is what I said to Harry about his principles of child-rearing:

> Harry—I admire your clearheaded approach to questions like these. One answer I particularly like: "No rush." That says a lot. Write it over the door!
>
> One thing that puzzles me: How do we draw the line between "personal force" and being "stern"? I realize there can be a huge difference, but there can also be a strong resemblance between these two methods. How do we keep them separate? Is "no rush" a clue here?

Luis is in his mid-twenties, a recent father, growing serious and thoughtful, but his mind isn't made up yet about many important things in life. Harry is probably forty, with several children and lots of decisive choices already under his belt. He knows what he thinks, and his writing comes in precepts. Rather than musing or puzzling things out, he makes lists. What distinguishes him most of all is that Harry automatically assumes that our questions refer to his own responsibilities as an adult and a parent, whereas Luis remembers what it once felt like to be a child and is asking himself what it means to leave childhood behind.

A few weeks after this meeting we asked the class to describe some important lesson learned in childhood, and Harry, who has so many such lessons behind him, began by exclaiming, "I'm still learning! Every day." These two perspectives, looking forward or looking back, parent and child alternating in the same person, can play out in remarkable ways over a semester.

The same dual perspective will surface much more ambivalently when we confront certain contentious matters addressed in our homework:

> *Can a genuine desire to be "good" be encouraged through force?*

The class is very much of two minds about this one, since it puts in question their status as probationers—enjoined to reform themselves, *or else!* By raising the issue indirectly, as one of child-rearing, we can talk about a touchy subject without shame or anxiety muddying the water quite so much. Luis remembers his own childhood as a pretty good one, but he is willing to probe the tender areas when he wonders how much a child can learn from advice or warnings, how much must come from painful experience. Characteristically, Harry is less in doubt about where he stands. His cardinal virtue is "hard work," tempered by patience and self-control, and he preaches moderation: "Teach your children that things get better every day," he writes. "No rush." In his homemade parents' manual it follows that "My own personal force is never the key." But Harry is not arguing for complete permissiveness: when children disobey or seem headed for trouble, "Being stern is the way."

Neither Luis nor Harry has said anything here about crime and punishment, probation and rehabilitation, yet it's not hard to read between the lines. Like the boy who burns his fingers once too often, Luis has learned his lesson, and he plans to avoid being "locked up" again like "an animal." Harry's attitude toward probation can be inferred from what he says about the importance of hard work, self-discipline, and facing stern realities. It's significant that he doesn't rely on institutions like church or school to teach his kids right from wrong but takes the responsibility on himself. In making peace with society, Harry has not handed over his autonomy to the powers that be.

Others in the class are much more conflicted over these issues, as indeed are most people in our self-indulgent, self-righteous, punitive society. It's only too easy to get probationers sounding off indignantly about a parent's "right" to discipline (slap, spank, or even beat) a misbehaving child, and the thought of a twelve-year-old "blowing the whistle" on his parents outrages them. But as we debate the legitimacy of coercion in such cases, the men begin to realize that attitudes toward obedience and punishment have implications not only for the dilemmas of parenting they face, and for their own misdemeanors and beatings as children, but also for public policy issues that affect them, all the way from plea-bargaining encouraged by incompetent lawyers or differential enforcement of drug laws with mandatory sentencing, to Civil Rights legislation, Affirmative Action controversies, the Patriot Act, or massive military responses to terrorism. Glimpsing the confusion of principle and pragmatism behind exercises of private and state power can produce a healthy sense of uncertainty, sometimes leading to valuable new insights.

As seen in Luis's case, passages from Douglass or Malcolm can serve as a springboard for writing, but we do not count on it, nor do we leave behind those who haven't done the reading. Homework questions are framed so that they can be answered without referring to our texts at all. Moreover, when we present a second set of questions as an opening exercise on Tuesday nights, it gives everyone in the room another chance to think about the issues before we start to talk. Thus, after a homework assignment calling for their views of how people "learn to face the things that life will demand," we ask students to decide which is the most important influence on a child—parental guidance, institutions like church and school, peer pressure, or relative wealth and poverty.

After fifteen minutes of silent thought and writing, the rest of our evening is typically devoted to conversations in small groups, where we begin by reading out loud from our bluebooks—a move from the personal to the public that we repeat many times before the semester is over. Asking probationers to write about how people "face hardship and temptation" or learn "the difference between right and wrong" invites the airing of long-standing grudges and complaints, baggage most of us carry from childhood. Talking afterwards with three or four other people who have been thinking about the same things helps us see that old patterns of misbehavior and punishment frequently replicate themselves and can even be passed on to a new generation. To imagine how the past might have been different is a step toward change in the future. To share memories and insights in a public forum helps create a new present to build on.

All this reading, writing, and talking converges unpredictably when we assemble in our small groups each week. Sometimes we ignore the reading or slide quickly away from the questions posed for writing, but no one worries about "sticking to the subject." Digression often proves the most direct path to what people are ready to talk about in our classes. The main thing is to speak one's mind earnestly, something that is hard to do if you think you have to say the right thing or display the correct attitude. It takes a few weeks for probationers to feel comfortable in the classroom, but even on the second night that I've been describing here, turning our chairs to make self-enclosed circles of three or four individuals immediately changes the atmosphere, allowing us to look one another in the eye and ask questions that don't echo against the walls. We begin to find the rhythm of conversation—still guarded conversation among strangers, to be sure, but not the stiff recitation of the schoolroom.

Tonight I sit down with the two Hispanic guys who were the first ones in the room at the opening class, obviously drawn to one another by age and ethnicity as well as serendipity. Luis wears a black do-rag tied tight to his skull in the accepted cool manner. His round expressive face looks tender as well as intelligent. José sports a leather cap with a narrow bill, equally cool but less dramatic. Behind his gold-rimmed glasses José's eyes look to the side, not eager to meet mine. Luis's gaze is open and direct, while José is slower to engage, more cautious. But they're both tuned in.

One question in the opening exercise tonight focuses on the role of peers in a child's moral growth. In his writing Luis has brushed it off as "not really important," though he adds, significantly, that "peer pressure leads to low self-esteem, and guess what else it leads to?" And yet, earlier in his bluebook he has written that "Friends build self-esteem too." There are some obvious contradictions here, and our conversation naturally gravitates toward them. José thinks that peer influence is invariably negative, always counter to the uplifting instruction in school and church, and much more likely to drag you down than poverty or even a rocky home life. Parents, backed up by social institutions, are seen as the first line of defense against the bad influence of other kids. Luis agrees, forgetting about his statement that "Friends build self-esteem too."

I ask if there might not be a positive side to a child's interactions with other kids. In my own childhood, for instance, friends and enemies played a huge role in the acquisition of social skills and my sense of myself as a moral being. This has been the main topic in my own bluebook tonight. Memories come flooding in on me, but I don't want to dominate the conversation, so I stop talking after a single example. Luis and José aren't really convinced. Yes, they can see how other kids might sometimes be a positive as well as a negative force, but their view is polarized another way, with kids (good or bad) on one side, and society with its institutions and enforcers (especially parents) on the other. In their experience, you have to choose, and they have cast their lot with the grownups. No doubt they're right about this generational divide, yet I'm more inclined to sympathize with the kids' point of view than they seem to be. Luis and José were children themselves not so long ago, but now they're determined to be adults, renouncing their own past. Past seventy myself, I bite my tongue.

Luis and José never quite realize that in my defense of "peers" I am talking about their "boys," as they call them significantly—that is, the friends they "hang with" today. All these words have positive and negative charges for them. "Peer" probably gets its connotations from the jargon of worried social workers, guidance counselors, and juvenile probation officers, a usage that Luis and José, like most people, accept unthinkingly. Their friends, if we call them peers, immediately seem less trustworthy, a source of temptation to be wary of. But we don't talk about this.

When we shift our focus to a related topic, the age at which friends turn into peers, our conversation gets much livelier. Here they know a lot more than I do, and they are interested in looking closely at the phenomenon. "High school?" I suggest. "Middle school," José says, "ten, eleven, those are the years when kids change. Before that they're. . . ." He falters, searching for a word, looking up at us expectantly. Luis finishes his sentence for him: "innocent."

All three of us are momentarily struck by this term, which seems to draw an all-important line across the past—the end of childhood. José immediately accepts the word, and we launch into a discussion of why things change so dramatically at that period of life. It's not quite puberty yet, though some of the social effects of growth and hormones are already apparent. The new factor is not so much awareness of some particular aspect of life as it is just plain awareness—call it self-consciousness, or in the social worker's jargon again, "adolescence."

I'm reporting the drift of our conversation here, not the exact words we used. Soon we're talking about the way that self-consciousness gives peer pressure its purchase on young people waking to the social world for the first time.

Once we begin to consider how wealth and poverty enter into this equation, Luis and José take complete charge of the discussion. Clothes—that's the key symbol of status in peer society. Wearing the right clothes is the sign of belonging. Both of them are knowledgeable about pricing and merchandizing techniques used by manufacturers, the manipulation of fashion. Personal style can be somewhat invented or creatively adapted, Luis suggests, but having the money to buy certain things—like the right sneakers—is essential to membership in the peer group, no matter what the brand-name or gang colors. I find myself eyeing their hats again, and the rest of their garb. Luis and José are wearing the uniform of their age-mates, adapted creatively to their own self-image. But I'm not going to bring *this* up—not on the second night of the semester anyway.

Our conversation has covered a lot of ground by this time, moving in fits and starts, finding the groove for a while, running out of steam, reviving—all of it tentative and a bit ill at ease, yet never quite going dead, and sometimes very lively. By the end of it we've accomplished more than any of us expected, following our noses into topics that click for all three of us, finding common ground and exploring new territory. The way we go at it is probably more important than what we talk about, but tonight in fact the two have come together: we've discussed how individuals form social connections that are not really bonds of friendship, even though they have extraordinary power in determining attitude and behavior; meanwhile, our discussion itself has been an exercise in finding one's place in a group.

Tonight's conversation is a perfect illustration of how our program works. The object is not to make friends but to establish a new kind of peer group, one not based on intimidation or the pressures of popular culture but on the sense of belonging to a representative social body—you could call it citizenship or community. José and Luis may know each other from other programs for probationers, and they certainly have a lot in common, but they won't become friends. In fact, so far as I have seen, no new friendships have grown out of Changing Lives in all the years I've been teaching it, not one, despite the fact that these men live in the same neighborhoods and may sometimes meet on the street or at the courthouse. They don't want to make friends with "criminals," and in fact the terms of their probation forbid it—though a friendship growing out of our course would not be frowned on. After all, these people ought to be friends, because they really understand each other, as few others do.

Ironically, a vital element in the genuine bonding that does occur in the Changing Lives program depends on the absence of ordinary ties of friendship. The work of the semester—reading stories of uplift and despair, writing responses to the concerns raised in them, sharing these thoughts with each other—this complex sequence of shared work gains in significance because it is carried out in a public way, by a group of men especially qualified to judge and understand, and without the bias of personal attachment. Just as their bluebooks never fall into the tones of letter-writing between friends, so too the conversations in small groups stay on the level of public discourse, with its sense of responsibility to ethical and civic norms. This is a public world few people in our society spend much time in, and some of our probationers have experienced it only in the courtroom, under very different conditions.

The small group discussions are the key to everything else in the program, but their full effect as public discourse depends on our moving from these more intimate exchanges, where everyone takes his turn in the conversation, to a brief open forum at the end of the meeting, when either Bert or I will moderate a general consideration of issues that have come up. We often begin by asking someone from each group to tell the rest of us what they've been talking about. This simple report has the advantage of giving everyone a stake in the general discussion, whether or not he feels comfortable speaking in front of what is now, suddenly, an audience. Some people who might otherwise avoid the spotlight are not so shy once they have spoken in a small group, especially if a group opinion has emerged for which each member is a potential spokesman with others backing him up.

Merely asking for a group report creates a retrospective point of view, and sometimes an interesting division of opinion, either of which will help us circumvent the awkward classroom ritual of questions and answers no one really cares about. Once people know what they think—because they've announced it—the ideas themselves become more important and interesting, and it feels very different to speak from a position of commitment than it does to recite when the teacher calls on you. Of course, this method of canvassing the small groups also gets us quickly to the issues that have been significant for this class on this night, not necessarily where we started with the homework. Often it turns out that several groups zero in on the same thing, from slightly different angles.

Tonight, for example, Harry's group has also been thinking about the question of peer pressure, including the way that clothes can serve as marks of belonging.

But in my group both Luis and José see the problem through the eyes of youth, remembering what it's like to feel that your sneakers, or hat, or haircut may be out of fashion, whereas Harry's group is full of fathers, who regard the peer phenomenon from an entirely different perspective. One of Harry's three kids is bused to a wealthy suburb for school. His daughter is only six but is already old enough to be envious of the fancy clothes that other kids wear, and to tell her parents so. For her, long before middle school, the conflict of peer pressure and parental guidance has come to the crunch, against a background that includes both school and income level—all four of our questions this week twisted into a single knot.

Harry has written in his bluebook that "It doesn't matter if you're poor or rich, show your kids the meaning of life as a whole"—a sentiment that we can all agree with but are liable to file away as too vague to be of any real use. Group discussion brings it to life. I don't know what Harry said in his small group, but once we begin to talk about peer pressure in an open forum, he goes right to the heart of the matter with the story of his daughter: "How do you explain to your six-year-old that you can't afford it?" Writing is useful for meditating on a subject—sweeping away distractions—but public exchanges are more likely to raise the complicated problems people actually deal with.

When someone like Harry offers his experience for the rest of us to consider—a dilemma that no one can really solve, but one that all of us recognize as confronting the facts of life—the effect is often great relief rather than frustration. Just getting the truth before us, with all its bite, allows us to say to ourselves, yes, that's the way it is, and we've got to live with it if we don't change it. This kind of recognition is fostered in the larger forum, where the mode is not conversation but public testimony, individuals speaking for us all, as if we were watching ourselves think something through. Harry is masterful at this because he seems so completely at one with himself. The dilemmas of life certainly haven't eased or vanished for him; on the contrary, it's because he sees them with such clarity, in their full and immediate actuality, that he seems capable of coping with whatever is demanded of him. Sitting there in the middle of the room, his lean body and likable countenance seem at once animated and relaxed—so unlike Albert's stiff and worried look—and I for one could listen to his quiet voice all night. In fact, we all do listen to him with unusual attentiveness, taking in his stoic wisdom, almost basking in it.

That's how our session ends on this second Tuesday of the semester, our first time discussing what children need to grow up "normal," and how the lives of Frederick Douglass and Malcolm X illustrate what happens when the cards are stacked against you, when things go wrong. In response to crisis some people can take charge of circumstances, changing history as well as their own destinies.

Although I've called it a typical class, no one class and no one semester in our program is like another. What I've tried to show in this chapter is how the basic format of reading, writing, and talking can engage students in questions of mutual concern, fostering more self-conscious commitment to shared attitudes and a growing sense of public responsibility. I wanted to move through this typical pattern for the reader, just as we need to do for each new group of probationers at our second meeting. In tonight's consideration of how peer pressure affects the young we've probably touched some sore spots and significant memories that will give rise to later insights and understanding. But to my mind the most useful work we've done has been tacit and implicit rather than directly addressed. We've begun our modeling of a public world in which everyone has his place.

# Part Two

## *In the Shadow of School*

# Chapter 4

# *Encouraging Failure*

From what I've said so far, it's obvious that ours is not a conventional course in literature, nor is it designed to sharpen basic literacy skills, encourage further schooling, or promote any particular views of history or society. We use reading and writing chiefly as a means to conversation, the vital center of the program. When we assess the careers of Frederick Douglass or Malcolm X, we are sorting out our own ethical positions, using these heroic figures and historic events as a means of building mutual respect and a collective public conscience, taking responsibility for the ideas and opinions of one another. Something like that, of course, is what the businessman I've quoted earlier learned in his ten weeks. He did not need our course to teach him how to read or write more fluently, but to see himself from a new perspective, part of a wider community than he had imagined.

Nevertheless, literacy itself, the ability to read and write, is more than just a point of departure for us, and I want to say something here about how it matters. As teachers of language know, there are kinds as well as levels of literacy, often matters of cultural savvy more than linguistic expertise—everything from being able to read the street signs and fill out a job application to mastery of the specialized jargon of computer programming or the protocols of international diplomacy. Each variety and grade of literacy has its symbolic as well as its practical value, and in our program we are more concerned with how students perceive their abilities than with assessing or upgrading them. They are often proud of their "street smarts," which can include important language skills, but they are usually ashamed of their reading and writing—even though a majority finished high school and are not really "street people," but have jobs and families and can keep their heads above water in the dominant culture of paper transactions. Experience has taught them that the world contains two kinds of intelligence—the lawyer's mind that allows people to manipulate the system from within, and the hustler mentality that works the system from outside, milking it at greater risk, for less profit, but equally dependent on the ability to use words expertly. Many probationers have fantasies of living in both worlds, and actually live in neither.

In recruiting students to the program, probation officers try to screen out anyone who doesn't have at least an "eighth-grade reading ability," but this is an impressionistic label at best. Although we've never had a student who couldn't read Frederick Douglass, some of them have a lot of trouble with Anton Chekhov, whose prose is steeped in irony and indirection, cultural nuances that can be hard to grasp even in a good translation. We've dropped Chekhov from the curriculum recently and added a Tolstoy parable instead, "God Sees the Truth but Waits," crafted for the newly literate Russian peasant late in the nineteenth century.

Although very few of our students have read any book at all since they left school, this is not entirely bad news. The stories they *do* read make a greater impact. I remember one evening when three students, triggering each other's memories, jointly reconstructed the plot of Richard Wright's *Native Son.* The leader of this conversation had read the book some years earlier, not in school but in jail. They were surprised and pleased by their feat, and others in the room were impressed and envious.

By the end of the semester we can count on every student taking satisfaction in knowing some famous authors like Malcolm X and Leo Tolstoy, and being able to retell the story of Frederick Douglass's life in slavery. Along with diplomas at our graduation exercises, we present each student with a fat clothbound edition of all the major *Slave Narratives* (courtesy of the Library of America), and the fact that this compilation includes Douglass's classic text means that it can go on the shelf as a reminder of accomplishment. Perhaps in some homes that volume will foster important bonds between fathers and children: "Oh, yes, I've read that. You should try it." So reading has symbolic significance as well as practical relevance as a jumping-off place for classroom discussions.

Writing, the other face of literacy, has even more emotional weight for our students, because there is a tangible product involved, something created and objectified that feels "personal" to its author, a measure of worth. This cuts two ways: you can feel bad as well as good about what your thoughts look like on paper. For our program both outcomes are opportunities. We want people to be proud of themselves, and so we praise them, and publish their writings for others in the class to see—always a big event. Even more important, however, is the shame that inevitably surfaces on that first night when we ask everyone to write in a bluebook. Feeling incompetent and small has little to do with what they actually write and everything to do with sitting in a classroom with a blank page in front of you, which you must cover with your own handwriting while a teacher stands waiting.

Bringing probationers back to such a desperate moment, anywhere from two to fifty years since their last encounter, is guaranteed to call up many of the old feelings that were crucial in determining their fate. Consider, for instance, the indelible marks teachers left on two of our probationers:

Luis

> In school I had this reading teacher, in her 30s, well-pampered and taken care of. She was the nicest, easiest person to understand and get along with. I get all my righteousness from her. She made me feel good about being good.

Neville

> I would say I'm a weak person, and only because I really never learned how to read or write like others, which has kept my self-esteem down for many of years! And I really don't know how to spell. I believe if I was strong like others that really don't do anything with the smarts they have—Me, I feel like I was let out somewhere along the line.

Neville and Luis represent two extremes of self-confidence, and you can see it in their writing. In fact, Neville is not so weak a writer as he thinks, and it's our job to help him realize this. Improved literacy for him will be a matter of getting past his shame. The passage I've just quoted was written halfway through the semester. Up till then it had been impossible to convince him to hand in anything—not homework, not even the class exercises that we *saw* him writing each week. He took them home crumpled up in his pocket. I will have more to say about Neville's writing later in this book, but for the present I want to elaborate on one aspect of it only, as a literacy issue.

Most men in trouble with the law have been poorly educated and possess limited vocational skills, and now their criminal records are likely to prevent them from getting any job that is attractive or a step up. Improving their literacy levels might help, but probably not much. We've had students with college degrees and real eloquence as writers who can't get white-collar jobs because they are black men with felonies that show up when Human Resources does a background check. And if the aim is simply to train a confident writer, we're talking about years of effort, and constant correction of "failings"—something very few egos can handle. Moreover, by this time Neville's failings in school have spread inextricably into every part of his life. As with most of our probationers, difficulties in school have coalesced with problems at home and trouble with the authorities. The usual pattern established by middle school is that every act of defiance, every avoidance, every mistake and punishment has ramifications through the boy's whole life. Whether it originates in school, family, or the streets, soon there is no real distinction to be made.

What Neville needs now is something like a complete overhaul, starting with his smoking habit and his eating disorder. Improving his writing skills seems like the least of his worries. Nonetheless, changing his attitude toward what he has to say and its worth in a public forum might make a big difference. The public I'm imagining is our class, of course, not the traditional schoolroom with its tests and grades, making demands that have already strained Neville's faith in himself to the breaking point. Going back to school would be a bad idea for Neville, certainly at this point and probably at any point. But the symbolic value of the literacy skills he already possesses can be honored in our classroom.

Now let's look at Luis. He already has most of the skills that make a successful student. He's alert and quick to engage any challenge, bold and confident. His writing ability is probably above the average of entering college students, and he can handle abstract ideas even though he is not practiced or accomplished. The "Writing Proficiency Exam" administered at my university would give him little trouble. He's had a few good teachers, starting with that "nice" reading teacher, and so he doesn't hate school. In all of this he could be considered the ideal student for a program called Changing Lives Through Literature. But Luis is the *only* such student in the room this semester. There are several others just as intelligent, in ways that count for them, and some are much more seasoned and sagacious, yet no one else is "college material," and if we think of our program as primarily designed for the likes of Luis, we'd better close shop.

I do not mean that no one else could make it through to a college degree, or that we never have more than one Luis in a semester. At least half of our probationers could do the work if they had the same incentives and support systems provided college freshmen. Indeed, Anthony, who is only eighteen, may end up in college if his mother has her way; but his situation is unusual, almost unique, in the Changing Lives program. Over the years we've had a few probationers coming to us with degrees already, or at least a semester or two of course work, perhaps accomplished in prison before education programs were shut down by the "no frills" penology in ascendance today. Yet by and large the Dorchester program does not send students on to the higher education track, and despite their general intelligence, I think it would be a guaranteed failure experience for 99 percent of them.

If I am skeptical about the promise further education holds for our students, so are they. "I'm too old to learn" is a common response, and for most of them it is certainly too late to take advantage of the elaborate indoctrination process that prepares the young for a place in our social order. Some finish high school, some don't, but almost no one gets what he needs to fit in—neither the middle-class information and literacy skills that make up most of the curriculum nor the habits of prudence, diligence, and conformity that are the true "social studies" of American classrooms. Without these, as one of our students says, children "will lag behind and somehow fall through the cracks."

This is Albert speaking, one of our "true believers" in education, responding to a set of questions posed early in the semester when we first begin to discuss "normal" childhood:

> *What are the most important things a child needs in order to grow up "normal"—a healthy, happy, worthy person?*

To help probationers zero in on these essentials, we also ask them what should be done when parents see their children failing in school, disobedient, headed for trouble. Although Albert counts himself among those who have fallen through the cracks, he still believes in the system, and he can parrot the advice that might be given young professionals in white suburbia: "I think the parent should seek help for the child as soon as possible, because as soon as they get help for that child, the better it will be for the whole family. To put the child back on track before it is too late, he or she should receive counseling."

Of course, this is not the treatment our probationers met with when they brought home a bad report card in elementary school, and Albert's suggestion seems naïve to me in two respects: first, in assuming that such counseling is available to families at the bottom of the economic ladder, living in neighborhoods where the schools are run like prisons and homes are often so full of noise that the bathroom is the only place a studious child could sit quietly to read; and second, in imagining that counseling in itself would solve or circumvent any of these problems.

Albert's faith in the system is not limited to the early grade levels when his own troubles began. He was the only probationer this semester to voice a hope that he might use our class to get himself "back on track" and into college. Would Albert actually be able to profit by the traditional education he says he wants? Let me ask it more inclusively. Who among our probationers could realistically be expected to improve his lot by going to college? I'm not asking who should have the right to it, but only who among our students has a chance, at this stage of life, of getting some advantage from further schooling?

Each of our classes includes a few men in their late teens or early twenties who happen to have no one depending on them financially, no children of their own, but who do have a place to live and food on the table, parents or grandparents supporting them, perhaps a mother saying to her son, "Stay in school, keep out of trouble, make something of yourself." (Mothers are the last ones to give up.) Here's what one eighteen-year-old says about his situation:

> Anthony
>
> I go through a crisis with my mother every day, always talking about getting a job, going to college, or moving out of the house. But now I have a part-time job, and I'm going to school part-time, and my mother ain't harassing me no more. And that makes me want to do more for myself.

Although he is lagging behind, Anthony hasn't yet fallen through the cracks. For him and others like him, finishing high school and entering college may offer a way out of the fate that older probationers in our classes have already met. It's a matter of timing and luck: having come to a crisis early in life (Anthony has been stealing cars) and recognizing that his future is going to be determined by his next step, the probationer of eighteen or twenty may have enough ability, desire, and support to change direction and devote himself to some pursuit that will give more shape to his world. School is one way to start.

During the semester we don't talk much about such choices except by indirection, as when we discuss how Frederick Douglass and Malcolm X taught themselves what they needed to know. At our first or second meeting, however, we do offer help exploring various educational avenues, and we sometimes make special overtures to probationers who seem as eager as Albert, or who show the kind of potential I've described in Luis and Anthony. This is always a very serious moment in our classroom, everyone listening intently. Although very few ever take the next step, the important thing is to feel you have a choice.

Sometimes we merely plant a seed. I remember one shy fellow in his early twenties who played basketball for his high school team and "did all right" in the classroom, just as he did in our program. He had been lucky enough to get into an electrician's apprenticeship program, liked it, and would ultimately make good money. No advantage in going to college at this point, but our course reminded him that books can be interesting. Without a teacher making assignments, however, he didn't know what to read, so we gave him a couple of paperbacks that fit his aptitude and taste, not urging him toward an academic career but simply feeding his curiosity. Maybe someday it will make a difference, positioning him for a major change he would not be able to imagine without books to suggest it. But maybe not. He was doing all right as it was, or would be, once off probation.

Another sort of student for whom further education might be a good idea comes from an opposite situation and faces a much more desperate moment of truth. We've encountered very few such cases in all the years we've run the program, but the example sheds some light on the limits of our students' ability to reconsider their options. One semester a functionally illiterate man slipped past our eighth-grade competency check. His probation officer was persuaded by his client's appetite for conversation that the course would be good for him.

Jason was a garrulous fellow, perhaps as a compensation for his lack of fluency as a reader and writer. Arriving early the first night, he sat in the front row and began talking nonstop, to no one in particular, until Bert called us to order. As the reading and writing requirements were explained, Jason began to fidget, and finally blurted out, "I can't do that."

"Oh, sure you can!" said Bert and I in one breath, and Bert assured everyone that homework needn't be more than an honest attempt to say what you think in a few sentences. To demonstrate how painless it would be, he immediately handed out the class exercise I mentioned a few pages back:

> *What are the most important things a child needs in order to grow up "normal"—a healthy, happy, worthy person?*

Jason signed his name on the attendance sheet that night, but he sat staring at his hands while the rest of us made our lists.

The following week Jason came running into the room out of breath and late for class, just as Neville used to do. We were already handing out bluebooks when he slid into his seat, and we greeted him with a grin, "Okay, time to write." At once Jason began to cough—a strange dry cough brought on, I supposed, by running from the bus stop in the cold weather. It sounded like it would work itself out, but Jason jumped up and left the room to get a drink of water. We were busy writing when he returned a few minutes later to gather up his belongings and hurry out the door, saying he had to go home, he was sick. Early the next day he went to the courthouse and confessed to his probation officer that he could not write.

At our next meeting Bert took him out in the hall for a one-on-one session, Jason dictating while Bert wrote. After this warm-up exercise Bert handed him the pencil, and Jason froze.

Jason's immobility/flight reaction had nothing to do with his ability to form letters and words. He could sign his name and produce a flowing cursive, so long as it wasn't "writing"—just as stutterers can often sing or recite poems, words not "theirs," with fluency. What Jason couldn't do was put his own thoughts directly on paper. We decided to keep him in the class anyway, taking the pressure off by telling him to concentrate on reading, which he did conscientiously. Often he was the first to raise his hand and ask what an author meant in some passage from our homework.

But Jason really did need to learn how to write. His panic reaction in our class was not new to him. On the contrary, the demand for words on paper was almost a daily occurrence in his life, as it is in all of our lives. Diversionary tactics, practiced for forty years, have taken over Jason's entire character, with disastrous consequences. His irritating loquaciousness, for instance, was obviously a smokescreen of words to hide wordlessness. After we made it clear that he would not have to write, he stopped babbling and his face cleared. Behind his frantic performance, Jason was an intelligent and likable person, however devious and self-thwarting.

After learning to trust us a bit, Jason asked for a list of adult literacy programs, determined to sign up. Here was a case where we felt that further education made sense, and his probation officer resolved to push him in that direction. But Jason's fear and evasiveness were stronger than his will to change his life or our determination to help him do it. Although the class seemed to bring out the best in him, he never could work up the courage to make the phone call. Within a few weeks after graduation he was in front of the judge again for driving with his license suspended, a crime that would probably lead to sixty days' incarceration. Would his resolve to learn to write be forgotten now, or would he build up his courage, like Malcolm, while doing his time? Maybe Jason is too old to learn, but I wish he could spend those sixty days in a literacy group instead of jail. Getting past his writing anxiety would probably bring an avalanche of other changes for him. Jason's been out of work for a year. If he could apply for and get a decent job, that would lead to other breakthroughs.

But his arrest for driving without a license indicates how the cards are stacked against him: although Jason may have kicked his marijuana habit, like other probationers who have served mandatory sentences for drug charges in our state, he isn't allowed to operate a motor vehicle for at least a year. Even if he does succeed in filling out a job application, without transportation and a clean record he's going to have a hard time finding work. Although success is not an impossible fantasy, the odds are very much against him.

Jason's case reveals some of the concerns we have in steering a probationer toward more schooling. How desperate is the need? Would school really help? Would it be worth the price? Can the probationer afford the time and effort? What about the pain of repeating old failures and facing new humiliations? Does a man like Jason dare to give up his defenses and become a vulnerable child again? Worse even than the shame, he exposes himself to the risk of a final defeat, inadequacy confirmed once and for all.

Let me return now to the case of Albert, who told us he wanted to go back to school to study "child development"—that is, to become the counselor he had imagined might help a "troubled" child. How could we not admire such an ambition? And yet, what if his hopes were based on a false conception of what school would actually do for him?

I've titled this chapter "Encouraging Failure" to highlight a disturbing irony built into the very idea of Changing Lives Through Literature, especially if we think that this implies further schooling. Let me conclude by looking more closely at Albert's fantasy of a college career that would lead to his working with children who might otherwise fall through the cracks.

Do we do a disservice to probationers by encouraging them to think that further education would improve their lot? By framing our program as a curriculum—reading and writing and discussion in a campus classroom—and by offering help getting into college, are we just setting these men up for another failure experience? I am not only thinking of those who decide to apply and then discover they can't afford it or are turned down. What about the ones who get in and find it's too hard, or not the boost they'd hoped for? What about those who decide against even trying, who say to themselves that it's too late, they've already fallen through the cracks? If they see themselves as having failed our "prep" program in advance, then instead of encouraging them we will have undermined their determination to change their lives.

Take the question one step further. What if a man succeeds in changing? What if school gives him new ways of thinking, believing, being in the world? What worries me is how such students might react when their changed selves are challenged by life—as they will be, for the society they must live in is not going to change. How many of us end up falling back into what we know best when life starts throwing curves at us? I'm not saying that the risk of change is too great to be taken. But let's be realistic—no one's basic character or lifetime habits are completely altered by higher education. And even more important, as our students who already have college degrees have discovered, a CORI file (Criminal Offender Record Information) trumps a Bachelor of Arts diploma every time when you're looking for a job. In short, society must change before our students are guaranteed a place in it by the usual routes.

When I first laid eyes on him, Albert seemed like a relatively young man to me, not much older than Luis or Anthony—still "college age." Later I realized that he was actually in his mid-forties. My mistake had more to do with Albert's demeanor than his face: there was something adolescent about his mixture of embarrassment and almost rapturous zeal. His speech was never quite under control, and, like Jason, once he got started he didn't know how to stop. Other students were impatient with him. They heard him out politely, but no one ever seconded anything he said, and when he began to talk you could see their eyes go blank. The classroom itself seemed to make him anxious, but his reaction was to cling to what he saw as the goals of the program—not a good sign.

So far as I could tell, Albert had no real aptitude for anything college offers or requires. His literacy level was probably adequate, but he wrote in clichés, and began repeating himself after a few sentences. His announced desire to study child development didn't seem to come from any actual experience with children so much as a yearning to redeem his own calamitous past.

At that first class, even before I knew any of this, I flagged Albert along with Trevor as someone to worry about, because his best hopes for himself seemed so unrealistic, and I went home that night wondering once again whether our program was misleading in its format and nominal aims. The solution for someone like Albert is not more schooling. School is part of his problem, and more schooling, even *better* schooling, isn't going to solve it.

A few probationers might blossom in a university setting and even crank up their earning power and self-esteem a notch or two, as the average college graduate does, but having a black face and a felony conviction makes it a gamble that looks bad to men who know how to calculate the odds. Whether deterred by the high stakes or by unpleasant memories of previous schooling, the great majority of probationers are not going to take the risk. Given their official designation in the system, it's only natural that they think of themselves as failures; society has judged them just as their teachers used to do, all the more insistently because their mistakes have escalated to offenses.

In our program, then, let's not punish them further but try to help them see that academic failure is not a reliable measure of intelligence or an insurmountable barrier to useful and responsible lives. Traditional schooling, with its tests and ranking, guarantees that most students will be disappointed, not just the least prepared or docile. Not everyone can get an A or even a B or C. Some will fall even lower, under the arbitrary level of "normal" on the so-called curve of best to worst.

If we hope to make our program a success for everyone, without exception, we must avoid this conventional model of performance according to standards set in advance. Encouraging students to regard Changing Lives as a stepping-stone to further schooling will send some students back into the trap that guarantees relative failure for all but those at the very top, while the rest will have already "failed" by refusing to try. Our challenge is to bypass the punitive criteria of success without undermining ordinary human powers. Instead of encouraging fantasies about the future, we must help our students take advantage of their present strengths—intuition, curiosity, and mutual aid—which can be put to use, here and now, exploring new ideas and sharing new feelings, perhaps in the long run establishing new habits and goals in life.

# Chapter 5

# *Sentenced to School*

We begin, as I have explained, with an emphasis on childhood and its vulnerabilities. Although we follow the probationers into whatever concerns them—parents or peers, Frederick Douglass or Malcolm X—sooner or later our reading brings us to the question of how people learn what they need to know in life, and how much of that knowledge comes through compulsion or punishment, aimed at instilling discipline or exacting obedience at home, in school, and on the streets.

These are not abstract ideas but the conditions of our work—where students are coming from, what they are reading, where they are headed. The relations between self-discipline, coercion, and obedience were key issues for Frederick Douglass and Malcolm X, and learning how they dealt with them gives each probationer a new perspective on his own life, a chance to examine how those same concerns have led to the present crossroads—and to think about what can be done now, to make a fresh start. The really sore spots—what it means to be sentenced by a judge, how it feels to have your freedom taken away, to be treated like a child—we leave to each man's private consideration. Our formulation is framed impersonally, a series of leading questions about schooling and its lessons:

> *What is society's responsibility in setting and enforcing educational standards? Is the use of force necessary to make children learn? Can a genuine desire to learn be encouraged through enforced attendance, assignments, etc.?*

This way of putting it draws attention away from their present plight, but as we talk, it dawns on some students that these issues have a direct bearing on our program, where punishment and schooling seem once again to go hand in hand. Although no one has been forced to join us, Changing Lives Through Literature certainly constitutes "serving time" since it is a substitute for six months on probation. Newspapers delight in such headlines as SENTENCED TO SCHOOL, or THROW THE BOOK AT THEM, where the doubled-edged irony should remind us that compulsory education can make school feel like prison too.

In many of the courts where it operates, Changing Lives is literally an "alternative sentencing" experiment, beginning when judges offer the option of school instead of jail. In the Dorchester program, however, students are not enrolled from the prisoner's dock. They have already received their jail sentences—sometimes long ones, sometimes suspended ones—and are on probation by the time probation officers identify them as men who are in earnest about changing their lives, and literate enough to read a book. This recruiting process helps set the tone for our classes. Students may come to us full of doubt, but they've chosen to come, they're already moving their feet in a new direction. Both the desire and the doubt are essential if they are to take their studies to heart instead of simply going through the motions.

Most probationers are willing to make the bargain: ten weeks in school for six months off probation sounds like a good deal. Many of them feel accused every time they pass the metal detectors at the courthouse, to report with proofs of residence and employment, pay their fees or restitution installments, and maybe have a surprise urine test sprung on them. They'd prefer the vague anxiety of school, where there is always a seat in the back of the room. That's not the only advantage. Although any restitution ordered by the court must be met, other payments may be waived for students in our program. Checking in with a probation officer simply by coming to class means they do not have to pay the usual interview fee, as much as $50 a month (or the equivalent in community service at minimum wage rates). That's $300 saved when they complete the program.

Without these incentives we'd have an empty classroom, for the average Dorchester probationer would never go back to school by choice. There were metal detectors at some of those gates too, and authorities constantly checking up on them. On opening night of Changing Lives everyone is braced for the chill that comes when a dungeon is unlocked after a long time. Once we get past that first shiver, however, it's not so bad. Although we do in fact transport students back in time to the schools they hated in childhood, it turns out that confronting the bad memories is a way of laying them to rest.

Half a dozen years ago something happened in one of our classes that dramatizes how these elements of past and present, hope and dread, can come to a new resolution. One of the probationers that semester was responsible for child care—I think his wife worked nights as a nurse—and so each week he brought his two kids with him to class. They were both boys, about eight and ten, and while we talked about Frederick Douglass and Malcolm X, their father gave them books to read, or pencils and paper just like everyone else. The boys busied themselves diligently, and so did we, each very much aware of the other generation, but they had no way of knowing the effect they were having on us. Our conversations were more focused than usual, all of us more thoughtful and more circumspect in our speech. We could show respect for these youngsters by straightening up in our chairs and being serious.

But their presence also revived the past in a particularly vivid way. Their father always brought them to campus a good half hour early. When the rest of us arrived, we'd find the boys standing in front of the blackboard eyeing a sentence chalked in big block letters, with a blank to be filled in. There would be hints for the right word—a couple of letters as clues to its spelling. Sometimes the game was easy, sometimes hard. We'd guess, silently, along with the boys, until it was time to start class.

What a strange combination of past and present! Detachment mixed with strong feeling. Becoming small again, yet no longer afraid of getting the wrong answer and being humiliated in front of friends. This was the perfect prelude to our discussions of schooling and its consequences, a "play within a play" that helped us reconnect with our childhood selves. It was fun, but we also found ourselves confronting painful memories when we turned from the children to our books. An excerpt from Richard Wright's *Black Boy* would remind us that standing at the blackboard can be a terrifying experience too:

> "Write your name," the teacher called to me.
>
> I lifted the white chalk to the blackboard and, as I was about to write, my mind went blank, empty; I could not remember my name, not even the first letter.

With or without Richard Wright to prompt them, probationers have their own memories of intimidation and panic in the classroom. Consider, for instance, the following episode from Neville's elementary school years. He unearthed it late in the semester, long after Luis and others had written up "one big lesson you learned in your childhood." In answer to that hopeful question Neville had nothing to say, but when we asked him for "A Crisis in My Life," he gave us this response:

> I loved school, but I just felt like I couldn't learn for some reason! . . . I had so many dreams as a little boy. I will never forget once when school was just about to let out, they passed out report cards in the Third Grade. And all the kids, my friends, were so happy about what they had gotten. And I couldn't wait to get home to show the family! When I opened to see what I had, which were all Fs, my teachers saw me just cover my face and say NAW! They let the class out and came to me, and gave me a long talk about trying a little harder next time if it meant so much.

Neville's crisis epitomizes what has happened to many of these students more gradually over their years in school. No matter how well-intentioned most teachers may be, the system itself, through its lockstep sequence of drills and tests, grades and report cards, is designed to kill the spirit and blame the victim. When his teachers convinced Neville that his failure was his own fault, the result was not that he tried harder but that he gave up trying altogether. And that's why he was so reluctant to hand in written work to us on Tuesday nights. Back in third grade again for ten weeks, he wasn't going to make a fool of himself this time if he could help it.

Expanding the headline writer's joke about school as a form of incarceration, we might dub our pedagogic experiment "returning to the scene of the crime": the windowless room with blackboard, desktop chairs, bluebooks, and pencils. Pencils! The word itself was enough to start someone like Jason desperately confessing his guilt, just as the dread of being confronted with evidence of his own stupidity rendered Neville speechless night after night. Don't say anything that can be used against you! Actually, Neville was secretly doing his homework—reading the assignments and even writing a few sentences every week—but since he rarely took the risk of turning anything in, we soon gave up on him as a reader or writer and concentrated on bringing him into the small group discussions, where he also kept a low profile. Until his "crisis" paper late in the semester, we simply assumed that, like Jason, he was permanently in hiding.

I need hardly point out the continuity from flunking in third grade, to being interrogated from a police cruiser, to facing charges at the courthouse. One thing leads to another; your report card becomes your rap sheet, with escalating consequences. Looking back, the path from stubbornness to felony may seem preordained. That's what many criminal sociologists think, a statistical slide from "Incorrigible" to "Recidivist." Although most of the probationers admit their guilt, they usually resist such labels, as baffled as Neville staring at the row of Fs on his report card. However pigheaded he may be, a boy of eight or ten is innocent—although not so long ago, believe it or not, a boy in third grade could be sent to Reform School for "stubbornness" (1940). As a grown man in front of a judge today, he may have done something truly reprehensible, often breaking his own moral code as well as that of society. And after years of failing to meet society's demands, first as schoolboys and now as adults, they come to our program dreading a new tribunal combining the worst of school and court. What could Changing Lives offer them that would not threaten their autonomy and self-respect, once more taking their fate out of their own hands?

Our challenge is to halt the cycle of demand, disobedience, accusation, and chastisement these men have been repeating since childhood. But where to begin? Mandated programs for alcoholics, drug users, and batterers tend to focus on symptoms rather than causes, rubbing their noses in their vices and crimes. Even if they've asked for it and deserve it since they're not children anymore, if the point is to change who you are, does it make sense to begin by giving up personal dignity and accepting the identity inscribed on a criminal record?—

poss cont sub

poss to distribute class b

disord pers

drinking alcohol in public

larceny mv

a&b

assault dw

Our approach in Changing Lives begins at the opposite pole, inquiring into innocence, not guilt. Probationers need to see the pattern in their history of "failure experiences" without letting their most recent trauma blot out everything else. We begin at the beginning, asking what every child needs, and how we acquire our righteousness, courage, and self-esteem. Where do these virtues come from? This leads us by the second week to the central issue of the entire program, although we do not proclaim it as such:

> *When is the use of force necessary to teach the difference between right and wrong? Can a genuine desire to be "good" be encouraged through force? What role should society (church, school, government, courts) play?*

When such questions call forth memories like Neville's, of how things originally went wrong, we try to frame them as problems of ethics and public policy rather than personal history. Obviously, there are implications for our immediate situation as well, since we are questioning the use of coercion as a means of rehabilitation while we are experimenting with it practically. In class discussions we talk about child-rearing and schooling in an analytical way, thinking of our childhoods or of how we want to raise our own children. No one ever mentions how it feels to be back in school, with demands altered and stakes reconfigured, but that is our real concern.

Thinking about how children learn what they need to know, and the part coercion and punishment may have played in their own cases, students often find they are not the dismal failures or miscreants their report cards said they were. It's not necessary to talk about it directly. We can count on ordinary common sense, colloquial eloquence, and the give-and-take of problem-solving quickly reasserting themselves in our classroom, once students realize they don't have to jump through the hoops of traditional schooling.

Our aim is to give each man a chance to think better of himself while simultaneously dispelling the illusion that success in school is the only route to respectability. We aren't trying to get people back on the educational track, but to let them judge for themselves what it would mean to return to school, a question that asks them to assess their own lives—*Who am I, really, and what kind of future do I want for myself?*

In provoking such reflections we send probationers mixed signals. Is it school or isn't it? Although we tell them that there will be no tests, corrections, or grades, they can see for themselves the familiar schoolroom. When we pass around pencils and bluebooks, they all begin to wonder: *Maybe six months on probation would be easier after all?* On the other hand, every one of them is fed up with life on the streets, where they have to be constantly on guard just to stay out of trouble. Though wary of our program too, they're looking for an escape route, not only off probation but out of the maze of folly and vice most of them have been wandering in.

Keep in mind that these are not hardened men, TV mobsters. Although some may arrive with an "attitude," no one has been recruited to our program unless his probation officer thinks he's ready to turn a corner—fearful of another term in prison or simply soul-sick. A few are still cocky, but most probationers come to Changing

Lives deeply shaken by their encounter with judgment and punishment. The majority have been incarcerated, some for long periods, and everyone has had at least a taste of "lock-up." They all agree with what one student wrote recently: "Being in jail is like being dead with your eyes open." When they join our class, these men already know they are at a critical moment in their lives. It's up to them to decide whether they're hearing a "wake-up call" or merely facing another ten weeks of "being dead with your eyes open."

Changing Lives Through Literature meets their ambivalence with ambiguity. Our schoolroom confronts them with a "safe emergency situation"—someone has dialed 911, the alarm bells are ringing, but there's no fire, no police cars racing to the scene. Although challenged by homework, recitation, and writing in class, each student can move at his own pace, without anyone breathing down his neck. Our program intentionally triggers anxiety and self-doubt, but by contacting those panicky feelings in a safe, supportive atmosphere, we hope to tie them down to reality, the first step in laying them to rest.

To create a truly *safe* emergency means avoiding the temptation to encourage someone like Albert, who wants to return to the *actual* emergency of school. He won't be ready for that until he finds his own solid ground, rather than capitulating to institutional authority, which is Albert's first impulse. Over the years we've discovered that strong initial resistance to the Changing Lives program is much more promising than eager acquiescence. There is a huge difference between learning to take orders and learning what you need to know. Probationers who come with a chip on their shoulders are frequently the ones who make the ringing valedictory speeches at the end of the semester, full of pride and determination.

Before that can happen the student must have already taken charge of his own learning experience, just as Douglass taught himself to read and write. It is of no use whatever to force a man to read a book "for his own good"—not even if it mirrors his life in every detail. A book can play a part in self-discovery only if students can make it truly theirs, not just another instrument of indoctrination. Each man must search out his truth for himself, just as he must find his own courage to change.

In order to work through a new set of attitudes, students must start where they really are, understandably suspicious of the book we put in their hands. One or two may have read Frederick Douglass in some college course, or in jail, and a few others will have heard him praised in church as a culture hero, like Dr. King. But no matter what fanfare introduces it, all these students are leery of homework. When we hand out copies of the *Narrative* on opening night, there's always some rebel who mutters, for all to hear, "You mean we have to read *all this*?" Looking round the room, I see other faces brightening with interest. He may not speak for everyone, but his challenge is what they've been waiting for, someone to confront the authorities and test the limits. It's what we're waiting for too.

On the first night of each new semester almost all the questions about Changing Lives have to do with the amount of work it will entail, the exact nature of the reward, and the precise provisions of the contract—to them, like the terms of their sentence. Puzzled by our motives and reluctant to commit themselves without first reading the fine print, the men want to know just what we mean by "Changing Lives," and why we're there—what's in it for the teachers? These are not questions they ever thought of asking in high school, and once they ask them now, they have already begun to understand that this class will be very different from anything they're used to.

Such questions contain a challenge: Who are *you* to say that *my* life needs changing? Unless we can answer this challenge, it will be hard for probationers to accept their own desire to change. If you suspect that someone is trying to manipulate you, the natural response is to dig your heels in. And indeed, these are questions that teachers *ought* to ask themselves before daring to meddle in other people's lives.

When it's my turn to field questions, here's my answer: I believe racism has always been and still is the most urgent problem Americans face, and that it's largely responsible for the current crisis in our criminal justice system. So this is a place to work for change—change in the whole system, beginning where we're sitting right now. That's one answer, the starting point for me. Later on in the semester, more personal motives will come into play, and I tell them that too: I expect to enjoy their company, and value our weekly meetings, talking seriously about things that matter to us. If we take the risk of trusting each other enough to really listen, then we may all grow and change in important ways.

They also want to know what our relation to the system is. Who pays? Why would the courts spend money on them, and what have we promised to do for that money? In short, isn't Changing Lives just another cog in the machine that teaches obedience through punishment and humiliation?

Although politicians in the State House are careful to maintain their public image of being "tough on crime"—here as elsewhere, they have passed the mandatory sentencing laws that fill our jails with first-offenders convicted of nonviolent crimes—nonetheless, in good budget years the legislature has been willing to spend a bit for our alternative sentencing experiment—anywhere from $50,000 to $100,000 for the dozen or more Changing Lives programs in our state—less than what it costs to keep a handful of men like these in prison for a similar amount of time. The program runs mainly on voluntary labor, so this has been enough to provide small stipends for instructors, along with books and other class materials, and some overall administrative assistance so that the various jurisdictions can keep in touch via a newsletter and annual training conferences. Depending on the appropriation, a teacher gets anywhere from $500 to $1,500 for a semester's work. Bert and I take turns doing the typing and feedback, so one of us is always sitting in as a volunteer, and in times of fiscal crisis we both donate our time. Others who help out have all been unpaid, though in recent years probation officers have been awarded "points" toward the extramural obligation that comes with the job.

Truth be told, I'm uneasy taking any pay at all from a "law and order" regime biased against people of color and the poor. Can such a system be reformed from within? Where should one draw the line between reform and complicity? These issues complicate the social meaning of our program, and probationers are always surprised and interested to hear them spelled out. For some it's a way to gain perspective on their own problems of change and their own attitudes toward Society with a capital "S." They come into our program brooding on their personal experiences in court or jailhouse, and it can be a salutary shock to realize that the criminal justice system is not a rigid and unrelenting instrument of retribution but an evolving institution, deeply flawed but open to criticism and change.

Whatever their opinion of the courts, there are always some students who view the entire social order as rigged against them, though they rarely have more than newspaper headlines for arguments or their private lives as evidence. For these angry men—and perhaps even more for those who passively accept their fate—the very notion of a comprehensive critique of society can open up a new perspective. The point is not to condone or make light of criminal acts they may have committed, nor to weigh them against their consequences, but to challenge these men to climb to higher ethical ground than anger or despair. They are not the only ones whose lives have been hard, and thinking about how justice is dispensed to entire social classes that they themselves represent is a step toward taking responsibility as conscientious members of the larger society, rather than viewing themselves as its victims or outcasts.

While hoping to promote a new attitude toward their situation as criminal offenders, we also attempt to demystify the system itself by presenting ourselves as its personal embodiment—a little group of real people who serve as teachers, probation officers, and judges in society's impersonal institutions. For many of these students, this will be the only time in their lives that a teacher or other authority figure enters into open-ended dialogue with them, outside the rules of role and format. This too is part of what I am calling the safe emergency situation. Although we may share our experiences of growing up, being schooled, and dealing with what life demands, authority relations have not vanished in our classroom—a teacher is still a teacher, a judge still a judge.

Teachers and probation officers inevitably remind students of all the admonishers out of their past, but it's much more emphatic when we add a judge to the row of authorities. Our judge has been the Honorable Thomas May, sitting at the Dorchester District Court.

Although he waits a few weeks before making his appearance, letting the men get comfortable with each other first, Judge May attends every session thereafter, and he has been doing so for half a dozen years, outlasting several instructors and probation officers who have come and gone.

Tom May is not a formal man, yet his presence changes the atmosphere in our classes. By virtue of his title and office, he certainly does represent the court, and some of the men in our group are likely to have been tried and sentenced before him. But Tom's authority sits so lightly on him that students are not intimidated. His bearing is confident and respectful, and his role is simply to be who he is, without his black robes and not towering over us from the bench, but on equal footing in discussions and doing the homework like everyone else.

Here then is the very epitome of a safe emergency situation: the judge in his sweater and slacks, deep-voiced but not commanding silence, white-haired but vigorous and trim as anyone in the room, and like some of the students half his age, an ex-Marine and proud of it. Yet reminders of his authority hover round him like an aura. For instance, he's the only one in the room to be addressed as "Judge" rather than called by his first name—but it's the actual man who responds, and not "his Honor." Students sit across from him in the small groups and look him in the eye, argue with him, listen, and judge for themselves.

Tom May grew up in a working-class family in the Boston area, one of nine children. He put himself through school, worked as a police officer while in law school, raised his own family of six kids, served in the military in the early 1960s, and came to the bench with a wide knowledge of life. Dorchester is the busiest criminal court in Massachusetts, yet he has devoted one night a week, semester after semester, to the men in our program. In our graduation ceremony at the courthouse, he tells us why, explaining to the probationers and the entire courtroom that contact on a personal level with those who might come before him to be judged, as many as sixty a day, reminds him that he is dealing with human beings, not "cases." Guilty or innocent, their lives are full of pain and suffering just like the rest of us, mistakes they regret, anger, and self-pity they yearn to be done with. Tom brings our semester to a close with these sobering reflections on the nature of public justice, those who administer it, and those who come before it as offenders. Half an hour later, the safe emergency situation will have become a real emergency for the courtroom audience listening to him, all those who have come that morning for justice. And as we listen to Tom's farewell to the graduating probationers, we all know that some of them might be back again before the year is out.

In our weekly sessions Tom rarely speaks in the free-for-all discussions we sometimes convene at the end of class, but sooner or later everyone gets a chance to hear his voice in the small groups. I think it's important for each man to have several sessions with him, especially the younger ones, whose relations to authority are more likely to be prickly. To a twenty-year-old black probationer who has been in trouble half his life with teachers and principals, social workers, police, and judges, Tom May represents the entire social order and its power to decide your fate. He can be a cautionary influence without robbing a young man of his pride. A dude like Trevor can ask the judge about his own experience in the streets, in the Marines, as a father, as a citizen angry at the politicians, as a judge worried about injustice. He can argue with him about Malcolm X or the plea-bargaining system. Often the liveliest conversations occur in Tom's small groups, where some probationers are finding their tongues for the first time in a classroom. From across the room in my own group I can hear Tom's even voice alternating with their excited speeches. To my mind this is the nitty-gritty of a safe emergency situation, in which a man on the defensive can feel his way to a new attitude toward old enemies.

Ironically, the presence of so many kinds of authority in our classroom has the effect of reducing the level of anxiety rather than increasing it. Any single one of us—judge, probation officer, or teacher—might well loom in a threatening way, but as a group we tend to cancel each other out. No one person wields ultimate authority here: the judge takes a back seat; the probation officers announce the rules but then become members of the class, reading and writing like everyone else; and even the teacher's voice is muted by the fact that there are two of us, one in front of the class, one sitting with the students.

This fragmentation of authority is another way that the emergency situation—being in school, confronted by a judge, reporting to a probation officer—can be made safe for these men. It's a bit like having no father but five uncles, all of whom share authority over a young boy. With so many father figures in the family, the power is diluted and less fearful. There's always someone to take your side—at least in the imagination, where it counts most.

The doubling of teachers and probation officers in our class illustrates how this works in practice. If I'm up in front moderating a discussion, Bert is in a chair with the class, reminding everyone that a teacher is just another person, only temporarily in charge. With the probation officers, it's even more dramatic, because of the character of our particular staff. Bert and I have our own styles of teaching, but the difference is negligible compared to the marked contrast of demeanor in the two probation officers who work with us, John Christopher and James "Bobby" Spencer.

John Christopher stands straight as an arrow, strong and handsome, alert to everything going on around him and even a bit steely-eyed. He's the one who announces the rules at the beginning of every semester, and if need be, enforces them:

Attend class on time
Read the assignment
Turn off all cell phones
Respect everyone in the room
Arrive sober and straight

Most important of all for him is respect, the foundation of our democratic classroom and the reason why everyone is expected to come on time, sober and straight, and prepared to take part in the discussion. John's insistence that each man give others the respect due them is a reflection of his passionate concern for social justice. Students soon discover that his stern countenance is not bent on them but on the social order that has failed them, in its persistent racism and its neglect of problems that all the poor face—the cycle of inadequate schooling, housing, health care, and employment.

Bobby Spencer comes from the same world of hard knocks that John grew up in, but his attitude toward it seems quite different, at least on first impression. He too is disturbed by the way that bias in social and economic realities can lead to repeated confrontations with the criminal justice system in a long downward spiral. But Bobby's posture is not as intimidating as John's. His optimism and good cheer are irresistible, and the probationers seem to trust him immediately, putting aside their usual suspicion of all those associated with the courts. They quickly realize that he is on their side. In Bobby's view there's not a probationer who can't turn his life around, get a better job, work things out with his family, go to college, shake his bad habits, and find contentment. Bobby's serious practice as a Buddhist no doubt contributes to his equanimity, but the buoyancy seems to come from the depths of his character. He himself has been through a lot—most recently a kidney transplant after several years on dialysis. Absent a year while recuperating, he came back weak and emaciated but the same cheerful, upbeat Bobby, sure that the world is okay and that people can bounce back from anything. Probationers in his discussion group are liable to get pretty boisterous, and at graduation ceremonies, it's Bobby who brings the camera.

I've described our volunteer team here in order to suggest how a Changing Lives class might feel to a probationer whose past experience with institutions like school or court has taught him to expect the worst. Just as the probationers come to the first meeting wearing "masks" of impassivity, so do staff members have the impersonal look of our official roles when we walk in on opening night—teacher, probation officer, judge. After a few weeks all the masks and roles are put to one side, but not forgotten. Of course it makes a difference who actually stands revealed—the personalities we bring to the encounter—but the outcome is not determined by any particular style or attitude so much as by the sheer fact of close contact. Many different character types would serve the same ends of mutual discovery and reassurance.

The essential ingredients of the safe emergency situation are structural rather than personal factors. What is necessary for fruitful exchange is a format that gives everyone a voice in conversation about matters that have brought us together. The "emergency" comes from awareness of power relations always hovering in the background, and the sense of being trapped that every probationer feels. The "safety" of the classroom is only provisional, and to some it may seem merely a pretense, but a few weeks of earnest talk are enough to establish a network of mutual trust with its own strength and stability, as real as the institutional structures and social fabric that constitute the "situation" in which we all must live.

# Chapter 6

# *Let That Be a Lesson to You!*

At our fourth meeting we move from our broad inquiry into child-rearing and early learning experiences to consider a narrower—and very problematic—aspect of it, seen from two different angles: the sources of cruelty, and the nature of punishment. Children are often cruel to each other, or to helpless creatures in their power—and sometimes punished for it. Those who punish them are often cruel too—yet rarely punished. And, of course, cruelty and punishment typically take violent forms and are not limited to children, though most people get their first slaps and whacks before they are old enough to know the words for them. "That'll teach you!" "Have you learned your lesson now?"

Our readings include two chapters in which Frederick Douglass describes the bloody whippings administered to slaves by their masters, read alongside a passage from Richard Wright's *Black Boy* recounting how, no older than five, he strangled a stray kitten in a noose hung on a nail.

Cruelty was Richard's perverse means of defying his father, who routinely treated the boy with offhand contempt—as if he were a stray kitten. Barely awake after his night job, and disturbed by the kitten's mewing, his father had roared, "Kill that damn thing!" The boy has seen his chance to get even with his father, and now he exults,

> I had had my first triumph over my father. I had made him believe that I had taken his words literally. He could not punish me now without risking his authority. I was happy because I had at last found a way to throw my criticism of him into his face. I had made him feel that, if he whipped me for killing the kitten, I would never give serious weight to his words again. I had made him know that I felt he was cruel and I had done it without his punishing me.

That night, although his father has characteristically washed his hands of the affair, his mother insists that Richard bury his victim in the backyard, forcing him to deal with the consequences of his act—the stiff body of the kitten, the dark grave, the horror of mortality.

Next to these grim reports from real life we read a jailhouse fiction by Maxim Gorky, the great popular author of revolutionary Russia, who himself had served more than one prison sentence for political activism, though the charge might read vagrancy. Gorky's study of cruelty centers on the convict who gives his name to the story, "Notch." A practical jokester who dominates the prison yard, Notch finds himself upstaged one day by a stray kitten the inmates have adopted as their mascot. In a bid to regain the limelight, Notch proposes to dip the kitten in a bucket of paint—a bit of fun everyone laughs at, until it becomes apparent the poor kitten will die of his sticky green bath. Then Notch's audience turns on him, and they beat him mercilessly for what all had applauded at first.

These two stories shift uneasily back and forth—kittens, young boys, childish men; clowning and high spirits; nooses and beatings, scapegoating and mob violence; guilt intertwined with innocence, perversions of justice, torments of conscience, and utter moral obliquity side by side. Read against the background of slavery and its routine cruelty, Wright and Gorky fill in the emotional nuances of punishment administered to maintain order and authority.

To cap it all, we read an excerpt from another famous Russian author, Dostoyevsky's *The House of the Dead*. The passage describes running the gauntlet, a typical punishment in the Siberian prison camp where Dostoyevsky was sent for his revolutionary activities. Sadism grows like toadstools in such institutions.

All of our texts are written in the first person and based on real experiences, though Wright's childhood has been slightly reimagined and Gorky's anecdote may have been invented. Whether case studies or fictions, in these stories powerless victims are seen to be as cruel and vindictive as their oppressors when they get their chance, and the effect of reading them side by side is to merge the roles somewhat, suggesting that cruelty and the desire to punish are not limited to those in power but easily aroused in the weak and oppressed as well. Our homework question for the week addresses this confluence:

> *What causes cruelty? Why do people inflict pain on others? Is it out of anger and hatred, or for other reasons?*

Framed by this psychological inquiry, our opening exercise shifts the emphasis from causes to effects, and opens up the problematic nature of punishment meant to "teach a lesson" to someone:

> *What does punishment do to its victims? Does it make any difference whether or not the punishment is deserved?*

At one time or another almost everyone in our classes has been at the wrong end of a belt or a switch. What can be learned from it? Sooner or later we get people thinking about their own attitudes and behavior—toward children in particular—in the light of their current condition as disobedient offenders being punished. As the readings make clear, it is not easy for people to learn compassion for others from their own suffering. By the same token, belief in institutionalized forms of punishment, purported to correct but often merely brutalizing the spirit, goes deep in most of us, even though we ourselves may have felt its numbing sting.

I want to quote some of the comments on punishment students wrote for this class. The perspective that seemed to intrigue them most was that of the opening exercise—"What does punishment do to its victims?" and "What difference does it make if the punishment is deserved?" Given this emphasis, it is noteworthy how many shy away from any mention of their own experience of being punished, although of course it is always hovering in the background:

> Punishment can do a lot of things to its victims, because it could set them straight or make them just don't care about anything anymore. (*Willy*)

> What does punishment do to its victims? I feel as though some people learn from punishment and some don't care about the punishment because they've been in worse situations. (*Trevor*)

> I think it makes the victims angry and sometimes want to know why he or she is punished. In some cases victims do not know why, but if the punishment is deserved, I think it should be in a respectable way. Some victims deserve more punishment than others. (*Charles*)

> If you're being punished for nothing, it might make you turn out the same way, punishing others for no reason. (*Randy*)

> Being punished can destroy some people. Punishment can send them on a very revengeful path, so that they will always be in the situation to bear punishment. (*Deighton*)

> Punishment scars a person for life. It is pain that will never go away. I think punishment traumatizes its victims in a vicious way. (*José*)

> Punishment is to make a kid understand right from wrong, and it's also to teach a lesson to the kids when they do something wrong. But from what I know, punishment doesn't always work.
>
> Does it make any difference whether or not the punishment is deserved? Yes, it does make a difference, because if a child does something that isn't that serious, they don't deserve to get punished. Whoever punishes someone whether or not the punishment is deserved, they should get punished. (*Anthony*)

> People make mistakes. Systems can fail, and not give fair punishment. What is deserved punishment? Who are we to punish people? Who are we to say when punishment is deserved or not? (*Harry*)

Of all of these answers, Anthony's was the only one that concentrated exclusively on childhood, though he flip-flopped between identification with the child who receives punishment and the parent who administers it. "They should get punished!" One can still hear the angry little boy in Anthony, punished for "something that isn't that serious."

No matter what their attitudes toward punishment's long-term effects, most of these men are believers in its use "to teach a lesson to the kids when they do something wrong," as Anthony puts it. Moreover, when you ask men in our program what has led them, at least for the present, to want a change in their lives, many of them will say that being punished by imprisonment has furnished the impetus, as it did for Malcolm. If you pursue the question, however, it becomes a lot more complicated. I once asked a man why his first two prison terms hadn't taught him anything, only the third. "It's not just prison that makes the difference then, is it?" He thought a moment, taken aback. Finally he said, "You have to be ready. The first time I was incarcerated, I didn't take it seriously. I met my friends there, people I knew from the streets. I saw it as a playground."

A number of factors had combined to open this man's eyes during his third term. He was older now and had taken on family responsibilities he would be unable to fulfill in prison. That hurt. And this time his sentence had been longer, two years, harder to wait out, more time to think. There was one more ingredient that seemed to serve as catalyst for all the others. He mentioned it as an afterthought, a sudden flash of memory that shed light on his whole story. During his second imprisonment he had met an older inmate who looked at him intently and told him, "Young fella, you'll be back. I'll see you again here." He paid no heed at the time, but when he did in fact return for a third stretch, he found himself thinking about the prophecy. Somehow that helped the lesson finally sink in. At first I thought he was telling me that there was something mystical at work, the hand of fate, and maybe that was how he saw it, but the truth is probably much more prosaic: he realized at last that he had become a repeat offender, a recognizable type—the jailbird—whose future had begun to close in on him.

You could see it in his eyes. Yes, prison taught him a lesson. I don't think you could quite say that his spirit had been broken, but his new resolve didn't come without a price that was a good deal higher than the pain and suffering of two years in prison.

Many of these probationers have similar stories written on their faces, but not everyone knows how to read the moral in the mirror. For some like this man, it's essential to give it a name—"repeat offender" or, as our program proposes, "changing your life"—without which they might simply live it through without the self-recognition that shapes character. As José reminds us, in most cases there will be scars like the stripes on his back that Frederick Douglass used to bare to abolitionist audiences from the lecture platform. And others are surely reporting their own experience when they tell us that the punished man finds it hard to give up his anger and desire for revenge. Not everyone finds a cause like Douglass and Malcolm did.

Taking it out on others is already a pattern in some probationers, and not just those who are here because they are batterers or brawlers.

In all these cases the undesirable effects of punishment can coincide with a new determination to change one's character. That, of course, is the public justification for our punitive criminal justice system and the mandated sentences for first-offense, nonviolent, drug-related crimes. A beaten man finally decides to abandon the life that has led him to disaster over and over. The great risk, however, is that punishment can numb the spirit just as it can the body. It's significant that Willy and Trevor choose the same words for this result: those who succumb just "don't care about anything anymore." People in this state of despair sometimes lose touch with their own humanity. Then they can be ruthless, perhaps irredeemable. Despair is not called "the unpardonable sin" for nothing. We find relevant case studies in all of the authors read this week, in Wright and Gorky and Dostoyevsky. Even Frederick Douglass writes of being reduced, by unrelenting labor and repeated beatings, to the spiritual condition of a brute.

On the evening that we talk about punishment and its effects, I sit with Ross, José, and Trevor, each of whom has begun to speak more unreservedly by this, our fourth, meeting. Ross has been absent the previous week, and so he has not read the stories or written a response, but he has his own story of punishment to report to the rest of us.

Typically enough, our conversation wanders off almost immediately, following the lead of Trevor, who likes to avoid the subject even when—or perhaps especially when—he has something important to say about it. He's in a talkative mood tonight. He tells us that he has a twin brother and that his childhood was full of confusions of identity. Like other children, the boys were often punished, but in their case the point was blunted by the fact that Trevor and his brother were frequently blamed for each other's misdemeanors. What a multitude of lessons were thereby taught! He still revels in the fact that he could get away with something because of his face—not just a twin but a narcissist. And he is extraordinarily handsome. At one point he laughs, throws up his arms in a gesture of surrender mixed with glee, and exclaims, "No! I still haven't learned. I don't think about anybody but myself. People are always telling me I'm selfish. I am!"

He grins. "I'm no good in relationships either, know what I mean?" His revelation is half boast, half cry for help. For all his bravado, Trevor is desperate. Last time in Bert's group he talked about his lousy job, how he brings home in a week what he used to make in an hour selling drugs. Bert thinks he's teetering on the brink of going back to the streets. The jobless rate in our classes is 30 to 50 percent: for every eight employed there are usually four looking for work and four who've given up looking. How long before Trevor comes to the point of not caring about anything anymore?

In my group tonight all of us are fathers. José's girlfriend is eight months pregnant. Trevor has a young daughter, though he rarely sees her after splitting with her mother. As Ross tells his story, Trevor's giddy sense of his own folly gradually wilts;

he sinks back in his chair, frowning and at a loss for words. Ross is old enough to be Trevor's father, and his own daughter must be about Trevor's age. All of us are more and more aware of this generation gap, as we realize that Ross is offering his own life as a warning to these younger men.

Ross has been married thirty years. He's held a job, raised a family, survived. What he has to tell us is not framed as some lesson that punishment has taught him, but the truth of life itself, as he sees it. In his younger days, he used to think that he had done his job as a man if he provided the basics—a place to live, food and clothing, some money to spend. A man has those responsibilities, so he thought, but after that he can do what he likes. He bares his white, crooked teeth in a big smile as he turns to Trevor: "Once I was just like you, full of myself." Ross doesn't say what his vices were, but booze and drugs and women were surely part of the picture, just as they are with Trevor. Nor does he tell us how he got in trouble with the law half a dozen years ago, only that the experience was a terrible shock to him.

His jail sentence was six months, he says, which doesn't explain why he's still on probation. There's been some new offense—probably domestic violence—but no one asks about it. What he wants to tell us doesn't have to do with his vices or crimes. His message has to do with the other side of male pride and family responsibility. He repeats one sentence over and over, the big lesson life has taught him: "I should have listened to my wife."

Although he never says exactly what his wife said to him, it's pretty obvious that she said it many times over the years, and that he heard it as nagging, when he heard it at all. He's ashamed to admit that he sometimes hit his wife to shut her up, but that too is obvious. Anyway, what he's trying to explain to Trevor has nothing to do with specific behavior, and we seem to have moved a long way from talking about punishment by this time.

Ross is saying that he was too cocky, riding for a fall. Also, this is not a lesson you can teach someone else, and neither Trevor nor José seems likely to take it to heart. That's apparent from the way they listen to him. They're not asking questions or offering their own perspectives. And yet they are more attentive than mere respect for Ross's age would require. We all know he's offering us the deepest truth that life has taught him, a lesson in failure and humility. No one wants to think it's a lesson meant for him, but merely hearing it from someone else can be profoundly unsettling. I too am moved by Ross's testimony, but because I'm the teacher my job is to get him to tell us more about how his life has changed; I'm not curious about what got him in trouble, only about what got him out. This is a lesson Trevor and José might profit from.

So I ask Ross what helped him see the light—was it the time in prison or the effect on his family? "Both," he answers, but he has nothing to add about his six months in jail, or his wife's distress. Instead, he describes one scene in the courtroom.

Other men, if they speak personally about punishment at all, want to talk about the lonely desperation of being locked in a cell. What Ross remembers is his trial, and his daughter there, seeing him "in shackles."

"Seeing your humiliation?" I ask.

"Seeing *her* humiliation," he replies.

It was this experience that changed him—and nearly broke him. His jail time was relatively short, followed by several years of probation. But this was the end of his marriage, and perhaps that was the real punishment. Afterwards he could barely function. More drinking . . . drugs . . . another arrest that has put him in our class. He doesn't try to explain, except to say that he's pulled himself together at last, found new ground to stand on, which he sums up in the phrase he keeps repeating, "Listen to your wife."

Ross's courtroom crisis could be called "hitting bottom"—from which it took him a long time to return, a different man. His self-respect was shattered and had to be rebuilt around a new sense of himself as a man, a family man without a family. Does he still see his children? He doesn't tell us.

Important as this new perspective has been, it's also clear from other things he says that his recovery from the depths of shame and despair has depended on finding decent work, one of the central problems both José and Trevor also face. Ross is a manual laborer and says it's too late for him to learn a skill or craft, but he's managed to get in a union, and that gives him better pay and more job security—not easy to come by when you have a felony record. He's proud of his work, and after the collapse of his masculine prestige when he went to jail, belonging to the union has no doubt helped to repair the damage, a badge of acceptance as well as a means of livelihood.

Ross's testifying rings true to my ear, but to Trevor it must sound like faraway music. Trevor has already told us that he's "selfish" and "no good at relationships." No longer living with the woman who had his child, he apparently sees his daughter very rarely. She doesn't mean what Ross's daughter meant to him. Trevor has a new girlfriend, but that relationship seems pretty fragile too. He tells us how he storms out of the house in a rage, picks up "some ho" to prove he doesn't need his girlfriend. Then, after his tantrum, back on the street, the quintessential moment arrives—rage abated, lust depleted, the world unchanged. He tells us all this indirectly, in his own macho style, but there's no disguising his dismay. Much of his charm lies in his inability to hide his innocence, however hard he tries. Behind his bluster a childish grin is always ready to spread across his handsome face, but his good nature won't last many years if he has to use it to defend his pride. Gloom comes fast on the heels of giddiness in his moods, and soon both will turn sour.

Others in the class, especially the older men, seem to be drawn to Trevor, and they too want to pass on lessons they've learned the hard way. Last week in Bert's group it was Albert who tried to teach *his* secret to him—work and determination. Like Ross, Albert is another man who has hit bottom, though it's not yet clear to me that he has found a mantra to serve him, like Ross's "listen to your wife." In any case, neither Ross nor Albert has managed to penetrate their classmate's pretense of not caring about anything. Trevor may suspect that he needs to find a similar meaning in his own life, but he doesn't believe he ever will. He doesn't even see the first step ahead of him. So what can be done? What is our class likely to do for him?

All through the telling of Ross's story José was no less interested than the rest of us, though the lesson was aimed straight at Trevor's predicament. Himself a young man about to become a father, and very much aware of the difficulty of finding work when you have a record, José has something to learn from Ross too, though his situation doesn't seem so desperate—not yet anyway. José is a very different sort of person after all. His face is solemn as Ross tells us the story of his humiliation in front of his daughter in the courtroom, an aspect of Ross's testimony that Trevor, with his highs and lows, has trouble hearing. I've already quoted part of what José wrote about punishment and cruelty for his homework this week. Let me now add the rest:

> What causes cruelty is the way you were raised. I think people inflict pain on others because, yes, sometimes it is out of anger, the way they feel at the moment. Hatred is such a harsh word. I think hatred comes from the deepest feelings. When you get that, you never show or express yourself to somebody.
>
> Punishment scars a person for life. It is pain that will never go away. I think punishment traumatizes its victims in a vicious way.

The emphasis José puts on hatred and its results makes me wonder whether he was treated badly at some point in childhood. The scar may have healed, but there's something that makes him reluctant to reveal himself, as I've seen now in two separate conversations, first with Luis when we talked about peer pressure, and now with Trevor and Ross. On the other hand, José doesn't tune out the way some probationers like Trevor do. And there is evidence that he knows how to use his close relationships as a safety valve—knows how to "listen to his wife," if you will. A few weeks later in the semester he would write a kind of sequel to his statement on punishment and cruelty:

> I think people cling to their anger because they don't really have anyone to talk to about it. They keep it to themselves. People like that have it hard. For you not to talk to somebody about your problem, it's pretty tough.
>
> Some people don't have parents, friends, or even a wife or a girlfriend to talk to, while others do. That's when the others come in, and they find something new to believe in, because they have people or family to talk to.
>
> I myself have hit rock bottom quite a few times. I, on the other hand, don't cling to my anger. I try something new to believe in—like try to find a new job or hustle, an environment I'm comfortable in.

All in all, I'd guess that José has figured out how to cope with the problems life has dealt him, certainly more than Trevor has.

In his own brief comment on punishment Trevor writes, "some people learn from punishment and some don't care." Trevor hopes that he's in the first category, but he's no fool; he worries that he may be sliding into the second one, the despair that afflicts so many men who have been sent to prison to teach them a lesson. Pride and shame play a big part in this balancing act, but Trevor hasn't yet confronted these feelings head-on, the way Ross did when he saw the pain on his daughter's face in the courtroom. That is not likely to come until Trevor's love for someone else obliterates his youthful infatuation with himself.

Ross is past all this, far beyond both José and Trevor in age, background, sense of self. He truly believes, with strong evidence, that punishment has made an all-important difference in his life. He wishes he'd "listened to his wife" many years ago, though now it's apparently too late. Although he's a changed man, Ross is still a little shaky. But he knows it, and he is determined not to go back to prison again.

* * *

Ross never returned to our class after this night. Perhaps he found what he needed in the conversation with Trevor and José. Perhaps he was too stirred by his avowal to risk another such encounter. In any case, we probably needed him more than he needed us.

By concentrating on his moment of truth in the courtroom, I've neglected another attitude toward punishment that many other students also hold, though only Harry was prepared to state it unequivocally:

> People make mistakes. Systems can fail, and not give fair punishment. What is deserved punishment? Who are we to punish people? Who are we to say when punishment is deserved or not?

Harry is not saying he or his fellow students are guiltless. No one ever says that. He is probing the authority relations involved in punishing or being punished, and raising the fundamental ethical question of whether justice is really served by chastisement. Here in our fourth week Harry has zeroed in on an issue that our curriculum will not formulate explicitly until the very last class: Who has the right to judge?

Although his distrust of "systems" hints at an underlying critique, Harry makes no accusations; rather, he frames the matter as one of ultimate ambiguity, positing a moral world where compassion is called for rather than blame. It is noteworthy that he gathers all of us into his "we"—drawing no lines between prosecution and defense in his courtroom.

From other things he said in our first few classes, I have no doubt that Harry practices what he preaches. He has as much to teach us as Ross, and it seems more than mere coincidence that he too left our class not long after Ross, having had his say about learning things the hard way. Harry and Ross seem to be in charge of their lives, though they've taken hold at different ends. Our program's goals might well be defined by pointing to their examples. They came to Changing Lives Through Literature with their homework already done, their lessons learned by heart. This semester they were our first graduates.

# Part Three

## *Old Lessons*

# Chapter 7

# *Street Smarts*

By the third or fourth week many of the probationers are arriving early and saying hello to one another as they walk in, a big change. A strange new appetite for school has been aroused in them, partly by the vital questions raised in our readings but mostly, I think, because they are drawn to our convivial classroom in the midst of bleak and arid lives—no mirage but a true oasis where food for thought is abundant, and drink for thirsty spirits.

It's a bit like going to church, a bit like a dinner party. Our opening exercise has the feel of saying Grace, prayerful meditation with pencil in hand. After that, meat and potatoes, the hungry clamor of four or five talk-fests in a small room. The hour goes by like a flash, and I have to shout to get their attention when it's time to clear the table for more formal speeches. Although consensus reports from the small groups are rarely so eloquent as the exchanges they have had among themselves, no one is afraid to speak up, and the occasion gives rise to testifying and advocacy of all sorts, from Pentecostal rapture and Quaker witness to the call and response of street-corner preaching:

> I can't get a job.
> *Neither can I.*
> The cops won't let me alone.
> *Know what you mean.*
> Why so many black men in jail?
> *Yeah, why?*
> I hit rock bottom there.
> *Just you and the Lord.*

I have also seen impassioned speakers rising to their feet or pounding on their desks, unforgettable moments of righteous anger, baffled and indignant at the same time. I remember a man in army fatigues who appointed himself tribune, the voice of all underdogs, a latter-day Garveyite who greatly puzzled his audience. And a man who striding back and forth said to our judge, "Give me a broom. Tell me how you want me to push it—this way, that way—I'll do it. Just give me a job!" During the semester I am writing about, most of our sermons came from unkempt and anxious little Albert, trying to find his voice by singing the praises of education, desperate to say the right thing and become one of the saved.

Although responses are unpredictable, there are nights when almost everyone is sitting on the edge of his seat, as if ready to jump up to testify. Even those who are most laid back, or who avoid the limelight entirely, often find themselves starring in some nonspeaking part—like Trevor slumped in his seat, or Neville, puffing into the room ten minutes late, making for the one deskless chair he can fit into. Each man's role is to be none other than who he is—acting in the drama while watching it play out.

If any lives are changed in the Changing Lives program, it's because of our ten-week crash diet of reading, writing, and talking—sustenance for the spirit that metabolizes in noisy spontaneous exchanges between men who are starving for conversation, for a new hearing, some evidence that what they think and feel counts, perhaps their last chance to salvage self-respect. There's no secret recipe, just a few basic ingredients: something to say, someone to say it to, an answering voice.

Because the colloquial impulse goes so deep in human beings, any four or five men gathered together invariably start talking to each other after a few minutes, even if they have no other motive than ending the silence. And when a genuine question has been asked, as in our small groups, someone is always ready to address it earnestly, and others will respond in kind, quickly drawn into the give and take. Not even the intimidation of blackboards and chalk can permanently squelch this impulse. In our classroom you don't have to have "school smarts," you just have to speak your real concerns, a challenge less daunting once you feel safe and know you will be taken seriously.

Ironically, openness to others in the room seems to depend on the fact that dangerous ground lies outside our four walls, the fabled "street" where vulnerability must be avoided at all costs and where a man's "street smarts" keep him ever on the defensive, braced against any new thing. A man on probation leads a life of chronic anxiety, always worried about his "back"—unseen threats coming from strangers, or police in cruiser cars beckoning him over for a little talk. Probation time is the period during which a former offender is officially—and statistically—most at risk, and it doesn't take much to put him behind bars. Of course, such a man is anxious about his "front" as well as his "back," the image he feels he must maintain with friends and family—and perhaps most of all, the self-image he thinks will help him face down old habits and temptations.

To fully comprehend the climate of distrust that surrounds our safe space, we need to keep in mind the shackled citizenship of men and women on probation—forbidden to associate with "criminal types" like themselves, subject to surveillance and perhaps curfew, routinely deprived of a driver's license, kept at the very bottom of the job market and barred from even the most menial work in hospitals, nursing homes, or any other state-funded "human services." Some states also deny felons the right to vote or hold office, no matter what their crimes, penance, or rehabilitation.

These civil disabilities loom all the larger when seen against the backdrop of ordinary life in the United States, where the traditional prerogatives of citizenship, which are civic responsibilities enacted through words and deeds, have been all but supplanted by passively enjoyed rights and entitlements—the freedom to associate with whom you please, the right to privacy, privileges of mobility, employment, Social Security, and the ritual of the ballot box. Granting the value of these automatic entitlements (and it is great), one must ask what happens to grassroots initiative, social conscience, and the legitimacy of statute and policy if ordinary citizens never come together in public to deliberate their real concerns and speak their own minds, not even in barbershops or beer halls, let alone civil assemblies? Some such forum for thought and action has served as backbone and nervous system of every truly democratic society from the Greek polis to the New England town meeting, and without it people come to feel powerless, and are soon reduced to cynicism or despair—the hallmarks of modern times in our vast and faceless bureaucracies.

It is against this background that we must understand the paradoxical mixture of wariness and trust I have been describing, as it plays out in our safe emergency situation.

So we come back to the actual men in our classroom, a dozen troubled souls from the streets and neighborhoods of Dorchester, almost all with prison time behind them, one or two with a bit of college experience but more who have never finished high school, less than half of them with steady jobs, and a full third living at the sufferance of family members, and many with alcohol or drug problems barely under control. Official statistics predict that most of them will be facing new charges before three years have gone by, yet every man is convinced that he has what it takes to survive if only he can get off probation. What makes them believe their "street smarts" could possibly offset CORI reports and domestic reprisals, not to mention their own defensive paranoia, and allow them to reenter the vindictive society that has cast them out?

From one perspective they may be right, for most of them are intelligent and resourceful men even though their histories seem to disprove it. In the past they have often defeated themselves by overestimating their abilities, or by demanding too much from our rich but stingy world. Long experience with frustration has made them impatient and bad judges. But they are ready for change. Looking back, they see their bridges burning behind them. "I should have listened," they say—listened to wives, grandmothers, older brothers. With a little luck and support, perhaps now they can listen, maybe they can change.

Many are hindered by their conception of what a fresh start will take. Pride has kept them from ever getting a foothold; many want to leap to the top in one bound. Their privileging of "street smarts" is an indication of how they misunderstand what the situation requires of them. "Don't trust anyone!" is their motto, and they all have convincing stories to prove its efficacy. They don't notice how this watchword contradicts their deeper wisdom about "listening" to good advice. Where will support and luck come from, if no one can be trusted and the world is viewed as a no-man's-land? To be sure, the streets *are* grim, but their own frightened and angry demeanor almost guarantees the slap in the face they are trying to ward off.

I am describing an attitude especially prevalent among the younger members of Changing Lives, men who have barely reached voting age. In our classes a generational divide invariably opens between three or four defiant young dudes like Trevor and Anthony, postured and costumed for the streets, and a few much more seasoned veterans of the courts and prisons like Ross, in their fifties or older, who show their broken teeth in a smile and say, "I was once just like you, full of myself." Raised in a vanished world, before the great backlash that followed the civil rights movement, these older men have a more patient and accommodating attitude toward the streets and the social order mirrored there. In between these opposite types we find men of thirty or forty who have had a taste of both worlds, today's and yesterday's. They can talk to both camps, though they live in neither.

In the remainder of this chapter I want to examine the attitudes embodied in three probationers who come from generations with utterly different experiences of the streets and their chances in them. Through their testimony and interactions I hope to show how provisional trust and fellow feeling can take hold in our safe space.

The speakers in what follows are men who haven't figured prominently in my narrative as yet—Charles (fifty-nine), Dave (thirty-five), and Anthony (eighteen). We sit together the third week of the semester, talking about childhood and what it takes to grow up "right" and function well as an adult. Each of these men made his break with home and family at sixteen, the great dividing line in American working-class society for at least a century—the age when in most states you can legally quit school, get a job, drive a car, go to jail. Even Frederick Douglass, an illiterate slave in rural Maryland, became a man at fifteen or sixteen. Like Douglass, each member of our group begins his story by telling us about his mother, and then, after a few decisive anecdotes of childhood, leaps ahead to his leave-taking and what followed when he said goodbye to home and family. These stories of coming into manhood, viewed from vantage points at twenty-year intervals, form my subject now. Charles, Dave, and Anthony have a lot to say to one another, and to all of us, about the destiny of the next generation in the streets of America.

Everything about Charles suggests a man trying to be inconspicuous. He wears the obligatory Red Sox baseball cap, the bill pulled so low on his forehead that it's hard to look into his eyes. With a little burst of courage he volunteers to read his opening exercise first, apologizing in advance for the few sentences on his page. Charles reads in a very soft voice, hard to hear in the already noisy room, and hasn't gotten very far before he falters and reaches for the glasses hanging at the neck of his sweater. "My eyes aren't so good," he says. Peering under his visor, I see they are old eyes, tired and cloudy.

Charles tells us that it was his mother who taught him to be a good person:

> In my life I've learned to be honest, work hard at what helps me and my family. I also learned that if you do good to others, good things will come to you. And I've

> learned to be respectful. I learned through my mother and other members of my family, and the help of God.

In four sentences Charles has touched on all four of the sacred commandments that would go up on the blackboard if I interrupted the small group conversations going on around us to elicit a general consensus on child-rearing. It's the old bootstrap ideology of Dick Whittington, Ben Franklin, and Booker T. Washington, minus only the ethos of frugality and ambition of those legendary poor boys who made good:

> Honesty and hard work are interdependent
>
> Doing right by others is an investment, with returns
>
> Respect starts with obedience to elders
>
> Look to your mother first for support and faith

Our students call this catechism *positivity.*

Coming of age when he did, Charles is from a generation that could affirm these rules of conduct wholeheartedly. Already pious platitudes in the 1950s when he grew up, nowadays such sentiments are hard to repeat without a smirk, and yet they still have force. There are very few probationers in our program who do not accept them as gospel, regardless of their absurdity in today's streets where "negativity" prevails. And indeed, if you turn this "positive" list upside down, looking for the principles of "negativity," it's apparent that not one of the key issues has changed, only the spin has been reversed. For a man with a criminal record in our society,

> Your CORI report makes you honest though jobless
>
> If you gamble and win, better keep it!
>
> Respect is what you demand from others
>
> If you ever find God, it will be in a cell

Charles grew up with the "positive" version of this outlook, Anthony with the "negative" one, and Dave has lived through the transition period.

Anthony is a good-looking, earnest youth—hardly more than a boy. "I'm not even nineteen yet," he says, half embarrassed and half proud to be in the room with all these older men. Although he's written three times as much as Charles, Anthony is just as nervous about how his opening exercise will sound to us; he reads it hurriedly, without looking up:

> As a child growing up, I wasn't what we would call now good. To make it better understood, where I grew up it was in an environment where it was like a community within a city. I had some family and was surrounded by a host of people and kids. I also grew up around positivity, and people who cared only for the benefit of me.
>
> Along with that, I was also around a lot of negativity. People who didn't care if I did wrong or right. I also grew up around issues that went deeper, like being

> involved with criminal acts, weapons, and drugs—which, little did I know, would affect my future—now!
>
> I am now faced with the question, "How did *I* learn what I needed to know in my childhood?" My answer is: back then, and now, "I guess I was learning to survive."
>
> I learned as a child, from my brother (and role model) that by keeping yourself busy, no matter what it was, as long as it was positive, you'll always stay out of trouble.

Anthony stopped writing just when his story began to get specific, but we question him further about "positivity" and "negativity," and learn more about his brother's place in his life. Four years ago, at twenty-three, his brother found himself in trouble with the law and resolved to turn his life around. Anthony was only fourteen or fifteen at the time, yet already following in his brother's footsteps. As he sees it, his brother gave him his wake-up call. Anthony had never listened to his mother's pleas to choose his friends more judiciously, take school more seriously, and spend his spare time in activities like sports instead of the streets. Only "now"—a word he repeats over and over—has he finally begun to hear with alarm that jail is waiting right around the corner. If he violates his probation, he'll end up "surrendered" to the House of Correction.

Like all the younger men in our class, Anthony blames the wrong crowd for teaching him to use and sell drugs, steal cars, and rob people on the street and subway platforms. No one mentions the fact that Anthony's brother seems to have been the original bad apple. Being older, Charles and Dave may see it differently, but they don't want to call into question Anthony's new relationship with his brother. Familial trust is sacrosanct in our class, and except for Randy all the probationers resist pointing the finger at family members, even if they have good reason to do so.

When one of these men voices regret that he lacked the guidance of either a mother or a father, he is usually thinking about a blank spot in his life, not an active force. Anthony never mentions his father, though he is quick to notice that Frederick Douglass and Malcolm X grew up without fathers and yet became great leaders. Charles still remembers "the day my father left"—but without rancor, as if it had been a mere climate change. Dave explains how "growing up without a father makes it harder for me dealing with my own children." The assumption most of them share is that a father should teach you how to avoid trouble—trouble that comes from your own generation—and you in turn teach your children the same thing. But for these men this lifeline has snapped. Those who did have fathers helping to raise them often report getting the belt for no good reason, yet almost everyone in our class agrees that it's better to have a father who beats you than none at all.

At graduation ceremonies over the years I have met quite a few mothers of these men, but only one father has ever appeared, and in the semester I'm now writing about, four men out of the dozen are still living with their mothers, while at least three others are partially dependent on female family members. One might contend that they've failed to grow up, cut the apron strings, and that the authority of a father is crucial to finding one's own manhood. Alternatively, I've heard it said that teenagers go astray because their older brothers, who might knock some sense into them, are all in jail. However that may be, in today's full tide of negativity, the only lifeline that seems strong enough to keep these men from drowning is maternal love, and they hang on for all they're worth. Once that tie is broken, if some new domestic attachment is not found, a man goes adrift. Even in a case such as Dave's, with his mother a drug addict who never paid much attention to him, her death seems to have been the great watershed in his life:

> I have a hard time remembering my childhood. Before the death of my mother, most of my memories are a blur. I don't remember when I learned how to ride a bike, or cross the street. I think I learned to read in school, probably in the third grade. Things like tying my shoes and making myself something to eat, getting dressed, cleaning my room, going to the store—I know I did these things with the help of my older sister. We went to the same school, so we walked together. She is a year older, so we did things together.
>
> Growing up without a father makes it harder for me dealing with my own children. But I'm learning as I go. It's hard, but I am willing to give it my best shot. I've had a hard life. I wouldn't wish what I've been through on anybody.

Dave is a burly man with an old four-inch scar down the middle of his shaved scalp, giving him a pugnacious look. But his frown conveys distress rather than belligerence, and though he doesn't smile often, his eyes are frank and his gaze is open. He's seen a lot of trouble, but he's not glazed over.

He goes on to explain to us what he means by "a hard life." His mother died of cancer when he was about sixteen, but long before that he had realized that his grandmother was the one who actually took care of him and his three siblings. The influence of this female household must have a share in the patient, sweet attentiveness he brings to our conversations, but the hit-or-miss supervision it entailed probably contributed to Dave's early troubles with authority.

Despite what he says about the "blur," Dave's most vivid memories of childhood seem to be of his mother. His grandmother was "always there" for him, but it's his "moms" who stands out, and whose presence seems to have been decisive, not invariably to his cost. For instance, he remembers being angry with her because she couldn't afford to buy him a bicycle like the kid next door, but his response was to build his own bike out of old parts he found in the trash. Dave's early experience of the streets was surprisingly positive—a place to search for what he lacked at home—but his resourcefulness could end up getting him in trouble. He recalls going with a friend to a department store and surreptitiously exchanging his old sneakers for a new pair, only to have his mother make him take them back. This time his enterprise earned him a beating—"I couldn't understand why."

His mother seems to have paid attention to him only when he misbehaved, and not always even then. She routinely refused to discuss his failing grades with his teachers, but on one occasion she appeared at his school without being summoned. Even though Dave was not officially on the carpet at the time, his reputation for "poor behavior" among his teachers earned him another beating and confinement to his room.

The only "positive" memory is of his mother enrolling him in art classes somewhere. He liked to draw, and he still remembers the thrill of learning to paint portraits, fruit, and pasture scenes. He now realizes "she did that to get me into doing something with my spare time, instead of hanging in the streets with my boys." Already the conflict between home and streets seems to have been fully established, and his mother was apparently looking for a way to change the dynamics.

In these memories Dave's grandmother is relegated to the background, yet he repeatedly speaks of her as the one who "raised" him and who supplied what others failed to deliver. "She was a teacher, a caring parent, a provider. She gave me shelter and protection, love and discipline." Because of her, despite poverty and a hard life, Dave's feelings about his childhood are essentially positive. "I can only really remember the good things. I was happy. Even with the beatings and punishments. And through it all, there was my grandmother, always there to talk to me." She told him "about everything, things I needed to know about life and growing up." Like so many of these probationers, his refrain is "I wish I would've listened. Sometimes I get into trouble when I think I know it 'all,' when I should just shut my mouth and learn something."

Not long after his mother's death, Dave's grandmother also died, leaving the four siblings alone in the house. Dave had already dropped out of school at sixteen. He never bothered looking for a job but was running wild in the streets and "knew nothing about paying bills." His younger sister was working and going to school. Their older sister found a man and moved out, while their little brother was following his own path—we hear no more about him. In short, the family quickly disintegrated. Dave now thinks his big mistake was not to hang tight with his siblings after their grandmother died, but "I didn't know anything about responsibilities. I stayed in trouble with the law!"

After the family broke up, Dave found himself essentially alone and homeless in the era of crack cocaine. As his drug problem escalated, his streetwise resourcefulness led him from shoplifting to car theft, and he soon acquired "burglarious" tools and skills. Larceny and breaking-and-entering did not pay well, so like many users he went on to small-time drug dealing, a more lucrative and more dangerous pursuit, with its free samples and mandatory sentences.

Dave's mother and grandmother have been dead almost twenty years now, during which time he's been constantly in trouble, often in jail. Things were going from bad to worse until he met his girlfriend half a dozen years ago. He had already been incarcerated several times, with no apparent effect on his downward spiral, but now there was something positive in his life again. Having a woman who cared about him made a difference, but he was slow to wean himself from the adrenalin and serotonin of the streets. Before their first child was a year old, he was back in jail again, with a two-year sentence. Providentially, his girlfriend waited for him, and when he was released last year, he returned to family life instead of the streets. He had a place to live, people who cared about him, and a motive to hunt for a job.

His daughter has already spent more than half her life without him, and Dave wants to be a father to her and to his infant son, born only three weeks before he started our program. "I'm a slow learner," he says, but in Dave's opinion he's "changing," not because his prison experience has finally taught him a lesson but because fatherhood has given him something new to build his life around. He loves being called "Daddy" and being run to "when they need me, or just for a hug." Having children seems to have led to the recovery of the child in himself.

Family comes with a price, however, and Dave has had to deal with his own anger and pride in order to reestablish domestic ties. The first crisis occurred last year when his girlfriend told him she was pregnant. At almost the same moment, they lost their housing. Now, instead of a single child there would be two, without a roof over their heads. Only recently out of jail at the time, Dave was not only on probation but also jobless. Each of them blamed the other, and the impasse might well have led to separation and permanent hard feelings. Here is what Dave wrote about it a little later in our semester:

> I didn't know who I could turn to. I felt helpless. Because of our problems, we weren't speaking. I was holding a grudge against her for not doing things to prevent us from getting into our situation. She was mad at me for whatever reasons.
>
> I had to let go of my pride (which I was holding onto). I asked my aunt, could I come and stay at her house. She had an extra room. Not wanting to leave my girlfriend with nowhere to stay, I ate my own anger towards her and let her come stay there with me. Forgiveness, for me, was to forget about my anger and my pride and do whatever I had to do for my "family." And to forget whatever it was that I was mad at her about.
>
> After making up with my girlfriend, I got busy working to help support my family and see what I could do to get us someplace to call our own. It's hard for me, being a "man," to give in to my girlfriend, just because she's a woman. I think I'm right—no matter if she's right and I'm wrong. I guess it's my stubborn pride. We still have problems, but we're working our way through them.

It's not hard to see that Dave will be wrestling with issues of manliness for a long time to come, but he's doing it now in the family, not the streets. And he's making progress, not only with his girlfriend but with other figures from his past. Dave's aunt was part of his childhood household, also raised by his grandmother. Identified with the older generation, she is generous but bossy. Moreover, her husband is slowly dying of bone-marrow cancer; moving into this troubled space has not been a simple matter.

Thanks to another relative, Dave has found a job doing house restoration, but ironically the pay for fixing up other people's premises is not enough to meet Boston rents, so they're still dependent on his aunt. When he finishes a hard day's work, Dave comes home to cramped quarters in a house full of tension. His girlfriend is irritable after being cooped up with two infants all day, his aunt "yells" at him, and the shadow of death itself lurks in the corners. He's looking for an apartment they can afford, but he works all day and goes to a drug treatment program one night a week, and our Changing Lives classes another. He does his homework with the baby crying and the television blaring.

Dave tells us his life is "crazy" and he's "stressed out." Nonetheless, he feels positive about his family—not just his children or his girlfriend, but other relatives who have come to his aid, including the sisters with whom he's reestablished contact after many years of silence. "I'm at a time right now when I'm desperately seeking help from family, so I'm reaching out to them, and getting good results." As he sums it up, "Someone, or something, comes along and offers you a helping hand (for a change), which usually touches you deep down in your soul."

He finishes reading from his bluebook and looks around at us with his worried eyes. "There's help for those who seek it," he says. Then he smiles and repeats his self-assessment, "I'm a slow learner."

Dave's earnest account of his life makes Charles more confident. He too has a story to tell, though he hasn't written much of it down on paper. I give him an opening by asking how old he is. Charles turns his sad, filmy eyes on me. "Fifty-nine."

"I'm seventy myself," I say. "How's your health?"

He's taken aback, not sure what to answer, gives his shoulders a shrug. "All right, physically," he says. "Except for my eyes." He fingers his glasses again, and holds out the bluebook in which he's written this week's homework. "I've got my story here," he offers, opening to the first page. But instead of reading aloud he follows Dave's example and tells us his story, in his quiet, uncertain voice.

Charles was born in Jacksonville, Florida, a Southerner like Ross, but without Ross's Southern accent. He's not a country boy, yet he has the shy, slightly formal manners of rural life. The primary facts of his childhood were no more propitious than Dave's, perhaps less so. "I remember the day my father left," he tells us. Charles was six when it happened. "I never saw him again." He had a sister two years older, a brother four years younger. "After that, my mother worked two jobs. She fed us, but we never saw her. She'd put out breakfast for us, and when she got home from her first job, dinner. But she wasn't there when we got home from school. She was always working."

At age eight or nine Charles began to contribute to the family income with a paper route. There was a morning paper and an afternoon paper, so like his mother Charles was working two jobs, one before school and one after it. He's proud of that, and says it twice. Unlike Anthony and Dave, Charles mentions school only to tell us that he dropped out at fifteen, when he went to work full time. There was no "wrong crowd" to lead him astray, and except for his pride in his paper routes there are no vivid memories, good or bad, in his childhood story.

He does speak of being "fearful" and "feeling inferior"—something he says he grew out of. Segregation and Southern racism must have had a lot to do with his early self-doubt, though he doesn't say so directly. In fact, he volunteers very little about the world he grew up in. It's as if childhood didn't matter. While Dave can tell us stories about envying the new bicycle of a friend next door and then building one for himself out of discarded parts, Charles tells us nothing about friends or bicycles, or any boyish exploits. Instead, we hear about his jobs. After outgrowing his paper routes he accompanied his mother to her work as a cook at the bus station. He would go "upstairs" to the white section of the segregated waiting room, where there was a bowling alley—and he was the pin boy. Did he like it? He doesn't say.

Unlike Dave and Anthony, Charles does not remember "the streets" as either tempting or dangerous. In his time and circumstances, the streets were simply not for the likes of him. To a boy born in the Deep South before the civil rights movement, staying out of trouble meant staying in your place, invisible except as an employee. At fifteen, when Anthony and Dave were being collared for shoplifting and various teenager street crimes, Charles witnessed his older cousin's arrest for using a whites-only restroom at a rural gas station in South Carolina. That was in 1957, the year President Eisenhower was forced to send federal troops to protect nine black boys and girls integrating Little Rock Central High School in Arkansas.

Those nine children were the only black students attending white schools anywhere in the South. But by 1957 Charles was not in school at all, and he was living where there weren't any streets to loiter in. That year his grandmother became very ill, and his mother decided to take care of her, which meant moving the whole family from Jacksonville to a small farm in South Carolina, seven miles from the nearest town. Here Charles would tend rows of cotton and beans instead of bowling pins. Although he met a few people his own age, his cousins and a girl he liked, it was lonely work, and he missed city life. After only three months he decided to run away.

Self-effacing people like Charles are often surprised by their own acts of daring when they share them with our small groups. In the mirror of other faces their lives become luminous and poignant in ways they never quite realized. Charles tells us this part of his story with increasing excitement in his voice. He has Dave and Anthony and me on the edges of our seats.

Charles saved his money till he had a few dollars, and then one morning he walked the seven miles to town. The bus for New York City wouldn't come till six that evening, so he hid in the woods, a fugitive like Frederick Douglass on his way to freedom in the fabled North. As with Douglass's railroad car a century before, the bus Charles was waiting for would be segregated until it crossed the Pennsylvania state line, but that did not worry him. If asked who he "belonged to" as he tried to board, it would be his mother who had reported him missing, not his master, and that was very unlikely. His real problems would begin when he arrived at his destination. He had the address of a relative in New York, but he didn't want to contact him until he had gotten settled. He was afraid of being sent home. Despite eight years of holding jobs, he had never been on his own. He had never lived in a city that was not completely segregated, and he had no notion of how to behave, no "street smarts"—a phrase that had not been invented yet.

He arrived in Manhattan in the middle of the night with two dollars left in his pocket. A friendly (black) man who worked in the bus terminal offered to take Charles to see his boss about a job when he got off work at seven a.m. "But don't go to sleep," he warned, "or they'll throw you out." Charles tried to stay awake, but the next thing he knew the Port Authority cops were rousing him and putting him on the street. "You can't sleep here." His chance was gone.

He walked the pavement till dawn, fingering his two dollars. He decided to go to a public employment agency, but when he got to the front of the line, he was told he couldn't apply for a job without a Social Security card. His card was back in South Carolina. He walked away disconsolate.

The woman who had just officially rejected him called him back. "Wait a minute," she said, "I have a cousin who has a little restaurant. Do you know where Jamaica is?"

Of course she was talking about Jamaica, Long Island, not the Caribbean, but Charles is reminding us of his youthful naïveté. She told him what train to take, and before long he was at the restaurant. The proprietor looked him over and put him to work. She served soul food—"greens and stuff"—and Charles went to the basement where he washed collards all day, something he knew how to do. When it was quitting time, his new boss asked him where he was staying. She had a friend who owned a rooming house, and soon Charles possessed a room as well as a job. The big city had welcomed him with open arms.

Charles lived in New York a couple of years, gradually getting on his feet, learning how to survive in that vast, turbulent city. Those were the years when Martin Luther King Jr. was filling the jails of the South with his followers, and Malcolm X, having served his time for burglary, was calling for armed self-defense in the streets of Harlem. It was also the period when urban youth gangs first entered public consciousness, so that by 1959 the term *juvenile delinquent* had become familiar enough to be shortened to "JD" for the headlines. But Charles was neither a freedom rider nor one of those teenagers who was doing battle over little squares of asphalt "turf."

He made contact with his relatives and moved in with them. For a short time he even went to school, but he needed to support himself and wanted to send money home. He wrote his mother to tell her he was safe, and he also began to correspond with the girl he had met during the few months he lived in South Carolina. The girl wrote back, and finally, when he turned eighteen, she promised to meet him in Boston. So Charles left New York and came here; they married, lived together thirty years, and had eight kids.

And then they separated.

Charles's story ends in a sudden collapse, like a child's popped balloon. Thirty years go out with a whoosh. After all that prelude he has nothing more to say, and we look at him dumbfounded. He doesn't tell us when or how or why he and his wife separated, and we don't ask, just as we don't ask Anthony too many questions about his brother, or Dave about his mother. What happened next? When I get home I do the arithmetic: born about 1942, left South Carolina at sixteen, two years in New

York, thirty years of marriage. He's fifty-nine now. That leaves nine or ten years unaccounted for. The marriage must have failed years ago.

Charles doesn't explain why he's on probation, except to say that he's never been in trouble, only this once. At the end of the semester he will write that he has "cut back on drinking alcohol almost to the point to stop," and there is other evidence that this has been a problem. Did the drink come first, or the collapse of his marriage? Is the implied moral of his story "I should have listened to my wife," as with Ross? All we can say is that it's not the lesson that Anthony thinks is most important, to stay away from "the wrong crowd."

All three of these men came to major turning points in their lives at age sixteen. That's more than forty years ago for Charles, twenty for Dave, and only a few for Anthony. Regardless of time and circumstance, they all remember the crisis of cutting loose from family ties, and sharing those memories has turned out to be what is known in the black community as "testifying." We might well adopt the phrase since it also fits our special circumstances: each man has his day in court returned to him, with the opportunity now to explain himself fully, to say everything he wants to say about the path that brought him to this place where once again his fate is in the balance and choices must be made. This time around, the judge is not passing judgment; it's a jury of peers whose opinions really count, before whom a man pleads his case, not trying to justify himself but to be truly understood. Perhaps it's this moment that is the key to Changing Lives—the discovery of support and community backing, not from friends or family, not from teachers or probation officers or judges, but from fellow citizens who are necessarily strangers to you but also your comrades in the fullest sense.

Is there a single pattern in these three lives that allows each man to see himself in the others? Yes and no. Sixteen seems to have been the turning point for them, the age when their primary reference group changed from family to peers, from home to the streets. But the shift had begun much earlier in each case: when Charles's father left and he began to earn a few dollars with his paper routes; when Dave's mother told him she couldn't afford a bike or new sneakers and he found other ways of getting them; when Anthony began to imitate his brother and hang out with "the wrong crowd." These early events were personal, shaped by family circumstances and individual character, but they were also sociologically and historically determined, and each man is a product of his times.

Charles grew up in a world that made sense to him. Although his life was a hard one, with no father, a mother working two jobs, and the culture of segregation hemming him in on all sides, nonetheless he was able to find a well-defined place and hold his own with the limited possibilities open to him. When he stepped into the adult streets at sixteen, he was not only well-prepared but also found a welcome from perfect strangers, good Samaritans who did not begin by running a CORI check on him. Up to this point his life was surprisingly similar to that of Frederick Douglass—hardship he was equal to, a moment of crisis and decision, and flight to the North. And like Douglass he was then united with the young woman who had encouraged him in his passage to independence, and he raised his own family with her. But something went wrong, and he lost his grip on things: the marriage failed after thirty years, he took to drink, looking for courage or oblivion, and he's ended up here.

Dave's life has been very different, full of paradox and ambivalence. He grew up pushing the limits, stealing what he couldn't buy, punished without understanding the rules. His independence was forced on him, with much less moral clarity than Charles found in his world. Life gave Dave mixed signals, teaching him how to take advantage of the urban wealth that surrounded him even though he had no legal right to it. But the lessons he learned were survival tactics rather than solid truths he could count on. Childhood beatings, school detention, and repeated incarceration failed to break his spirit, but neither did they teach him how to make peace with the social order that was stacked against him, or to come to terms with his own desperation. What finally pulled him out of this whirlpool was family feeling—the original source of his ambivalence suddenly reasserting itself as unconditional love when Dave became a father.

In Dave's case the powerful draw of street life with its highs and lows seems to have abated at last—but now what? Instead of the no-man's-land of the streets, Dave faces the closed doors of respectability and job discrimination. In criminology research literature there are two major factors that determine whether a man desists from his crimes or not: a positive domestic relationship and a decent job. Dave has got the family support now. What about earning a living? He works hard at his job in construction, which brings home $200 or $300 a week, but he'd like to get something better so as to save enough to have his own apartment and be more self-reliant. This is not going to be easy. In Massachusetts as in most other states, Criminal Offender Record Information (CORI) is not only mandatory screening for all jobs with state-funded "human services" but also available to all prospective employers, and cranked out at a rate of 100,000 a month. Nowhere on Dave's CORI is there any mention of his change of heart, his new relationship with his family, or his love for his children. A CORI report is solely a badge of shame, one that every person convicted of a felony must wear around his neck when job-hunting in America. And as Dave puts it, "People look at you differently when they see you as a criminal. They treat you different." His challenge is to maintain his confidence when the world seems never to trust him—a problem that Charles was not called upon to solve in his generation, and one that Anthony's generation has agreed in advance to regard as insoluble.

When Charles was first on his own, looking for work, he was handicapped by class and education and color, but it was not assumed automatically that he was a criminal. At the other extreme, in Anthony's world, the climate of distrust and cynicism is everywhere—in the streets and in the personnel offices as well as on the talk shows and at the State House. Anthony grew up among "people who didn't care if I did wrong or right." The fact that his mother and his brother kept nagging him—"always talking about getting a job, going to college, or moving out of the house"—has never felt like genuine love to Anthony, insisting that he play a game that seems meaningless to him since nothing he sees around him works that way. Ironically, he chose the streets because they seemed more honest and "the wrong crowd" because it seemed like the only game in town. "I guess I was learning to survive," he says, with the implication that survival is the best one can do.

The phrase *wrong crowd* has little substance when every man's hand is raised against you. From the start Anthony's watchword has been "dog-eat-dog." On his streets there is rarely a glimpse of human solidarity, not even a society to be at odds with or a bandit gang to belong to. Those would at least imply a moral dimension, albeit that of the outlaw. But these days you can't trust anyone, whatever "colors" are worn.

Strange to say, today's metropolitan streets with their traffic lights and shop windows have evolved to the State of Nature posited by Thomas Hobbes three centuries ago, the primordial pit where human bonds count for nothing. Without a basis in mutual trust and obligation, all ethical criteria melt away and concepts like crime and sin become utterly meaningless. The distinction between being locked away in prison and being free in the streets becomes merely ironic. Same friends, same enemies, same rules of the game: *Trust no one. Demand respect from your friends, fear from your enemies. Keep what you gamble for. Step over the bodies as if they weren't lying in your path.*

This life is beyond the reach of either remorse or fear of punishment, utterly reckless and fatalistic. It is what our probationers mean when they speak of "negativity" or "street smarts," their lingo for nihilism and despair. For those who must live this way there is no such thing as trust or betrayal. Today's young hoodlums have become brazen and savage because they no longer believe in the possibility of human affections. Breaking the law means nothing if one has no conception of law and lives by calculation and fear instead of conscience. In the absence of social bonds, all virtues and ideals fall away.

Teetering on the brink of this abyss, Anthony has pulled back in the nick of time. Dave has actually passed through the no-man's-land; he grew up in another time and has returned to it. Dave's attachment to family and to his own child-self has revived his faith in humanity, concretely embodied in his love for his children and their unquestioning love for him. Those bonds sustain him as he struggles to establish new ties with society. As long as he can come home to them every night, he'll be able to keep at his job, look for better housing, and resist the temptation to lose his temper with personnel interviewers who treat him as if he were nothing but a smudged CORI report.

Charles grew up in another era entirely and remembers a world that has vanished in urban America. When he left the close-knit, segregated society of the Deep South to take his chances without family or friends in the metropolis, he went with trepidation as well as hope for an open future. Fortunately for him, in 1957 the streets of New York were not yet a battle zone. The city was still full of paths one could walk, and if one stumbled there were helping hands. Charles encountered obstacles and confronted the Northern variety of racism, but he also found a welcome from trusting souls—all of them black like him—who ignored the fact that he had no money, no Social Security card, no one to vouch for him. In 1957 it was still possible to find work without a CORI check, a place to sleep without first and last months' rent in advance. Even if you were poor and black, you could live in decent poverty without being humiliated by not having a TV set, a car, and the right brand of sneakers. By the time Dave was a boy in the 1970s this was rapidly changing, and it had completely disappeared before Anthony was sixteen.

The differences between these three men might be summed up in the folk wisdom young children learn about street luck and small change:

> For Charles and his generation, if you find a dime on the sidewalk, it's yours.
>
> For Dave and his generation, you look to see whether it's heads or tails, pick it up if it's heads and turn it over for the next guy if it's tails.
>
> But in Anthony's generation no one ever stoops for a dime.

All three are children of poverty, but with different attitudes toward the wealth they see around them. In the 1950s and 1960s Charles was ready to wash collard greens in a basement when necessary. He was not too proud to bend his back. In the 1980s, when someone like Dave stole a car, it was larceny, because he meant to sell it or its parts. His burglarious tools were the tools of a trade, full of risk and more exciting than pushing a broom, as well as more profitable. Today when someone like Anthony steals a car, or when Neville borrows one without permission, it's often just for a joy ride, or to display his "cool" in front of his "boys." And the vehicle, instead of disappearing or showing up by the side of the road stripped and sitting on its axles, will now be found a few blocks from where it was stolen—vandalized and abandoned.

Many of the acts that get teenagers arrested look like the bravado and display of eleven-year-olds, liable to dissolve into the tantrums of very small children, delirious with frenzy and frustration. These young men are not growing up into the adult world but are stuck in childish fantasy, played out with real weapons and speeding cars, with deadly threats and vows carried out the instant they're spoken. For a sixteen-year-old in today's streets, neither sin nor crime is a meaningful conception. Sin, the betrayal of one's own moral code, cannot exist without mutual affection, loyalty, and personal obligation to family and community—the foundation of all righteousness. Similarly, crime, disobeying the legislated and policed codes of behavior in society, doesn't signify when a young man doesn't have a place in society, doesn't fear its sanctions, doesn't share any of its ideals or genuinely aspire to its goods.

Despite the cocky boasts of the young, street smarts are actually the opposite of ordinary common sense and deeply antithetical to the shared humanity that all social endeavors and mutual aid are founded on. To contrast street smarts with school smarts is misleading—not because the polarity is false, but because neither phenomenon really exhibits intelligence; they are alternative responses to forced socialization. Either you learn to do what you're told and conform to the norms, or you practice defiance.

A more deep-going challenge to street smarts is found in the Changing Lives classroom, where the relentless vigilance of the streets and the coerced obedience of schooling are both in abeyance, and men in trouble can relax their guard and drop their masks of belligerence or indifference. Here their vulnerability is transformed into a bond of mutual understanding, and for not a few of them, into compassion. Thus did Charles listen to Dave's story and find the assurance he needed to tell his own. And Anthony, who began with a set of admissions and exculpations set forth as if a courtroom defense, ended by dropping his script and betraying a boyish relief in having finally found a way to give in to his mother's admonitions. By relaxing his street-smart posture and accepting the embarrassment and docility of his situation honestly, Anthony was able to step across the line into adult self-respect and manliness at last—something that would hardly be possible for him in the streets or in school, but was quietly accomplished in the little circle with Charles and Dave.

It's important for Anthony to listen to his brother when he warns him to change his ways, take a new path, but it's even more essential for him to hear the stories of older men like Charles and Dave, because they may be able to convince him that there *is* a path, that life is more than just grabbing what you can for yourself from the goods on display in the me-first society. Anthony is at the point now that Dave went through twenty or twenty-five years ago, when he was being exhorted by his mother and grandmother and even his older sister to behave himself. Dave didn't listen, but Anthony seems to be able to hear the warning: "I go through a crisis with my mother every day, always talking about getting a job, going to college, or moving out of the house." Finally, he says, "I came to my senses. Now I have a part-time job, and I'm going to school part-time, and my mother ain't harassing me no more. And that makes me want to do more for myself."

Anthony may be right to turn away from the streets and try the more conventional route to the American Dream of wealth and ease. But the grim negativity of today's streets reflects a more widespread public despair he is sure to meet on his new road, the feeling that "nothing can be done" by individuals to counter the massive forces that seem to determine their lives. Even the successful and happy feel powerless in the face of the organized system. The lack of youthful idealism in the new generation is ominous. With Charles and Dave it seems to me that their struggles have kept them hopeful and forward-looking, even while burdened with shame or frantically scrambling to stay afloat. Life has given them something hard to do, and they're doing it. They have stories to tell that are not over. Anthony, just starting out, has no stories yet. Just to "be" in school, to "have" a job, isn't going to save him from the chronic desperation that lies beneath the surface pretty much everywhere in our society, and certainly in the black community, with so many of its young men caught in the criminal justice system.

# Chapter 8

# *The Moral of the Story*

The week after our hard look at the effects of punishment, we take up a new group of texts that direct our attention to lessons brought about by means other than systematic coercion in schools, courts, or prison. Life has many ways of teaching us what we need to know.

The stories assigned now are moral tales—a set of anecdotes from Frederick Douglass, Richard Wright, and Malcolm X that could be given titles like "How I Learned to Read." The real story in each case has to do with the determination these men brought to their quest for literacy, wresting this skill from a world of hardship and oppression—Douglass in slavery, Wright in desperate poverty, Malcolm in prison. It is worth noticing that two of the three, after finishing their self-education and freeing their tongues, also chose the names they would henceforth be called by. We add a fourth man, Cassius Clay, whose literacy level remained far lower than the average of our probationers, but whose self-mastery and eloquence became legendary, and whose insistence on his autonomy and the right to be called Muhammad Ali is summed up in his celebrated sentence, "I don't have to be what you want me to be."

Side by side with these heroic tales, which never fail to stir powerful feelings in some members of the class, we juxtapose a sample of the use of language and schooling as a means of social control. Bill Russell's sobering discovery came in his teens, at the public library, when he realized that some of the history books he read with such pleasure contained lies. The whopper he could not swallow was the assertion in one of them that slaves had a "better life" in America than in their native Africa.

We are not urging probationers to line up behind any particular notion of what it means to be educated, but to look at the evidence in their own experience. We call for examples from their past not to prove the irrelevance of schooling but to illuminate the important things they know, and how they learned them. If there is an underlying message, it is that people must work hard for any lesson worth knowing:

*How did you learn what you needed to know in your childhood? Make a list of events in your childhood when you learned something important.*

Not everyone in the class is ready to address such questions seriously. A few of the younger men like Trevor and Willy are still clinging to childish attitudes despite the fact that they have adult bodies and responsibilities—a refusal to grow up that can be appealing, though I must admit I was often impatient with it. Here, for example, is Willy's list of things he learned in childhood:

Ride a bike
Tie your shoes
Look both ways when crossing the street
Respect your elders
Don't talk to strangers
Don't touch nothing that doesn't belong to you
Learn how to read and write
Learn your ABC and math
Learn not to play with fire
Wear clean underclothes when going to a doctor's appointment

Trevor's list was similar, though lacking Willy's playfulness. Willy was our class clown, the one who would collapse on the floor in mock asphyxiation if someone near him let a fart. His pratfalls reminded us that we were back in school, just as Trevor's frequent trips to the men's room did.

In this week's opening exercise we asked for a detailed account of a single childhood lesson, a memory triggered by these lists:

*What have you learned in your life that seems especially important? How did you learn it?*

Up until this class exercise our requests for writing have left it to the probationers to decide how much personal experience to include, but now, almost halfway through the semester, with the testimony of Douglass, Richard Wright, Malcolm X, and Bill Russell setting an example, we invite everyone to think back to significant turning points or revelations in their own lives. This exercise, culminating the first month of our course, asked each man to consider how his childhood has influenced who he is today.

I want to present two such memories written this semester. The first is by Deighton, a tall, almost languorous man of around forty, raised in Jamaica and with the rhythms of the *patois* still in his speech. As Bert says, you can't be in Deighton's presence without feeling comforted. He's like sunshine. But despite his irresistible warmth, something in Deighton's past has made him wary of other people. Of course, most of the probationers have the habit of being on guard. You can see it in

José's averted eyes, Willy's clowning, or the way Charles always sits near the door. In Deighton there are no visible manifestations, only a few bitter proverbs he favors, about friends disappearing when you're broke or in trouble and coming back if your luck changes.

Here is Deighton's childhood memory:

> I was playing marbles with my friend. I ended up winning all his marbles. He was upset and wanted to fight me. I ended up giving him six marbles out of twenty. We started playing again. This time he ended up winning all the marbles from me. I got upset. Now I wanted to fight, since I know I gave him back six marbles. Would you believe that my friend went home with all twenty marbles, and refused to give me even one of the marbles. So if I had known that he was going to do something like that to me, I would never give him any marbles.
>
> The lesson is, when you gamble and win, keep it!

I was a little surprised to find this comic scene among the responses, because most students take our opening exercises as an occasion for solemn pronouncements and conclusions—often "the moral" without the story, as in the following earnest paragraph from José:

> I learned that in life you must do right, so you can be successful most importantly, and get some education, or pick up a trade while you're growing up. That way you'll have the skills to make up your own business or be smarter than the rest, or even the boss.

It's hard to break free of moralizing when you start with the idea of "learning your lesson." Trying to make sense of our lives, most of us rely on the past to rationalize how things have turned out, or like José, use it as a goad to self-improvement. But when Deighton draws his moral at the end, he seems quite free of the urge to say something uplifting or contrite. Indeed, at first glance his little exemplary tale may seem trivial, its moral almost beside the point. But as we will soon see, the chord struck here echoed much more somberly in Deighton's attitude toward all experience.

Although I have quoted only one so far, Deighton recounted three separate "lessons" in his opening exercise this week. Here are the other two:

> Passing a lady's house on my way to school one morning, I did not say hello. The woman told my parents and I was scolded. I learned that it is very important to have good manners to other people.

> My cousin's mother who was in England sent him a very nice and sharp suit. When I saw my cousin in the suit, I told my mother that I wanted one just like my cousin's. Not that my mother could not afford to buy me one—but she got upset and yelled at me, saying, "don't be grudgeful!" I learned that not everything you see someone with, you should want. Instead of being jealous when someone

> has something nice, you should be happy for them. I learned to do unto others as I would like them to do to me.

Later in the semester Deighton would come back more than once to the themes clustered here: honor and deference, generosity and envy, trust and betrayal. As the moral of his first story sums it up, life is not just a game but a gamble, and although it may not be sporting to begrudge others their luck, the winner had better take his marbles home with him while he can. On this occasion Deighton tells his story humorously; at other times melancholy overtones predominate and an ominous note may sound, as in his reflections on punishment written only a week earlier: "Being punished can destroy some people . . . can send them on a very revengeful path."

I will return to Deighton and his grudgeful character shortly, but first I want to look at another story with a comic climax, presented the same night by a probationer with a very different sort of magnetism, no less compelling. When Deighton speaks, he bends his head to you, smiling. When Randy talks, he stares straight ahead, hollow-eyed, as if reading something off a screen inside his head. Deighton tells a story with obvious pleasure, working you toward the punch line. Randy remembers and recites every detail in a kind of rapture—eyes front, shoulders at attention, like the ex-Marine he is—with the barest hint of amusement dimpling the corners of his mouth. Meticulously rendering every twist and turn of plot, his deadpan delivery can be unsettling. Randy soon has us on the edges of our seats:

> When I was seven or eight years old, my mom could not afford to buy a lunch box, so a friend in our building gave my mom two lunch boxes. One was square and one was oval.
>
> The square one was a boy's and the oval looked like a girl's. Anyway, she gave my brother the square one and me the oval one.
>
> I hated it, it looked just like a girl's lunch pail.
>
> Everyone teased me, called me a sissy every day, until one day a kid was following me home, teasing me, calling me a sissy with a girl's lunch box. As I walked home from school, he was behind me, ragging on me, and really pissing me off, so I turned around and hit him right on top of his head with my oval lunch pail. Well, the pail just exploded and broke apart, and he ran home crying. He never teased me again after that day, and I took a paper bag for the rest of the second grade.
>
> What did I learn? I didn't like to be teased.
>
> What did others learn? Big things come in little packages.

Randy portrays himself here as the victimized "little brother" familiar in *Peanuts* or *Little Lulu,* second choice at home and a sissy at school, teased until he explodes with the satisfying "Ka-boom!" of a comic strip. But no matter how funny, this childhood misadventure was as prophetic for Randy as playing marbles was for Deighton. Like Malcolm X, Deighton learns to be suspicious of smiling faces; like Frederick Douglass or Muhammad Ali, Randy learns to fight for the right to be who he is.

Randy sits in the very center of the room each night, the only white face among all these brown ones, the only man who knows the Frederick Douglass story by heart, and perhaps the only one of us with personal knowledge of what it means to be a slave—to heroin. In any case, he is who he is, let others take him as they may!

Whatever the challenge, Randy always seems to win his battles for dignity. Played out against the background of a lifelong feud with his older sibling, the scenario never changes: honest effort is frustrated by unfair competition and bad luck, but then his temporary setback is unexpectedly transformed, like his oval lunchbox, into the roundabout means of final victory.

Soon we will look more closely at Randy's soap-opera life, but first let us revisit Deighton's gallery of grudgeful self-portraits. Our next request for personal stories with a moral was not scheduled until several weeks later, when we asked for an adult memory with lasting impact:

> *The readings this week are about self-discovery and self-fulfillment in conditions of crisis. Can you tell a story from your life that would fit in?*

It takes some confidence to share such stories with strangers, but two-thirds of the way through the semester our students trust each other to be sympathetic listeners. Here is what Deighton wrote that night:

> Working in the construction field, sometimes a worker does not work all year long. In the middle Eighties things were real hard as far as finding work. I was living with my son, his mother, and my stepdaughter. My girlfriend at the time worked part-time with the telephone company. Her income was just from hand to mouth. I used to always get a small job sometime, basically carpentry work, as I know the rent has to be paid every first of the month.
>
> Some weekends we used to keep parties to help our financial situation. She always quarreled with me, telling me how lazy and worthless I was. That did not help the situation. I was doing all I think I could at the time to provide for them. I even got a temporary job paying me eleven dollars less than I used to get on my regular job. It hurt to go to work every day, but I stuck with it.
>
> The bills were being paid on time, and a stable meal was able to be put on the table each night. Still, all this was not enough. Now she wanted me to leave the house, because she felt things were not working. This was the hardest thing I feel I had to do—leave my son—considering the fact that I did not grow up with my father. I got a room not too far from the house. Not to watch her, but to be able to see my son when I can. I provided for him on a weekly basis.
>
> Now that I was on my own, I gave up the temporary job and started cooking in a restaurant. I still have to pay my rent, and a part of hers, just to keep a roof over my son and his sister's head. At this point I did not give a shit about her, but I had to do this. Things kept getting better and better for me, because I have faith and I do believe that things would change. Things worked out in my favor—that my son ended up living with me, and that was exactly what I wanted.

No doubt there is more to this story than Deighton tells us—much that might be said against him and many angry scenes he chooses not to report—but as he sees it now, his girlfriend took advantage of him just as his friend had done in their boyhood game of marbles. Male pride and honor under attack, Deighton retreats with as much dignity as he can salvage, brooding, bitter, and grudgeful.

Upheavals like this often go hand in hand with domestic violence, substance abuse, and street crime, though nothing in Deighton's testimony suggests such conduct. Neither does he present his crisis as prelude to the offense, whatever it was, that brought him into our program fifteen years later. By the time we meet him in Changing Lives, Deighton seems as genial as ever, and is once again making good money as a carpenter. Since the breakup of his first family he has been involved with other women and fathered other children, though how he has fared in these subsequent relationships I cannot say.

Although Deighton liked to end his stories with an emphatic moral, he had little desire to reassess his past. Still smarting and stinging from what he regards as betrayal, he seems none the wiser. Nevertheless, in his next homework assignment Deighton would begin to imagine how things might have been different.

His new perspective was inspired by readings the following week that stressed the ultimate challenge facing all probationers—the difficulty of return and reconciliation, the possibility of forgiveness after transgression and punishment. Once again Frederick Douglass provides our positive model of courage and resolve in times of crisis. But this week it is Leo Tolstoy, instead of Malcolm X or Richard Wright, who delineates the desperate plight of the social outcast trying to find redemption—after a life of substance abuse, domestic violence, unemployment, homelessness, and moral collapse.

Though each probationer will have his own perspective, no one in our class is indifferent to this plight that sends as many to the bottom today as it did a hundred years ago, when Tolstoy wrote the story we discuss during our eighth week. Here is how Luis summarized "Korney Vasiliev":

> Korney, who was the father in this story, went through the good life, and then Kouzma, a poor old man who, by the way, disliked Korney, tells him about an affair going on between his wife and Justin, a laborer. At that, he also told him people are laughing, and Korney ventures home in silence, pondering over the information just received. Korney questions his wife and then beats his wife and breaks his daughter's arm accidentally, not meaning to, and leaves for more than a decade of years; then runs into his daughter and eventually tries to go home, gets yelled at, told to leave. He's very sick and dies in his daughter's house, and his wife Martha feels guilty of sin and tries to reach him, and while doing so finds her husband dead in her daughter's house.

Randy also summarized Tolstoy's story for us, focusing more narrowly on its moral dynamics as they emerge in two key encounters after Korney's return, first with his daughter:

> After he beat his wife and hurt his little girl, he fled the area, losing all he had saved. Now on his way back home, all he could think of is revenge. When he met the little girl on the road back, at first he didn't know it was his little girl, and in the hut when he asked what had happened to her arm, she answered, my daddy did it, and he said, you must really hate him for that, and she said, no, that she had forgiven him right after he did it.

and later with his wife:

> Then the next day when he finally got home, the revenge he wanted so bad was gone. All he wanted was forgiveness. And his wife threw him out. Was it right, after such a long time? Who knows?
>
> When he made it back to his little girl's house, he wept, telling her all. By now his wife had time to think, and all she wanted to do was forgive him and live out the rest of their lives together. But she was too late. Korney was already dead.

There are always a few close readers like Luis and Randy eager to retell a story in their own words, but most students use "Korney Vasiliev" as a springboard to dive into their own deep waters, where they too have "hit rock bottom." For Deighton this was a chance to return to the theme of betrayal and grudge-holding, examining it now from the higher ground Tolstoy afforded him:

> Some people find it very difficult to let go of the past.
>
> When a male and female are in a relationship and the male keeps correcting his partner about things that he dislikes or things she does that are wrong, it becomes a conflict. If they separate because of these reasons, then there is no solution to the problems. In this case, one can be angry at another for a very long time.
>
> Let us say they decide to go back together after years. If the male did not forgive his partner or let go of his anger, he will still throw the past back at his partner. This means he has not moved on. He is still fueling self-pity, because he feels that if she had listened to him in the first place, and done the right things, then they would not have had to separate and then get back together later.
>
> Forgiveness is letting go of the past and moving on. It's easy to tell someone that you forgive them, but it is hard to forget the things you forgive them for.
>
> True forgiveness lets a person feel like there is a burden lifted off their head or shoulders.

In this new look at guilt and recrimination Deighton has reversed his angle of vision. Instead of the woman telling the man "how lazy and worthless" he is, we find the man "correcting his partner about things he dislikes or things she does that are wrong." Whether or not Deighton is thinking of the mother of his son, he seems ready to accept his own share of responsibility for the breakdown of that relationship. This is not merely letting bygones be bygones. Deighton has not yet "let go of the past" despite the recognition that he too is to blame. Now that he sees forgiveness as an option, we might expect him to offer an opposite "moral" to his story, and he does weigh the possibility: "True forgiveness lets a person feel like there is a burden lifted off their head or shoulders." But Deighton has apparently not experienced any such relief, and so this insight derived from Tolstoy's parable cannot serve him in that way. Indeed, Deighton's new story offers no decisive moral. Instead he has written an unresolved case study that leaves the reader and author without closure: "It's easy to tell someone that you forgive them, but it is hard to forget the things you forgive them for."

When a personal narrative ends with a moral, we are being told where it belongs on the shelf of cultural wisdom, stored for possible future use. "This happened to me" is not just a way of saying who you think you are, but also an attempt to state what we must all expect from life. Everyday conduct and cultural norms are underwritten by such testimony, which collaborates with statutes and court decisions, newspaper columns, and ordinary gossip in recording normative acts, life's choices entangled with character and fate.

Personal narratives that are left open-ended are more unsettling. They leave us wondering, and thereby seem to undermine conventional wisdom about right and wrong. When a storyteller like Deighton decides to revisit the past in search of a fresh perspective or new evidence, things may not fall so neatly into place. Instead of a tidy lesson, the investigation may give rise to more questions than it answers and leave us looking life's contradictions directly in the eye. Each variation of Deighton's story finds him grudgeful, but only this final version probes his deep ambivalence about the past, entertaining the possibility that the outcome is still to be determined. This can be unnerving, or bracing, or both.

A week later we asked the class our last question of the semester: *Who has the right to judge?* The readings for that session raise some fundamental problems of justice in any society based on law, but our students inevitably take this question quite personally, applying it to their own experiences in actual courtrooms and to their own cases of transgression, punishment, and forgiveness. Although they very rarely speak of their own cases directly, what they do say is always weighted with unspoken feelings aroused by their earlier writings on punishment, crisis, and hitting bottom. From that last assignment, here then are Deighton's valedictory reflections on his own story, now thrice told:

> I think God is the judge of all men and all things.
>
> By society's standard, a judge in the court of law has the power to judge certain people.
>
> I can be a judge to a certain situation. Each individual at some point in life will judge some one, whether for the right or wrong reason. Eventually we all will be judged by the Almighty One.

Deighton's carefully balanced view applies with equal force to his private history of betrayal and vindication, and to his larger conception of human justice as he has received it in the criminal justice system. He speaks of "certain people" and "certain situations" but disclaims any certainty for himself as judge or judged. He accepts responsibility and also frailty, acknowledging society's standard and his own fallible conscience. At least for this moment, his private and public worlds are aligned and make sense to him.

At that final meeting, after talking for a while about the "right to judge," we also canvass the class for the moral to our own story, asking each man what lessons he will take with him from our ten weeks together, the "memorable things" that happened during the semester:

"This class has taught me that lots of people have it hard," said José.

"Now that I see what I have been missing in life," said Albert, "I am going to try and change my life for the better."

"I've seen changes in this class," Randy told us, "where others tried to help others."

"I'm not alone in my madness," said Dave.

In his turn, Deighton mentioned forgetting to come to class one night—significantly, it was the session when we talked about Tolstoy's story. He also revealed how apprehensive he had been at first about so much reading, more "than I have done in a long time." But he found it easier than he expected, and he thought the stories taught him something important: "After reading something you might just get yourself in a situation where you have to reflect back and apply what you read to such situation, to get yourself out."

When I asked Deighton which story he would remember longest, he replied, "The one about the man who beats his wife and hurts his daughter and comes back for forgiveness at the end."

As Deighton and others spoke, my eyes kept lighting on Randy, on whose face I could see a faint smile slowly spreading. Having been in our class two semesters in a row, Randy knows these texts almost as well as his own life. Is it a kind of nostalgia that brings the smile to his face as he listens to his classmates? I know he takes a similar pleasure in his own stories, of which he seems to have an endless supply: "My memories go back to having gone through so many things," he says. "As you get older, the more you go through life and its experiences, the more you have to remember. The same goes for reading."

For Randy both reading and storytelling are intensely social acts, his primary connection with his classmates and perhaps even the world at large. With his solitary habits—reading, fishing, drugs—Randy lacks opportunities to make contact with other people. He hasn't had a job for many years and is getting too old for active sports, but he is in counseling, and when he goes to his support group meetings, he brings his Changing Lives homework along. He reads while waiting for these sessions to begin, and he is pleased when others notice and "seem to envy me." Such mixed signals hardly constitute an invitation to conversation, however, and Randy ends up in fantasies of contact rather than the real thing. In our classroom too, he almost never initiates a conversation but uses stories, his own as well as our readings, to "intermingle with others and get to know them, your classmates, as a person."

Whether or not Randy really does "get to know" others through reading or telling stories, he seems much more eager for an audience than most of the probationers—as if he dare not believe in his own memories without witnesses. And yet he is proud of his memory—"my mind is like glue, everything sticks"—and he recapitulates the plot of a long story, his own or Tolstoy's, in such minute detail that I find myself wondering what forest is hidden behind all these trees, why it's so hard to let go once he's got his listener's sleeve in his grip.

Such questions are double-edged for a program based on storytelling like Changing Lives, where we're often dealing with obsessive imaginations like Deighton's or Randy's, in pursuit of vindication.

Like his comic anecdote of the oval lunchbox, many of Randy's stories of adult life concern his mother and his older brother, a triangle taut with envy, resentment, and fantasies of revenge. Randy quickly spots a similar pattern in Tolstoy's tale of Korney Vasiliev, whose jealous anger poisoned his life for seventeen years—exactly the period that Randy's family feud has lasted. "Seventeen years"—I draw attention to this minor circumstantial parallel because coincidences and providential events are very common in Randy's stories, giving them a melodramatic aura.

It has been a melodramatic life. During a routine operation seventeen years ago Randy's father suffered a fatal heart attack, and then less than a year later his younger brother died of AIDS. In the interval between these two deaths, says Randy, "I get a really bad habit"—that is, his heroin use escalated dramatically. He found himself with multiple arrests and court cases—caught shoplifting, buying, holding, using.

His younger brother was not a needle-user but contracted AIDS through sexual contacts, and had admitted to his doctor that he was gay. In the final stages of his illness, he begged Randy for help in dying—a fatal dose of heroin. Randy had no money to buy it and suggested an overdose of his brother's pain medication instead, but this scheme was thwarted by their mother. At last, in a gesture compounded of compassion and despair, Randy told him, "if he was afraid of dying . . . as a brother I would go with him so he didn't have to go alone."

Randy needed to appear at the courthouse for sentencing but was granted a "stay" until Thanksgiving, so that he could be with his brother at the end. On Thanksgiving night, a week after his brother died, Randy shot himself with a one-bullet homemade gun. Another failure. Somehow the shot missed Randy's heart ("by centimeters") and he survived.

In the wake of all this high drama the dead man's property, a triple-decker duplex where their mother lived, ended up in a trusteeship controlled by Randy's older brother, the one with the square lunchbox. Perhaps this trust was a family strategy to insulate the inheritance from Randy's "really bad habit," but Randy never mentioned this probability. He merely stated that he now kept house for his mother while his brother (in Randy's opinion) took advantage of the situation to line his own pockets.

Up to this point, Randy had never been in serious trouble with the law. There was a single exception, some thirty years ago, when he was accused of home invasion or trespass and brought to trial by the mother of a high-school friend. As a result, he never finished eleventh grade, instead joining the Marines to avoid a jail sentence, and went to war—coming back with his "bad habit" and a disability pension. This part of the outcome, however, is omitted in Randy's account, where the focus is on the injustice of the adult world he entered at seventeen, and the roundabout way that he ultimately triumphed:

> I was told to tell the truth. It was a court case. I was 17 years old. The prosecutor asked me a question: Did this woman give you permission to be in her house? I said, No, and that's all he asked. But the woman's daughter invited my friend and myself in, every weekend for a year and a half (to party). He did not go into the whole story.
>
> So there's the injustice. I had to quit school and join the service (U.S.M.C.) in which I got my G.E.D. That was during the Vietnam War, so I really did not mind signing up. But the fact is, he knew the daughter let us in. I was just young and naïve, to trust that maggot to tell the truth like I did.

As always in Randy's stories, whether it's a boy's lunchbox or a clause in a will, some legitimating credential is denied him, but in the end an even better authentication comes to him, providentially. Although without the usual pomp and circumstance, the GED is more to his credit than a diploma. The same pattern shapes the ongoing drama that begins with his father's death, his own attempted suicide, and his exclusion from his brother's will. Having survived it all, he now has his mother to himself and is waiting for the fifth act, which will climax when his rival brother ultimately hits bottom, a final judgment Randy solemnly predicts: "God will be waiting when he hits, and so will I."

This motif of illegitimacy and ultimate vindication appeared in almost everything Randy wrote over two semesters. One way or another, all of these accounts end with Randy saying, "If I wait long enough I win in the end." I've pieced together the foregoing overview from multiple versions, each of them fragmentary but fully consistent with the others—perhaps too consistent, as the recurrent number "seventeen" warns us.

In addition to the autobiographical material on which I have been drawing, Randy recorded four or five brief childhood memories of his father that contain the same themes—striving for recognition from authority, loss of credibility, and providential recovery of status:

> I can remember when I was young, about five years old, and my father would give me a kiss every day before he went to his second job. One day, I can't remember what I was doing, but I remember my father had left for the bus stop without kissing me goodbye. I remember falling down about seven steps and running for the bus stop just for that kiss.

> I would see my father on weekends and he did a lot of fishing, but you had to be up early. Well, I was up early but my brothers would rather sleep. I spent special

> times with both parents but being young I made more time for my dad than for my mother.
>
> Once in my life I went fishing alone. I was told to be home by 12:30 that afternoon. Well, I didn't make it home till 7 p.m. My parents were frantic. They thought I might have fallen in the water and drowned. I was only 10 years old. When I got home at first, I was comforted by my mom. But my father didn't want to hear the reason I was so late. He beat me with a belt. I'll never forget it. To top it off, it wasn't my fault I was late. I was never late again.
>
> One night my brother kept sticking me with a pin, so I got a big sewing pin and stuck it in his leg. He got out of bed and showed my dad. My dad took the pin out of my brother's leg and came in my room and beat me again. Earlier that day he stepped on a pin and it stuck in his foot, so he thought I was playing with the pins and I caught hell for it.

Of course, the premise here is typical of childhood stories that every one of our probationers can tell. A boy gets in trouble and is punished, through no fault of his own. Very rarely does the outcome favor the boy instead of his father, as in the "kitten" episode of *Black Boy*—only once in Randy's recollections:

> Another time he came home feeling good and he had me in a corner and he kept telling me to fight him. I would have my hands up but I did not want to hit him at the time. My mother would be out but that one time she came home as he was saying hit him, so I did. He never played that game with me again.

As with Richard Wright, or in his own saga of the oval lunchbox, Randy relishes turning the tables on power and intimidation—"he never teased me again"—but more often he gets the belt. Fighting back is risky.

I want to present two more elaborate stories from Randy's adult life that pick up the thread where his childhood anecdotes end. In these new stories he was also balked in the attempt to achieve something worthy. Having suffered some physical blow that temporarily incapacitates him, he serendipitously finds himself in a situation where endurance and good intentions are finally rewarded, empowering him in an unexpected emergency.

Significantly, both of these trials and vindications occurred before he turned thirty, when family catastrophe plunged him into the life of a junkie. Although his heroin use goes back at least another decade, to the war years, in his stories the habit never seems to have prevented normal functioning. After his discharge from the Marine Corps Randy went to school on the GI Bill, learning business and clerical skills; he spent time in the construction trades as a carpenter, a welder, and a sheet metal expert; he drove a taxi, worked in hospitals, and experimented with still other ways of earning a living. When necessary, he always had his disability checks to fall back on.

This start-and-stop job history may have been drug-influenced, but Randy's stories of that period rarely hint at the cycle of getting high and coming down, petty crime and jail, reform and relapse, that makes a junkie's life so miserable. Instead we read of efforts to find a legitimate place for himself in society, how they were blocked or derailed, and then come to paradoxical fruition. Here is one such story, which involves both his "good" and "bad" brothers and also mentions the number seventeen, popping up in the barrage of dates and designations that make all his writings sound like testimony from the witness stand:

> I can't remember the year, but I took the test to become a firefighter. Everything went well, I passed everything, and was 22 on the list. That year they were to hire 50 firemen. But it was a voting year, and I'll never forget "Vote No on Question 2½." Well, everyone voted Yes, which froze the list.
>
> Two of my brothers were firemen, and they encouraged me not to give up, so, two years later, I took and passed the test again. This time I was 17 on the list, but prop. 2½ was still in effect, and the list remained frozen for four years. I remember the dates now, from 1979 to 1981.
>
> In 1980 I started working at Boston City Hospital. I pinched a nerve in my neck in November 1981. Now I'm out of work. I needed money for rent so I started driving a cab. May 2, 1982, 5 p.m. Sunday evening, a young guy jumped in the front seat of my cab, held me up and shot me.
>
> I got out of the hospital May 26. I had a good cat down my place. Some time in August I saw smoke coming from a house down the street. I went down and a young girl said, "My father is up there on the 3rd floor." Fire was coming out of the back of the house real good, so without thinking I got to the stairs leading to the 3rd floor.
>
> The smoke was getting real heavy. I went up anyway and felt the door. It was hot. I called in once but no one answered. I was low to the floor, where you could breathe anyway. Forgetting I just got out of the hospital, I stood up and kicked the door once. The door and frame fell inside. Ahead of me was flames, to my left a doorway. I yelled in again—no answer. Then a kitten came out as I was about to leave, so I grabbed it and left.
>
> When I got downstairs the girl hugged me and said her father was already out of the house, and thanks me for saving her kitten.
>
> Later, my brother said knocking down that door stopped the fire from coming to the front of the house, and tried to put me down in his captain's book as being a hero.

Randy starts out to say one thing but digresses to another, in a narrative that may seem haphazard yet drives relentlessly toward its heroic ending. Interruptions and detours may threaten the progress, but ultimately they too are woven into the destined outcome—that cat he had "down my place," for example, becoming a little girl's kitten. The climactic events are all the more compelling after such a buildup, yet nothing seems contrived or artful. Luck is with him after all, and he lives up to his second chance gloriously.

The way that Randy's imagination transforms the raw material of memory into a single mythic drama becomes more evident when we have a second narrative to compare it with, written in the same roundabout, circumstantial style. One of Randy's persistent desires has been to serve others—surely a factor in the last seventeen years with his mother, during which time their care-taking roles have slowly reversed. "As a kid," he writes in one early memory, "I learned . . . manners, and helping old people in my building by taking out their trash or going to the store for somebody." This impulse to help those in need, especially people in desperate circumstances, led Randy to seek training in emergency medical care, and for a while he tried to follow that calling:

> Back in 1976 I took an EMT course at Bunker Hill Community College. I was very excited that I had passed my test and now I was a certified EMT. The next day was registration. When I got to Bunker Hill CC, the fire department was there showing us all these new gadgets they had. Well, registration was put off for 2 days.
>
> That night at 8:30 p.m. I was sitting in the passenger's seat (front seat) when my friend who was driving was going way too fast for the main intersection. As I looked to my right I noticed a car coming down D Street—we were on west 7th Street. Anyway, my friend had the stop sign and it was a blinking red light. D Street had a blinking light. Anyway, my friend did not stop. He thought he could make it through the intersection. Well, he didn't. The car coming down D Street, his hood ornament hit dead center in my door. If not for the fact that I had seen the other car, I would have been killed that night, because I tried to get out his side. I took the impact on my rear end and back.
>
> Needless to say I never got registered. . . .

Although by 1976 he was already using heroin, Randy doesn't mention it as a factor in his failure to register for official EMT status after recovering from his injury; nonetheless, his addiction and his CPR training now intersect providentially:

> One day I was on Dudley Street, looking for some . . . (I'll call it candy). I gave a friend my money, and he went up to an apartment to get it. A little while after, he came down and told me to take off, gave me back my money, and said a guy just OD'ed up in his friend's house. I asked which apartment was it. He said the one at the top of the stairs, but the guy is dead.
>
> With that I ran up the stairs, opened the door. About five people were trying to get the guy back, putting ice on him and other things. I said, "Get out of my way." I felt his neck for a pulse. There was none. He was a big white guy. He had foam coming from his mouth, so I cleared his airway and started CPR. After about the fourth time I did compression on his chest, I had a pulse. I told everyone to pick him up and let him stand on his own. We did, but he kept bending at the knees,

> so I slapped him as hard as I could. It seemed like forever, but he finally came around and was walking on his own.
>
> The man who owned the apartment picked me up and kissed me—he was a big Afro-American—and thanked me for saving this man's life, and his too. And with that I left.

This rescue predates Randy's adventure in the burning building and already contains all the essentials of that later story, from the familiar bureaucratic snafu to the act of daring that reestablishes his worth. Even the digressive subplot is repeated in both stories. A near-death experience in an automobile, followed by hospitalization, results in the loss of Randy's legitimate claims. In each case, after temporary physical incapacitation comes the test of his mettle, the same rushing up stairs into danger, knocking down doors, pushing obstacles aside—and even the same hug of gratitude afterwards. The convoluted path of cause and effect, with all its roadblocks and detours, finally leads to the saving of another life, by virtue of the studies for which he never received proper credit. And here once again his good and bad brothers hover auspiciously—a Fire Department demonstration having interfered with EMT registration. In the end Randy is a hero embraced by a black "brother"—for "saving this man's life, and his too." But of course it must all remain unreported and unconfirmed, for the same complex reasons that would prevent his being written up as a hero in his brother's "captain's book" or mentioned in his will.

What's going on here?

Ask anyone who works closely with addicts. Men like Randy often have ingenious stories to explain why they have their particular need, how they acquired it, and what they're doing about it. Or to show who is really responsible for it, and when it will no longer be a problem. Or to prove that their addiction isn't really an addiction, can't really be treated, or has turned out to be a blessing in disguise. Randy is a confabulator.

Of course, confabulation is not so very different from the private fantasizing most of us rely on to explain, not necessarily to excuse, our own weaknesses and vice. The main difference between Randy and you or me is that he has only one story to tell, and he tells it over and over again. Self-deluding as it may be, this story is his attempt to make sense of his life and justify himself in front of others. Confabulation is the work of interpretation, selecting and arranging the facts to confirm a point of view. Are we to say Randy is making things up? Is his story of the oval lunchbox to be dismissed as a junkie's fantasy? The load of circumstantiality, the marvels of coincidence and serendipity, must not be dismissed as mere fabrication any more than his mastery of pace and proportion should be dismissed just because it is naïve.

The "moral" of many a tale is an ethical construction forced on a plot that twists and turns as the author tries to get a grip on it, himself wrapped ever more tightly in its coils. The question is not whether or not to believe Randy—I for one do believe him—but whether it is productive for him to tell these stories. With most probationers, I feel certain that reading, writing, and talking about lives at risk in moments of crisis or change help them think about their shared problems and reconsider their responsibility for the fate that awaits them. Individuals like Deighton are sometimes able to use storytelling to shift perspective in explaining who they are and how they got that way. When we first ask students where people get their courage, self-esteem, and righteousness, their answers tend to be conventional and impersonal, but as the weeks pass, they begin to tell stories to match those we are reading.

Everyone has a little bag of treasured moments, brooded over in fantasy and already polished by many tellings, each of which plays a part in maintaining courage, self-esteem, and righteousness. Having recently faced judgment, and now asked to probe and prove himself, a probationer's trust in these old myths of selfhood has been severely shaken and put in doubt. It is frightening to expose them to public view, but once dared, the thrill of self-revelation can be transforming. A new confidence may emerge, infused with unexpected insights and ambitions, and ratified by the circle of readers or listeners.

As it happened, Luis had a rescue story to match Randy's. Putting them side by side is instructive:

> During a summer, like 2½ years ago, I had the job of a lifeguard, and I had never ever ever thought anybody would drown, or even come close. But me and a senior lifeguard had an incident we had to attend to. There was a six year old stuck in the six foot part of the pool, doggie paddling, and he had dropped so quick my heart fell into my ass. But anyway, I jumped in, and I could not see the boy under water until the other lifeguard jumped in, and I found the kid. But then the lifeguard jumped directly, straight for the kid's ass, which my arm was around, and BOOM the senior lifeguard landed head first into my right arm, and gave me the most painful frog it had ever had. And the kid dropped and I was going down, so now there were three people going down. And then my feet touched the floor of the pool, and jolted, with the kid in my left arm and my right clenched on the senior lifeguard's neck and arm. Soon the kid—after CPR by another lifeguard—was all right and breathing. The lifeguard told me I was remarkable, and they all clapped for me.
>
> This was a 2½ minute rescue mission, and I never felt better about myself before. This was really a "flinch" reaction basically, but what is really important is I have saved at least one life.

Like Randy, trained but not legitimated as "senior," and frustrated by accident and injury, Luis proves himself a hero. This memory of crisis and glory gives Luis something to pin his hopes on. Here is the kind of person he can be, even though at times he may find himself "going down," hitting bottom. But Luis is not a confabulator, and he does not tell the same story over and over, obsessed with explaining himself. Exactly how such stories are used depends on character and luck, but we all construct a past and a self out of such materials. If Randy seems to be trapped in a-thousand-and-one nights of the same old excuses, costumed as heroic exploits, who are we to lift the veil? This is the way Randy keeps himself going, on a path that has taken him through hell and out the other side. Whatever else we might say about his life and the stories he tells, Randy is a survivor. I would be extremely wary of any attempt to shake him out of his dream.

But then what *should* we do, in a program like ours, when writers seem to be deluding themselves? With someone like Luis, it might be productive to put some pressure on, perhaps asking him to say a little more about the competitive context of his heroic feats, his need to prove himself better than some rival. With Deighton, simply mirroring back what he wrote each week, in a typed version, was all that was necessary to position him for a change in perspective. Once he had the sight-line from Tolstoy, he was able to reconsider his old resentments and revise his life story, leaving it open for another kind of ending.

In Randy's case there was less likelihood that patiently listening to his tales of self-vindication would ever change anything. He was too practiced and skillful a confabulator, and life itself conspired with him in furnishing yarn for endless variations on the same pattern. Nonetheless, I can offer one final example that I believe does justice to both the weakness and the strength of Randy's storytelling, and also indicates one way we found to respond to him without directly calling his bluff.

Let me recall the anecdote of his failure to come home on time from a boyhood fishing expedition. "It wasn't my fault," he writes, but his father "didn't want to hear the reason I was so late" and beat him with a belt. Randy doesn't say why he was late—there is no equivalent here to the car accident or the one-bullet homemade gun. We only know that he had been out all afternoon and arrived home seven hours late, to "frantic" parents who "thought I might have fallen in the water and drowned." And there is no final episode in which Randy is somehow vindicated and becomes a hero. Actually, his vindication did emerge a few weeks later, but not in his homework. It came up in a small group discussion between Randy, Bert, and Neville.

By this time in the semester we had given up hope that Neville would gather the courage to hand in any writing, which he stuffed in his pockets every week instead. But he was still attending, and perhaps the small group conversations might get him thinking constructively about his addictions to the commonplace dangerous substances of our culture—television, junk food, and tobacco—that led to his obesity, asthma, and insomnia. Bert had established strong rapport with both Neville and Randy in previous classes, and one night we decided to pair them in a small group with him, to discuss that week's topic—the opportunity for self-discovery in times of crisis. For once Neville had come to class in time to write the opening exercise, and to start off their group discussion Bert asked him to read it aloud, even though he probably wouldn't hand it in:

> For me, my crisis started when I went to jail. Putting on all this extra weight that I cannot get rid of has caused me to have a very bad sleeping disorder. I tell you! you talk about punishment! I just pray that this crisis ends some day for me. It's like I am a walking zombie with no life.

Neville gets small disability payments and lives with his family. With no job, and not really looking for one, his self-destructive routine is to hang out with his friends, avoiding food all day, and then at night, alone, when he can't sleep because of his asthma, he binges on TV, cigarettes, and junk food.

Bert asks him if he is getting any counseling, and it turns out he isn't. This is why we've paired him with Randy, who immediately begins to offer names and addresses, telling Neville where he can get free counseling from people Randy trusts.

Neville hasn't read the homework for the week, so Bert asks Randy to tell them one of the stories. This is the kind of challenge Randy loves, and he goes through the plot episode by episode, gradually drawing Neville in, while Bert remains quiet. Before long the story has led them back to the problem of addiction and how to find the strength to fight it. Neville speaks frankly about his smoking and eating disorders as a part of some conflicted stubbornness deep in his character. He knows these indulgences aren't good for him, but he can't summon the will power to change. In prison, life was eating and watching television. That's where he gained all this enormous bulk. But he's been out of jail for a year now. His mother thinks he should be in a hospital, but he wants to do it his way. How does someone conquer an addiction? Randy makes suggestions:

> Try AA
>
> Try a gym
>
> God's right at your shoulder
>
> Open yourself, you're ready to change

Neville says he prays.

I overhear their conversation only in snatches, but it's obvious that Neville is moved by Randy's concern for him. He's not just another well-meaning probation officer, counselor, or family member urging him to seek help. Randy has been there. He's still there. When he tells Neville that his own secret is "the power of the mind," Neville listens hard, for he knows it's true. Randy's is a kind of ecstatic personality, filled with visions. Somehow he is able to survive in the center of the same world of suffering and disaster that Neville inhabits, turning stories of failure and defeat into victories.

I hear him beginning a new tale, seemingly irrelevant to Neville's problems. It's about fishing, one of his solitary substitutes for drugs. Randy is explaining that he goes fishing every chance he gets, right here on Dorchester Bay, in fact, casting in the surf for striped bass, the great eating fish that poor folks from the neighborhood try to hook every spring. Once again he is the hero, only this time it is not a story about coming home seven hours late and being beaten for it while his mother stands by crying. That time there were no fish to show for his trouble and no listeners willing to hear his excuses. Now Neville and Bert are all ears—and so am I!—as he tells how, on one fine day not too long ago, he hooked a 32-pound striper. Now that's a big fish, and it didn't get away like so many things in Randy's life that he almost had in his grasp. He sold it at the supermarket for $87. But that was only money—the fabulous striper is still thrashing in his memory.

Suddenly I see where it's going. Like so many other stories Randy tells, this one is going to end in a rescue. At this very moment Randy is inviting Neville to come fishing with him—any time! Just say the word!

Will Neville take him up on it? Probably not. There are too many obstacles, not least of which is Neville's spiritual sloth, the weight that Randy is trying to lift and drag to safety. Nonetheless, the invitation is sincerely meant, and wholeheartedly accepted. Neville agrees to come out to the Point some day, before sunrise, to try his own luck in hooking a big one. And of course it would be a fine thing for both of them, a storybook ending for their separate narratives that begin with unfulfilled hopes. But the likelihood of these two meeting at the crack of dawn to go fishing is miniscule.

So what is to be said of this fantasy invented in our classroom on the spur of the moment? Is it really any different from the confabulations Randy spins out to prove that despite his bad luck and thwarted ambitions he has triumphed?

I think so. As with Deighton's discovery of a new perspective, from which he no longer saw himself as the victim in a story with a tidy moral, so with Randy in this final example—there is no climax neatly restoring the hero to his rightful status. Instead the story is magically lifted out of the literary medium of plot, character, and representation, and into the realm of life itself, where a gesture in the living moment contains its own generous meaning and also offers an open-ended affirmation of further possibility—active hope for the future rather than triumph confined to the imagination.

All of us constantly invent stories about ourselves and what happens to us, making sense of the past as best we can, in order to meet the demands of each day without flinching or despair. As with Randy, we begin with "facts," the raw material that experience offers us, and the invention comes in the way we select and put together the pieces into sequences of motive and act, cause and effect, where we play the primary roles of hero, victim, or chief witness for the prosecution. Writing it down, even in the few sentences most of our probationers produce, inevitably leads to moralizing, just as putting any event into words fixes a particular understanding of its significance. But once you begin to think hard about something in the past, there is always the possibility that processes of recapitulation will sort things out in new ways, that outcomes will be assessed from a new perspective—perhaps only gradually and unconsciously, yet threatening to break into awareness at last—and surprise us like an uncanny yet transparent dream.

Whether or not we can learn from such stories depends in large part on those we tell them to. How honest can we be with this person? In his presence, how do we sound to our own ears? Some people make you think about that. Sitting in a classroom with three or four other men, each of them telling his story in turn, uncensored or guardedly, with the buzz of other conversations coming from similar groups in every corner, what version of your childhood self will come out? This is not something you can know in advance.

The uncertainty may be frightening and tempt a man to fall back on safely packaged memories with their lessons stuck on them like ready-made bows on a Christmas present. Or it can happen that someone like Neville needs encouragement and advice so desperately that you look into your own life anew and pull out some old story still alive with possibilities, a story you can offer up, inviting Neville to imagine himself as the hero of this one.

# Part Four

## *Responding to Crisis*

# Chapter 9

# *Standing Up for Yourself*

In this chapter I want to look closely at a single case of a violent man, as defined by the statutes and the courts, and follow his progress in our class as he gradually got to his feet, found his balance, and contemplated a new way of life that would lead him away from situations where he might lose self-control and lash out destructively against the world.

Although it would be possible to start by asking what drives such men to violent acts, we prefer a less accusatory approach. Instead, we begin by puzzling over dilemmas parents face in guiding and perhaps punishing children, when the resort to force may seem justified as a response to blameworthy behavior:

> *What should a parent's role be in teaching morality?*
>
> *What is society's responsibility in setting and enforcing moral standards?*
>
> *When do obedience and disobedience come into play, in learning the difference between right and wrong? When is the use of force necessary?*
>
> *What rules should govern the use of force or punishment in teaching morality to children? Can a genuine desire to be "good" be encouraged through force?*

Sometimes our discussions break through to an underlying question: Are the parents' powers, duties, and disciplinary choices—all founded on physical force—any different from those of institutions like schools, courts, or prisons?

These conversations usually end up in debate over the ethics and efficacy of punishing children for misbehavior or disobedience. Although most of them start from the common ground of having been chastised or beaten themselves, probationers disagree vigorously on the use of corporal punishment in disciplining their own children. They are not ambivalent but adamant, caught in the middle of a great cultural shift. This discussion leads the following week into broader questions of social control, seen from the perspective of schooling and its role in developing, or undermining, inner discipline and self-determination, and argued against the background of Malcolm X's story of self-discovery in prison, where he set himself the task of mastering the means of his own freedom in the midst of institutional coercion meant to break his spirit.

Considering violence as a means of self-defense, with the possibility of refraining from it as well as giving in to it, we raise harder issues for ourselves. When is it essential to stand up for yourself, and when is it not worth the price? We ask this question in the context of Frederick Douglass's fight with the slave-breaker Edward Covey, but we complicate the picture by considering the nonviolent practice of Dr. King, as well as examples of self-defense from Richard Wright, Bill Russell, and Malcolm X. Our texts can be read as moral dilemmas as well as exemplary tests of manly pride and self-respect.

In our classroom students do not view Frederick Douglass as a violent man even though he fights back rather than submit to a whipping, and will ultimately advocate armed resistance to slavery. They believe in the right to use force in self-defense. Although somewhat less approving than the general public of the coercive power of the state—to maintain its laws or prosecute its wars—most of these men approve of violence used in the right cause or for the right motives. "When I know I'm right," says Charles, "then nothing else matters."

In discussing issues raised by the problem of self-defense, the question we begin with is this:

> *After Douglass refuses to be whipped and risks his life in fighting the slave-breaker, he wins not only the fight but his manhood. Is his experience a useful model for men today?*

Although most of the probationers believe that the terms of the struggle have altered radically since slavery times, their consensus is that men today should "fight back," as Neville puts it, "when you feel that your rights have been violated." Again and again, Malcolm's famous slogan is quoted:

> Luis: When a person is going beyond your limit, you must protect and defend and whatever is necessary.
>
> Albert: When someone has threatened your life, such as trying to beat you with a bat or stick, or cut you with a knife, you have the right to defend yourself by any means necessary.
>
> Charles: I have faced a lot of injustice in childhood and as an adult. From my readings and listening to Malcolm X, I feel like he said: "By any means necessary."

When faced with a question calling for a public stand, these men think of familiar formulas like Malcolm's, or the traditional rallying cries of the American Revolution.

In contrast with their responses to Douglass's physical defense of his humanity, which they understand as a test of masculinity to be met by "any means necessary," most probationers view the issues rather differently when we frame them in a way that fits their own situation more exactly:

> *What can people who are "weak"—because of illness, poverty, prejudice, or a history of being in trouble with the law—do to change their lives and make themselves "stronger"?*

In discussing self-defense from this point of view, probationers are certainly influenced by the example of Martin Luther King Jr., but even more, I think, by the emphasis both Douglass and Malcolm put on self-realization as a means of empowerment—more effective in the long run than personal bravery under direct attack.

As the reader will have noted, we regularly ask leading questions to help students articulate their intuitions in such inquiries. For instance, in the passage I will quote next, when José speaks of "self-esteem" and "self-expression" as more important in standing up for yourself than knee-jerk violence, he seems to be picking up language from questions asked earlier in the semester. Is this what he really thinks, or is he only mouthing our pious phrases? For my part, I believe José is in complete command of his ideas here, whether or not he is right about the efficacy of self-confidence in crisis situations:

> People can defend themselves by trying to ignore the person that's making fun of them. Another way to be strong is to have high self-esteem. It is quite easy. I think, also, a person that is weak or oppressed can use self-expression.

We hear similar claims from Charles and Albert, who also regard self-esteem as the key factor, but they go into much more detail analyzing the obstacles and the means of overcoming them. They have come to a realization similar to Douglass's, when he overheard his master say that teaching him to read would ruin him forever as a slave.

> Charles: First of all, I think the weak should have knowledge, education, and self-esteem, and be able to associate with the strong without feeling inferior. In that way I think the weak can become strong as time goes by. In many ways I felt weak, but as years went by I began to feel stronger and stronger. I was fearful, but not anymore, thanks to family and the help of God, and friends.

> Albert: A weak person can defend themselves by leading a life based on their belief of truth and morals learned early in life.
>
> Also stand up, even if someone tells them otherwise, so long as that decision doesn't harm anyone.
>
> There are many ways of being oppressed. Being denied education, for one, by an individual or group for profit or personal gain. Leading one to self-doubt, low self-esteem, and poor health by denying basic human rights and equality. Being denied the knowledge of one's past cultural background. So, by living a daily life,

> the chance of being oppressed for many different reasons is only a step away. If not recognized by the individual, they will also be considered a weak person.
>
> Awareness of self allows one to overcome the oppressor.

As I have suggested more than once already, at this point in the semester I was still concerned that Albert might be using our class to construct a trap for himself. I might agree that "awareness of self" is essential in finding one's way from weakness to strength. But does Albert really know himself? He talks about studying "child development" and getting a college degree in order to devote himself to children. Does he realize how much struggle and discouragement he would face, just bringing his basic skills up to the level of college work? He may want what college offers, but I'm not sure how deep the drive goes. I don't see that he has Randy's passion for books, for instance, nor is there any solid evidence of a dedication to children. Albert is not a father and has never mentioned any children in his life. However heartfelt Albert's pronouncements on self-esteem and self-awareness may be, his confidence is likely to take another battering if he pushes his fantasy of further schooling too far. It's not clear how much his desire is based on a genuine calling in him and how much is but a desperate attempt to fit in and prove himself to the powers that be. In my next response to his homework I ask him, "What kind of self-awareness is the real solution?"

The truth is that Albert is still a mystery to me, and I'm reluctant to say anything that might undermine his hope. By this time I probably know Charles as well as will be possible in our classroom situation, but so far I haven't penetrated the surface Albert presents to us in his brave stumbling speeches that seem to confuse his personal yearning for respect with conventional notions of schooling as the high road to respectability.

On the night we discuss ways of defending oneself from violence I sit with Charles and Albert to hear what they have to say. Both have read the assignment but have written very little in response, scarcely more than I have just quoted. Albert has added a few sentences in his opening exercise that tilt the perspective toward his own preoccupations while keeping Douglass's practical realities at arm's distance. He volunteers to go first, reading his page aloud in a nervous monotone:

> In defense of oneself, you can respond to violence by accepting harm to yourself or to someone else, or to minimize hurt to anyone else by seeking help from law enforcement.
>
> If you do not stand up and fight for what you believe in, it says to me that you are a weak person. And that you will let the world pass you by.

Albert apparently has some personal experience in mind. Drifting further and further away from Douglass's example of physical bravery, he never quite embraces "standing up for what you believe in" as his own problem. Our question seems to have forced an answer from him before he feels it, preventing him from knowing what he wants to say. Once again I wonder whether we are putting words in the mouths of these men who are not comfortable in the classroom. For Albert, true courage may be finding the strength to speak in his own voice—instead of trying to guess what we want him to say—not so different from the bind that most students in American public schools find themselves in.

Although Douglass seems to serve him as a model for the heroism of free speech, Albert's notion of standing up for yourself is obscured by conventional rhetoric about manliness and democratic faith: "In some countries," he writes, "a lot of people do not have their freedom, and are still willing to fight and die for what they believe in." Underneath these clichés of physical and moral courage lies some deeper existential bravery that is real to Albert—simply to have a thought and speak it. However falteringly, his own call to arms is sounding here. His moment of truth is occurring right now in our little group, though he's barely able to identify it. The poignant turn comes when he remembers how life seems to be passing *him* by. There he sits—a frail black man with a worried face and anxious eyes, uneasily aware of the crossroads he has come to, and imagining his choices in the ready-made phrases of American manliness, from Malcolm X back to Patrick Henry. But he's mustered the courage to go first in our group, to speak his mind before "the world passes him by."

Now it's Charles's turn, and he zeroes in on Douglass and his personal crisis in a completely different way. "Man should not be beaten," Charles carefully reads from his bluebook, interrupting himself to explain that since Douglass was a slave, he had duties to perform. As long as he performed them, the overseer had no right to beat him. I am surprised by the obligation Charles apparently feels to *justify* Douglass's resistance to Covey rather than simply to applaud it. In this curiously legalistic reasoning there is no critique of slavery itself, though Charles also says—almost as an afterthought—that of course slavery itself was wrong. He reads from his page again: "Although he was a slave, there are other ways to deal with the matter. We all know that slaves were beaten or punished at some time, but some more than others. In Frederick Douglass' case, he fought and he won."

Charles assumes a status quo founded on the nature of things, whatever they may be, whether slavery or his own condition as a black man raised in the Jim Crow South. Although he doesn't like to talk about himself, after a long pause he suddenly comes to life and draws a line that marks the boundary of his own self-respect: "When I'm right—*when I know I'm right!*—then nothing else matters." Like Douglass, he too has his boiling point.

Several others in the class also conceive manliness as a matter of "rights" and "standing up for what you believe in," but Charles understands these principles in a special way. For him "being right" means being *justified.* Covey had no "right" to beat Douglass, who was guiltless, so Douglass was "right" to resist. Abstract as this may seem, when Charles applies his formula to today's world he seems to be recalling some particular event, and in fact he keeps looking toward an empty corner of the room, as if it were happening there. Perhaps Charles is inviting us to ask him what he is remembering, but all he adds is that on "a number" of occasions he has chosen to act without regard for his own safety. "Chosen" would probably not be his word—he simply *disregards* danger and risk when "I know I'm right." And yet he phrases it peculiarly, as if he were talking about a dispute over facts in a court of law, or the great American struggle over civil rights, or the ultimate sources of legitimate authority. Remembering what it feels like to "be right," he raises his head a bit. I can see his faded eyes under the bill of his cap, and his face set, determined.

To explore the issues in more mundane circumstances, I offer a challenge I have actually experienced more than once: confronting a drunk on a crowded subway car. Suppose a drunk is harassing someone—what do you do?

Albert has his answer ready—indeed, his opening exercise seems almost to have foreseen my question: "You can respond to violence by accepting harm to yourself or to someone else, or to minimize hurt to anyone else by seeking help from law enforcement." He now expands on those options: Don't get too close, he advises us, but sometimes you can reason with a drunk. If that doesn't work, it's better to step off the train, or try to persuade either the drunk or his victim to do so. Alert the police in any case.

Watching his face, I see Albert imagining these possibilities, thinking it through as he talks, and I wonder whether "reasoning" with the drunk also means reasoning with himself about how to deal with the situation. Albert doesn't strike me as someone who trusts his instincts, nor does he seem likely to step forward in an emergency. He has some *dos* and *don'ts* at his fingertips, but they sound like instructions posted at the end of the subway car, not based in real experience.

Charles has a very different approach. First off he tells us that he has often been in just this situation. Take the drunk by the arm, he says—raising his own arm to demonstrate—and lead him aside. If you get him alone, a drunk can be talked to. Charles is absolutely certain of this. Although I don't feel he's dismissing Albert's caution, he doesn't share his timid spirit. He too believes that reason can prevail, but his attitude is more pragmatic and engaged. For him, "reasoning" with a drunk has preliminaries and stages, not just an outcome.

When I ask him whether he can anticipate when it might be dangerous to intervene, Charles says he would know infallibly—and would never step into a truly dangerous situation. His examples from barrooms and the streets convince me that he knows what he's talking about. But quite unlike Albert, it doesn't occur to Charles to begin analyzing potential risks. On the contrary, he seems to be reliving actual events, not merely imagining what he might do. Once again his eyes lose focus, though the look on his face is not quite the same as his earlier inward gaze while reporting how it feels to abandon caution when he knows he's "right." I wonder what scenes from his past he is revisiting now.

Compared with Douglass's antagonists, my hypothetical drunk on the subway has lowered the stakes enormously, but some elements are the same—the threat of violence, the choice of resistance or acquiescence, the risk of losing self-control in the heat of the moment. These are major concerns for many probationers, whose tempers are short and whose cramped lives frequently bring them up against potential enemies, including authorities who wield absolute power—it isn't just drunks on the subway who present such challenges. Charles and Albert approach these matters in a positive spirit, but it's not difficult to imagine negative possibilities—losing self-control and then finding yourself in trouble with the very authorities that might otherwise protect you. After all, that's why many of these students are sitting here, and perhaps attending "anger management" programs as well.

As our conversation proceeds, I begin to realize that Charles and Albert have experienced both the positive and the negative. My example from the subways was spontaneously offered from my own experience, but it was surprisingly prescient, for it turns out that both these men are recovering alcoholics, and Albert has a history of violent behavior when inebriated. I don't know about Charles—domestic abuse maybe?

In considering such possibilities, it is worth noticing how easy it is to fall into conventional terminology for socially disapproved behavior, at once convenient and condemning. It's an easy step, too, from one to the next: alcoholic, violent, batterer. Let me also remind the reader that neither Charles nor Albert matches the public stereotype of the criminal offender—big, black, and fierce. Indeed, aside from skin color very few of these students fit this mythical mug shot, nor do those who actually have convictions for assault or violent crimes fit the typecasting of the "evening news." The truth is that, like most people, a probationer's main concern is how to avoid violence directed at him. To the degree that their lives in "the hood" have made them vulnerable, some of them have developed habits of self-defense that have the look, and sometimes the outcome, of thuggish behavior. But for most of them wariness and caution are more in evidence than belligerence. My guess is that the fascination with violence that grips the American imagination is less endemic among them, though they watch the same cops and robbers on television and devour the perpetual warfare on the sports page with the same avidity. Their attitude toward our country's chronic military violence is also atypical, for almost to a man they disapprove of our wars, despite the fact that quite a few of the older students, like Randy, have fought in them.

Although we've had our share of batterers and brawlers in class, it's been rare for anyone to talk about it. No doubt there's more than enough focus on violence in their anger management programs. The only extended discussion of actual violence and its psychology that I remember was provoked by my example of the drunk on the subway, which led finally to personal revelations from Albert. His story is a common one: When he goes "out and about town" with his friends, he's susceptible to pressure from them to have a drink. One thing leads to another and soon he's "pissy drunk," as he puts it. Then he gets into an argument—he doesn't even know who has offended him, or what it's about—and leaves his friends feeling angry and ready to lash out at anyone. Often it's his girlfriend who has to absorb his rage, but on one particular night he found himself staggering home to his mother's house. Suddenly he was being pushed by someone through a "picture window," presumably a plateglass storefront. He doesn't remember how it happened or why.

The next thing Albert knew, there were cops and medics and a crowd gathered. He was badly cut, covered with glass and blood, and in a daze. Although he doesn't tell us the upshot, it's not hard to guess that several such episodes have ended with Albert himself in jail for assault. Very likely he has provoked a fight, as a result of his drinking, though the deeper cause is not alcohol, as he goes on to explain.

"It is difficult for me to express my true feelings," he says. "When I feel that no one is listening to me, I get very mad and take all my anger out on anyone that is around at the time. It does not matter to me who it is. It can just be for them not understanding me or not seeming to care." "*It does not matter.*" This is Albert's version of what Charles says—that "nothing else matters" when you know you're "right." We are at the point where these men, drunk or sober, draw the line.

Our conversation has not really strayed from the original problem of violence as a test of manliness, querying Frederick Douglass's relevance for black men in today's world. Albert and Charles may quote Malcolm's "by any means necessary," but neither of them evinces the least bit of aggressiveness in their advice for dealing with potential violence from a drunk on the subway. They know well, from their own experience, what fuels a drunken rage, what can ignite or extinguish it. Albert can get so drunk he throws all of his characteristic caution to the winds, and in a crisis Charles is also in danger of losing his prudence—when "nothing else matters."

I ask Albert how he intends to deal with his drinking problem. He will surely find it hard to break out of the cycle he has lived with so many years, but at least he is not wandering in fantasies of self-renewal of the sort that tempt him when he talks about going back to school. I am asking him now about a minefield he knows intimately. In answering he makes an effort to communicate exactly what his past experience has been. He falters a bit because he wants so desperately to say it right:

> Sometimes people need someone to talk to, and when they do not have anyone to talk to, they tend to depend on their own thoughts. Maybe that person's thoughts are not the best ones in the world, but it is the only one at that time.

He gets this far, then starts again, from a slightly different angle:

> When people have anger in their heart, sometimes they will not let anything stop them from expressing the way that they are feeling. And that can be a loss to that person. Sometimes when my friends and I are out and about town, something happens that I had no part of. I get very angry at the time, but I do not show it. I just wait till I get to my girlfriend's house, and when she says something to me that I do not like, all of my anger comes out. I take everything out on her, even though she has no idea about half the things that I am talking about.

Once more Albert is not satisfied with his account of his behavior, and tries again:

> Sometimes in life, we all feel the need to lash out at someone, for many reasons. For me it can just be for them not understanding me or not seeming to care. Many times I am wrong and don't want to admit to that person that I was wrong.

Finally he has come to the point he wants to make about his cycles of isolation and self-doubt—how he holds everything in until, after an evening of drinking, he explodes in rage. He goes to his girlfriend's house, or worse, to his family home, "pissy drunk," and humiliates his old mother in front of his siblings. He realizes how much suffering he has caused his mother. He feels ashamed and is gathering the courage to change—no doubt with renewed insistence from the court.

> After seeing the hurt that I cause them, I open up my heart to them, to ask for their forgiveness of me, and talk things over so that we both understand each other. And when that happens we both feel much better. That's called love.

What brings any alcoholic to the decision to confront his problem? Many factors may be at work, and there is no sure formula. Albert has been avoiding his "bad friends" for some time now. He speaks of seeing them on the street, drunk and disorderly as he used to be. As Albert comes to the end of his story, Charles and I think our own thoughts silently. This once, Albert has moved far beyond his usual desperate need to keep talking. He too becomes silent. He has had his say; we have heard him.

# Chapter 10

# *Crisis and Self-Discovery*

Walking down the hall with Albert one night after class, I suddenly realized that he has a game leg—in old-fashioned labeling he would be called a "cripple." How had I missed that? I was taken aback. What did I actually know about Albert? Nothing, really nothing. In trying to tell his story perhaps I should have started here, at the point halfway through the semester when I finally began to see that he was not the befuddled person I thought he was, and that no formula would do him justice. He was not a "cripple" any more than he was a "recovering alcoholic" or a "violent man." He was not desperate to follow the rules or live up to expectations. He was just Albert, gradually coming into view.

Six weeks through the semester, addressing resistance to oppression by the weak and powerless, we reach the climax of our discussion of violence, while at the same time we introduce a new theme, first sounded in the conversation on schooling and self-determination, now brought into sharper focus when we invite identification with the victims of personal and institutional intimidation. This new emphasis colors everything we read and talk about from here on out, and it will bring another side of Albert to light:

> *In one way or another, all of the readings this week are about self-discovery and self-fulfillment in conditions of crisis. Can you tell a story from your life that would fit in?*

The readings referred to here have been chosen chiefly to shift attention from violence to nonviolence, and from personal self-defense to public resistance to coercive institutions—seen through the lens of the modern civil rights movement. What allows men and women like Martin Luther King Jr. or Rosa Parks—or Malcolm X for that matter—to turn oppression and defeat into new challenges and unforeseen self-discovery? To put it more pointedly than we ever actually formulate it, what can probationers hope to achieve, what can emerge from their harrowing experiences as offenders brought to justice and punished?

With heroic figures like Rosa Parks, a single dramatic act often lies at the center of the story, giving the career a literary quality, with a climax summing up the lesson that makes this life exemplary. For the most part, however, probationers telling their own stories do not remember vivid moments of crisis that became turning points, but only long periods of desperation. One might say that they are like Frederick Douglass, *minus* his great feats of self-determination—learning to read, or the fight with the slave-breaker—that put purpose and direction into a life over which he had little control. Just as Douglass recalls what it was like to live every day as a slave, or to witness the endless whippings administered by the master, so a probationer might reflect bitterly about his life on the street, or in "South Bay," the house of correction they're all familiar with, but when asked to write about "A Crisis in My Life," they are much more likely to choose things that happen to everyone, perhaps dwelling a little more than most of us on family upheavals. Here are a few examples:

Willy's grandmother was the one he turned to as a child when his mother was angry with him, and he still remembers how his "heart dropped" the day he came home from school and found all his family gathered outside her house because she had "passed away."

Similarly, Trevor misses his grandmother, who recently left for Georgia. Now his aunt is living with them, and "she really gets on my nerves." This shift in family dynamics seems to embody a "crisis" for Trevor, perhaps mirroring other undoings in his life—fights with his girlfriend, separation from his young daughter. His situation is not unlike Dave's chafing under his aunt's thumb, or Randy's ongoing feud with his brother, or even Deighton's obsession with the girlfriend who threw him out.

In all of these examples family crisis tends to modulate into job crisis, almost archetypically in the case of Anthony, who tells us he goes "through a crisis with my mother every day, always talking about getting a job, going to college, or moving out." Less obvious examples would include José's memory of how his mother longed for the heat of Puerto Rico and finally moved the family back home when he was sixteen, where José and his brother couldn't find work no matter how hard they tried. We have already heard about the day Charles's father left, which led to his mother's two jobs, his own two paper routes, and then striking out on his own at sixteen—another example of the rough passage from childhood security to the demands of working life, which seems to be replayed many times.

Although these stories are mostly about periods of crisis already lived through and hardened into fate, students also write about current predicaments, looking toward the future for resolution. In one of the few classroom exercises he ever turned in, Neville confronts his immediate plight, its origins, and his sense of desperation—high stakes again straining mother/son bonds:

> For me, my crisis started when I went to jail. Putting on all this extra weight that I cannot get rid of has caused me to have a very bad sleeping disorder. I tell you! you talk about punishment! I just pray that this crisis ends some day for me. It's like I am a walking zombie with no life. It also tears my mother apart, just seeing me like this. She wants to put me in a hospital so that I can get some help. She

really worries about me. I really pray to overcome this crisis that is in my life today, someday real soon.

Albert too regards his present situation as a crisis, and like Neville he imagines himself at the mercy of circumstances out of his control, with nostalgia for irrecoverable childhood certainties looming in the background. Here is the brief paragraph he wrote when asked for a memory of self-discovery in crisis:

> I believe that when it is time for me to get off probation, they should let me go and continue with my life, and not try to keep holding onto me. I am trying to go back to school and further my future—childhood development, because I would love to work with kids—that's my goal in life.

After six weeks in our program Albert is still clinging to the hope that he can pull out of his downward spiral by going back to school. "Going back" is conventional phrasing, but it is especially apt in cases like that of Albert, or even of Neville and Randy, men overwhelmed by adult life, whose mothers are still supporting and worrying over them. Albert is imagining starting over, twenty years after his graduation from high school, and perhaps he is stuck at an even earlier age of "child development," the curriculum he wants to study in college, "to further my future." Somehow this ambition is connected with his desire to make amends, like Randy, for the suffering he's caused his old mother, now seventy-two. Although I continue to be skeptical about Albert's goals, perhaps it would make sense to take his fixation on child development more seriously as a plan for self-rehabilitation. Several other aspects of his perilous balancing act also begin to emerge more clearly this week, as once again I choose to sit with him and Charles, to talk about self-discovery in moments of crisis.

At the start of the semester I had seen Albert as an unkempt, slightly glassy-eyed man of about thirty, somehow as wobbly on his feet as he was in his speech, not sure of himself but trying to line up where he thought we wanted him. Even before pairing them in a small group conversation, I was bracketing Albert with Charles, who also seemed somewhat at a loss, though much more guarded and reticent. In our full class discussions Charles never ventured a word from his place next to the door, but Albert was often fired up by the small group conversations and was among the first to try his voice in front of everyone. Others waited patiently for him to run out of steam.

After a week or so I had noticed that Albert was older than I first thought, by at least a dozen years. I have already described my next realization, that his unsteadiness on his feet was not simply a matter of demeanor but due to a malformation of one leg, causing him to limp noticeably. In short, by the time of the conversation I am about to relate, my impression of Albert had begun to shift. I was not sure how much could be attributed to changes in him, and how much to my own closer look.

Perhaps inspired by our earlier conversation about hypothetical confrontations with drunks in the subway, and with our reading about Rosa Parks also in the background, Albert now brought to class a "crisis" story that captures in a single incident his own self-image—as a person who, himself at a disadvantage, wants to defend others from the same abuse and shame he frequently experiences:

> The only times when I have trouble on the bus is when you get on. Sometimes people will not get up from the front seats and give them to people who need them, such as myself. When you ask that person, Could they let you sit in the front row seat, they just look at you like you are crazy. Seems to me that the bus driver should ask or tell the person to give the seats to the people who need them the most.
>
> There have been times when I was on the bus, and more people got on at the next stop. Sometimes people ask the driver what destinations is the bus going to, and the driver yelled at that person. I know that you should know which direction you are going, but sometimes the driver forgets to change the sign, and therefore we all have to ask questions at one time or another. So I said to the driver, when I was getting off the bus, that he did not have to be so rude to people—and the driver said back to me, If you do not like the way I talk to people, do not ride on my bus route.
>
> Hopefully I will not have to ride the buses after this summer. And then I feel that I will have peace of mind.

Despite his halting gait, Albert doesn't really carry himself as a cripple. This must be why people on the bus don't give up their seats but look at him as if he were "crazy" when he asks for the space reserved for the handicapped. To be frank, I catch myself wondering just how much he "needs" that front seat. His difficulty walking or standing seems to be very much in the background, not a pressing problem. These doubts may not be resolvable, but I am seeing him now from a new perspective. Does he get disability checks? How does the official world regard him? And the real question, for which I also have no answer, is how thoroughly he defines himself as a loser.

Albert's encounter with the belligerent bus driver was hardly a victory, especially when you keep in mind his advice about handling a drunk on the subway—"call the authorities." Just as in the South during the Jim Crow era in which Charles grew up, here too the relevant authority *is* the bus driver. And when told, "If you do not like the way I talk to people, do not ride on my bus route," Albert is simply receiving the treatment he imagines appropriate for a drunk on the subway. Meanwhile, silent in the background are two ironic shadows: on the one hand, the heroic legend of Rosa Parks refusing to stand up and move to the back of the bus; and, on the other hand, Albert's personal myth that the most important thing a man must do is to "stand up" for himself.

Memories of suffering and self-doubt are private matters, things that students may not want to talk about. Albert knows that no one is obliged to go into personal details, and our conversations, even when anecdotal, typically revolve around ethical and social issues considered as general principles of behavior, not personal concerns. Nonetheless, any discussion of crisis and self-discovery, no matter how impersonal, or conducted as literary analysis, is bound to light up an inner world full of ghosts and demons. For ex-offenders the shame and humiliation of substance abuse, loss of self-control, lashing out dangerously and futilely, are at least as hard to talk about as the public trial, judgment, and punishment they all share, for these private feelings darken the landscape they see when they turn their faces away from the hopes and dreams of their youth:

> "I had so many dreams as a little boy."
>
> "When we are young, it seems friendships are more real, more sacred."
>
> "I have always been an outgoing, free-wheeling type of person."
>
> "When I was a young boy, I always tried to look forward in life about how life would be and what I wanted to do."
>
> " . . . making my old-time dreams vanish."
>
> "I had hoped for so much more."

It's hard to "reform"—to kick your habit, give up your easy money, turn your back on your street friends—but it's even harder to renew lost hopes and ideals. Once gone, childhood innocence is gone forever. Perhaps the closest thing to renewal is fatherhood, the chance to give your own child what you never got. For some of these men—especially those like Albert, who has no children—the desire to go back to school often stems from a similar yearning, and our program can feed that little flame—riskily, since the world is likely to blow it out in one quick puff. This possibility poses a major issue for the Changing Lives Through Literature program. We want to foster self-confidence and ambition, new hopes and reaching out to the world, rejoining the society that has rejected every probationer. But are these new hopes practical? This is a question of fact as well as of spirit. Nothing will send a man back to the bottom faster than the crushing of renewed faith. And so I have worried about Albert and his ambition "to go back to school and further my future" by studying childhood development.

I do not know what will happen to Albert's ambitions once our course is over and he is allowed, as he says, to "continue my life." But whether or not he can follow through on his imagined path, Albert has most emphatically been changed by daring to formulate his hopes at all. Having publicly recounted his own crisis of defeat and self-recognition, he seems to be aware of new powers in his own character. These new powers are real, and everyone saw evidence of them when we began our general classroom discussion of crisis and self-discovery.

What happened then is also important in understanding how change occurs in the Changing Lives program, the delicate balance between the emotional risk-taking of small-group conversations and the public testimony and self-assertion that often grow out of that soul-searching when we reconvene as a more formal, public body. However intense their separate testimonies may be, in writing or in small group conversation, the turning point for most probationers comes in the larger, more public arena, where every eye is on you. The discovery that the soul-shaking personal experiences you've had can be talked about, shared with others, and are not shameful, provides new ground to stand on.

Already Albert has his hand up. I call on him, and suddenly he's rising to his feet, next to his desk, something almost no one ever does in our classes, his weight on his good leg, head held high. Originally so unsure of himself, he began the semester anxiously speechifying, worried that his opinion wouldn't count and that he would have to toe the official line, as he imagined it, if he wanted anyone to pay attention to him. But he's been trying out his voice every week in the small group sessions, discovering in conversations I've been describing that others are willing to listen to his story, not so very different from their own experience. Now he is ready to speak publicly to us all, not the conventional opinions he still thinks it's his duty to uphold, but rather his deeply felt desire to be taken seriously, to be "understood" and "cared about" when he finds the courage "to stand up for himself."

In the past Albert's classmates have sat patiently through his anxious harangues in front of us all, but with an unmistakable air of waiting for it to be over, giving him respect but not real attention. Tonight something new has come into Albert's voice, and it immediately registers with everyone. It isn't *what* he says this time, but the *way* he says it that makes us sit up and listen intently.

Taking a deep breath, he begins to speak of his own memories of hitting bottom—friendless, no roof over his head, living in shelters "without a cent." From there he goes on to tell us how his family, his mother really, took him in—no reluctance, no recriminations. Albert's theme is forgiveness and reconciliation. As in Tolstoy's story "Korney Vasiliev," our reading for this week, the cycle of hurt feelings, violence, and moral degradation could only be broken by hitting bottom and realizing that there is something more important than clinging to one's anger and pride. In Tolstoy's narrative the climax comes when the beaten and despairing protagonist returns home to his family and finds unexpected forgiveness. It was much the same for Albert, as for quite a few of our men. And for those like Albert who are still living with parents or extended families, this may constitute a return to childhood innocence—"starting over" in a symbolic sense, and even in a practical sense. Randy, for instance, the next to speak, will talk about his resolution ten years ago to rehabilitate himself. When I ask him what gave him the strength to turn his life around, he will reply instantly, "my mother."

From his rhythms and fervor I can sense that Albert is winding up his testimony. Like Randy he has often displayed a tendency to lose himself in these speeches, not knowing how to stop. Tonight, however, Albert has his story straight from the outset, and he is able to tell it without feeling that he isn't saying what he wants to say, or that no one is listening. I have been watching the faces in the room. Luis is sitting quietly in the back corner, his big, thoughtful eyes and full brows, usually so active, now concentrated in a frown, intent on what Albert is saying. No one is bored or glazed over.

Albert himself seems quite altered. Ten weeks ago he looked like he had walked right out of a shelter into our classroom. Tonight he seems taller, straighter, self-assured.

When I ask him if he can identify the moment he began taking himself more seriously, he knows what I'm driving at. He tells us that he came into the program because it was a chance to get some time off probation. When he found people giving him their attention, he began to think he might have something to say. Conversations in small groups made the difference.

I traveled more or less the same road with Albert this semester, not taking him seriously at the beginning when he talked about "furthering my education" in what seemed like someone else's words. What I didn't realize at first was how big a leap it was for Albert to say *anything at all* in front of other people, without a couple of drinks to fortify him. I needed to hear more of his story, in small group conversations, in order to understand where he was coming from.

Not everyone wants to speak about hitting bottom, but everyone seems truly represented by those who do, perhaps especially by what Albert has said. The last person to volunteer is Deighton, also sitting in the back of the room, twenty years older than Luis and more mature, a lot of life behind him. He too describes hitting bottom, his face very solemn. Although he doesn't speak as personally as Albert and Randy, his earnestness is equal to theirs, and I begin to feel that, if we had time, everyone in the room could speak this way, even Willy, whose clown costume is so hard to see through, to the real person hiding there.

This semester, our class valedictorian, if we had one, would have to be Albert, and in fact his speech on this night, very similar to what he later wrote in his bluebook for our very last class the following week, sounds like the hail and farewell that is traditional on such occasions:

> Since I have been in this class, Changing Lives Through Literature, it has changed my life. It made me see that I do have something to offer in life, outside of hanging out in the streets with so-called friends. This class made me want to go back to school and further my education.
>
> Because all I wanted to do in life was to help people, and by taking this class it helped me to know and learn that all things are possible. Just have faith in God and yourself.
>
> Classmates: Some of us will go on in life, and go for our goals if they really want it bad enough. I am sorry to say that most will not, because they do not understand what's really going on in the world. Now that I see what I have been missing in life, I am going to try and change my life for the better.

That last class would end with handshaking all around. Randy tells Bert he'll be back next semester, though he won't be getting probation credit for it—he's finished his sentence. Bert tells Randy we'll be glad to see him. Others promise to visit, or announce loudly that they won't be back! The last ones to leave are Randy and Albert, who walk down the corridor with us, Albert swinging along on his gimpy leg, all of us exhilarated. We'll see each other again in a few days, for the graduation ceremony at the courthouse, so it doesn't feel like a final good-bye.

# Part Five

## *Making a New Start*

# Chapter 11

# *Hitting Rock Bottom*

The fulcrum that does the heavy lifting for us all semester long is Frederick Douglass's *Narrative*, which shows us a man raised in captivity like a beast of burden, beaten and driven, who somehow summons the strength to break his bonds, escape to freedom, and become a leader of his people—author of one of America's great books and inspiration for later generations, including our own.

As we read the climax of Douglass's story, almost at the end of our semester, we bring in a second master text that throws a dark shadow across Douglass's narrative of hope—Leo Tolstoy's "Korney Vasiliev," a story of moral degradation and despair written near the end of Tolstoy's life for an audience comprised of barely literate former serfs and a new class of social activists who were struggling, partly on the model of American abolitionists, to turn legal emancipation into genuine freedom.

Tolstoy first heard this tale from an itinerant storyteller in 1897, framed as a "pilgrim" legend about a prosperous kulak who leaves home and family to wander seventeen years, finally coming back to die. By the time Tolstoy finished his own version of the story a decade later, it had become a parable of the plagues and passions of modern life—jealousy and domestic violence, alcoholism, joblessness, homelessness, suicidal recklessness, self-pity, and despair.

At the end of the semester when we ask probationers which of our supplementary texts meant the most to them, this is the one they point to, even though some of them can't remember its title or its famous author. For readers like Luis or Deighton it's the one about the betrayed husband, while for men like Charles and Albert it's the one about drunken violence, so familiar and so appalling. But there's something for everyone in this story, because Korney's terrible punishment mirrors their own condition—the loss of everything, especially self-respect.

Although Tolstoy's tale of human folly and moral collapse is full of openings for comparison to their own lives, we invite students to higher ground in our prelude to this week's opening exercise:

> Some people say you have to "hit bottom" before you can change. But it's dangerous—you might not come out of your depression. It's been compared to dying and being reborn.
>
> Hitting bottom helps you stop feeling sorry for yourself. One problem with depression is that you can't think about anyone but yourself. This kills love. But when there's nothing more to lose, it's possible to give up your anger and pride—and then suddenly the world brightens, there's something to live for after all. You are "born again."
>
> After he is sent to the slave-breaker, Frederick Douglass seems to hit bottom and completely give up. He becomes a mere animal, without a soul—"Behold a man transformed into a brute!" he exclaims. But then somehow he gets hold of himself. He prays for strength:
>
> > *God, deliver me! Let me be free! Is there any God? Why am I a slave? I will run away. I will not stand it. Get caught, get clear, I'll try it. . . . I have only one life to lose. . . . It may be that my misery in slavery will only increase my happiness when I get free. There is a better day coming.*
>
> He summons up the strength to fight back when Covey tries to whip him again. Douglass does not dwell in self-pity. And instead of clinging to old ideas of pride, he finds a new kind of pride in resistance to injustice. This is the beginning of his freedom.

This elaborate exegesis, full of assumptions and high seriousness, comes to the class with a jolt. Most of our opening exercises simply present some knot of meaning to be untied, letting students set the terms. There's always someone like Willy who blurts out, "What are we supposed to *do* with this?" This week we address what might be called problems of pastoral theology, picking apart the concept of despair and laying out the strands, expecting students to see their relevance to our previous week's discussion of "Crisis and Self-discovery."

Almost a third of our hour and a half will be given over to answering these questions:

> *How can people survive hitting bottom? Why do some people cling to their anger, pride, or self-pity in negative ways, while others are able to find something new and positive to believe in?*

After everyone has finished writing, we forego our usual small group conversations in order to conduct a freewheeling general discussion for 30 or 40 minutes, beginning with volunteers who read aloud what they have written.

By this stage of the semester almost everyone has become more comfortable with pencil and paper, trusting that his voice is adequate to his thoughts and will be respected by others. Because of the gravity of the subject, their testimony about hitting bottom has remarkable qualities of both self-revelation and collective wisdom—so much so that I have chosen to devote the rest of this chapter to it, with little comment of my own. I want to give representative voices, gathered here from several cohorts of probationers, a chance to speak for themselves about their darkest nights and new awakenings.

All semester long, students have been sounding religious notes, most often in traditional Protestant terms. Even so, the theological approach to despair takes some men by surprise, since it challenges everyone to reconsider the meaning of spiritual crisis, going beyond popular notions of "hitting rock bottom" and "bouncing back," for which our culture has all-too-ready phrases. This opening exercise complicates conventional formulas by suggesting differences between depression and despair, faith and grace, pride and hardening of the heart. This tangled nest of meanings will be explored in many bluebooks this week. Some of the terminology will be borrowed from the leading questions we ask about "being reborn," "dwelling in self-pity," or "clinging to anger," but these phrases are not empty containers in the soul-searching pages that result. Here, for instance, are half a dozen responses gleaned from the semester immediately preceding Charles and Albert's class:

> I think when a person is in despair, they've made up their minds and convinced themselves that there's no hope. Then they get mad at the world. I think some people cling to their anger and pride because they don't know where to turn when in despair. So that makes them angry and they don't want to ask for help because of their pride.

. . .

> Depression is like being in despair. When a person is depressed, he/she will no longer have self-control, and will not care for anything besides whatever is good for theirself.
>
> A person that is under depression is always "blameless," and it is never their fault, because they become so bitter that they care for no one. Being depressed or despairing is the lack of faith and hope for loving, and it turns one into bitterness and hate.

. . .

> You feel like everyone is against you, no one cares, wants to help, or can help. The walls around you start to close in, and all of the so-called good advice that everyone is trying to drill into your head just all seems to be wrong. Who should you listen to, when everyone says *that's* your problem, that you don't listen to anyone but yourself?

. . .

> Depression—a subject I know a lot about. Despair—even the word itself, "Despair," sounds forbidding, empty—Despair. It's a real bad form of depression. It's kind of like quicksand. You can see yourself going under, but you can't do anything about

> it. It's like a cancer—even worse. Sometimes you don't even know what's wrong. But there is such a hellish feeling about life. You don't even want to get out of bed or come in contact with anybody.
>
> . . .
>
> With hitting bottom, after you hit bottom you can at least say, well, I learned and now I'm ready to get back up and try again. When you're in despair, you tend to just give it all up, as to say, "I'm at the end of my rope so the hell with everything." It's like, why live? I have nothing to live for. I think that people who cling and stick onto his or her pride and anger are scared. It's like they're scared to let go, because sometimes letting go means change, and a lot of people are scared of change.
>
> . . .
>
> To me, Despair is when you've lost all your faith, your heart is cold, when you've given up, and you just don't want to be by yourself, just don't care.
>
> And Hitting Bottom is when you've done all your wrong, and now you're suffering because of it. You have people that love you and care about you, but at that time you don't really care about yourself. That's when pride kicks in—like you know that your people will help you, but you're too proud to ask for help, thinking that people will talk about you. But when you sit back and look at life, people are going to talk anyway.
>
> When you realize these things, you'll be all right. Just believe in yourself. All you need is that one thing to lift you up, and it's on! The thing about hitting bottom to me is, if you want to rise to the top, it's all up to you. The only thing that comes to a sleeper is a dream. I've experienced both and my worst was feeling sorry for myself and the way things were going. Now I'm trying to make a better life for myself, because I have kids that will need me. Plus I will not have my kids thinking that Daddy went out like a chump. My life is now on the rise.

The passages I've selected here are typical of all Changing Lives semesters. Very few probationers are without some experience of hopelessness and the temptation to simply give up—as Trevor and Willy put it, when "you just don't care anymore."

But not everyone emphasizes despair and its snares. Some gravitate to the theme of forgiveness, linked in the opening exercise to the psychology of anger, pride, and self-pity, and the counterforce of remorse—a realm of deep ambivalence for students who identify with Korney Vasiliev's jealousy and marital tragedy. We have already seen how hard it has been for Deighton to forgive his former girlfriend, even without the sting of jealousy. And José seconds his honest avowal:

> Forgiveness is a strong word. Sometimes you could forgive somebody, and sometimes you can't. For example, say if you have a wife and she cheats on you. Would you forgive her? I wouldn't.

Here are more examples from other semesters, showing how important forgiveness, or the lack of it, can be for men who have lost their spiritual equilibrium:

> Forgiveness is something I learned when I grew up. Holding a grudge is something that will never allow a wound to heal; it will only make it fester some more. I have always forgiven wrongs done against me, if only to let the situation pass. The only unforgivable wrong done against me was when I was in the hospital and my ex-girlfriend refused to bring my children to visit me. While I have not forgiven her for that (and never will, for that matter), I have learned to carry on despite that.

. . .

> We went through a very bitter divorce. It was kind of hard on the kids at first, but we both spent a lot of time with them, and they turned out to be good kids. I still talk to my ex-wife, and we became good friends again. It feels a lot better to have forgiveness in your heart.

Some men talk about forgiveness as a key to self-forgiveness, which is the final lesson of Tolstoy's story:

> I remember the first Christmas and New Years I was not drunk. I was out with the church in a van with big pots of soup and bread. It was very cold. But we found a lot of homeless people who welcomed us. As we fed them, we told them that God loves them no matter what their situation. Maybe I felt good about helping somebody that was less fortunate than me. I believe that if you think you're doing bad, there's always someone a lot worse off than you are.

Without forgiveness, the path to change often seems barred:

> Forgiveness is tough for me, because a lot of harm has come my way and it was forced forgiveness on my part in many situations, which left me with resentment. I'm a typical grudge holder; carry shit until it kills me. I had a fight with one of two brothers around the age of seventeen, and although we lived in the same house and saw each other day and night, I couldn't forgive. I went nine months without so much as a head nod being acknowledged at times, and was still unconcerned with the thought of resolution. Can one truly forgive without forgetting?

Forgiveness is not the only place where the ego can rear or balk. For men behind bars, facing the fact of irreparable loss, the challenge is to discover *any* support or meaning in life. Finding yourself utterly alone in a cell can feel like the abyss opening beneath you:

> My first time being locked up, I had known then that I had hit rock bottom, because my birthday was the next day after I had gotten locked up. I really didn't

understand why I was there, because I didn't think I did anything to be locked up. I was working and going to school, but I had a probation officer that felt as though I was hanging on the corner too much, and kicking it with my old friends too much, so I guess he thought, he has to be doing the same thing as these guys he's kicking it with. But he was wrong. I was actually doing what was right.

I think that's the point when I hit bottom, because my whole earth crashed before me in a matter of hours. But it's just a stone thrown to hold me down. I still see this person till this day sometimes, and really I've gotten over it—but deep down in my heart, not.

Another student tells how, on a downward path, you can suddenly realize that you are sinking fast, out of your depth, and call for help:

> You get to where nothing matters: you don't care if it is night or day, hot or cold. Nothing matters. This will affect the people around you as well as yourself. There could be thoughts of suicide, hoping you will die so the pain you're feeling will end your despair with a capital D. Nothing changes your feelings except for the worse, no matter what actions you take or are taken upon you. Alcohol or drugs may come into play and only intensify your depression. Bad things, one after another, will come your way, and you still don't care.
>
> Until one day, a silent alarm can go off inside of you, signaling that you have had enough, or the grace of God, which is what I believe helped me out of my depression and let me care about life again. Prayer truly helps, at least that is my experience. There is no other way to explain what I have felt in my life, other than a Divine intervention that allows you to reach deep inside and find the strength and meaning to pull yourself out of your troubles.

. . .

> You know, when I first got locked up, I felt there was no God. I sat in my cell asking myself, "How could God do this to me and why did He do this?" I prayed that I was dreaming, but woke up every morning in the same cell. My mother always made sure I was at church on Sunday morning, so I could not understand why God was doing it to me.
>
> As time went on and I prayed more, I realized that it was me that God was helping. Today I'm a better person for the lesson I've learned in prison. Thank God. Sometimes I feel I can be born again.

Typically the Word comes to these men when they're all alone but not necessarily locked up in a cell:

> I lived in the street for two years sleeping outside, in hallways, not working, partying all the time, until one day I hit bottom.
>
> I got up, stopped everything. For a minute there I lost all bearings—like something told me I could do it, go for it. I walked away.

. . .

> Regardless of how good a liar, fraud, etc., you are, you cannot lie to yourself. Reality hits you in the face constantly. Although one might choose to ignore the truths, it is only a matter of time before you have to stop running and face yourself totally. Sometimes we need depression, bad luck, etc., to build us as a person.

In some cases an intermediary makes all the difference, usually a woman, as in these two final stories of redemption found in the midst of suffering:

> Life has never been a bed of roses and, like Frederick Douglass, I was at one time in my life standing inside of his shoes. I was not a slave, but I was looking at doing time inside the prison system. Looking back on that time, all I felt was sadness, loneliness, and isolation just thinking this might happen to me. Every night in bed I could just picture myself driving a car through a ten-foot wall.
>
> I was angry at myself for my mistakes. I blamed others for selling me out. But in reality I could only blame myself for making silly mistakes. I turned to my parents for help, but they just knocked me to my knees with a long lecture about how they raised me and what they expected from me. My thoughts were on the impossible, and based on stupidity like running away to another state, my thoughts were not on facing the reality of my mistakes and the problems I created in my life. My thoughts were only on escape.
>
> One day, after going to court and coming home thinking about what's next, I turned to my wife and asked her, "Honey, what am I to do?" She just simply looked at me and said, "Baby, put your worries and your problems in God's hand. Get down on your knees and pray, and all those feelings of despair will go away. Just give God the glory."
>
> That night, before I went to bed, I read the Bible and I went on my knees and began to pray. I say, "Father God, you know my life story. Lord, I have sinned and now, Lord, I am about to be punished for my wrongdoings. God, you say if I commit a sin, Lord, and I ask you for forgiveness, Lord, you will forgive me for my sin. So tonight, Lord, I'm asking you, Lord, to ask the judge and the courts for forgiveness for me, Lord. Give me strength, Lord, and, Lord, never let my enemies reign superior over me. Just take my freedom from whoever has the power to put me away and I'll be most thankful. And Lord, if this is so, Lord, just give me a sign."
>
> The day of my trial when I went to court I didn't have all the money to pay my attorney. But I know God touched him cause he smiled and told me, "Don't worry about it. We have a very understanding judge; he can be reasoned with." Instantly I knew God was working His power. God had given me that sign, and today I am here in class sharing this experience with whoever reads this story.

And here's a story some modern Tolstoy might well have invented, except that it really happened:

> I never really had a good relationship with my mother. We had never really talked about why. Almost four years ago I had gotten myself in some real trouble when I was pulled over for drinking and driving, and was going to be going away at least three years. I was going to have to do time at a local facility.
>
> I started to do my time there, not telling my mother or any of my family. It wasn't too long, maybe a couple of weeks, when I got called for a visit. It was my mother. I wasn't too happy to see her, because I didn't know how to explain to her that I wouldn't be leaving here for at least three to five years. When I did tell her, I'll never forget the look on her face—like she'd seen a ghost. She started to cry. I remember telling her not to. That everything will be all right. Before she left that day, I hugged her and told her I loved her—something I hadn't done in probably ten years.
>
> Two days later I was called down to the Sheriff's Office, where they told me my mother was killed in a head-on collision with a drunken driver. Here I was trying to figure out how I was going to have to handle being in this place for three years, but now I would have to deal with something a lot worse than that.
>
> It is now four years later, and my life has changed in so many ways. When I think about that visit with my mother, in a weird way I am grateful that I was where I was, because it gave me the chance to say goodbye to her.

So many remarkable testimonies! I quote but a fraction of them, but I trust they convey the depth of response to Tolstoy's parable of despair and redemption. Of course, these flashes of illumination are not merely responses to the story we have read. By this point in the semester these men are ready to confront their own darkest moments, and Tolstoy merely provides a spark to ignite the fire already laid during eight weeks of trust-building in small groups, with listeners who understand "where I'm coming from." They've all been there, and by now they know it.

This mutual trust also grows as the cumulative effect of sequenced topics for writings correlated with Frederick Douglass's life story. Leading up to this session we've dealt with childhood and family, schooling, poverty and racism, confrontations with authority, punishment, manliness, violence, crisis, and self-discovery. All these simmering ingredients now come to full boil, suddenly welling up with great eloquence from men who were struggling for words at the beginning of the semester. By the eighth week they've also had a good deal of writing practice, certainly beneficial, though that in itself doesn't really account for the sureness of tone in the passages I've been quoting. The secret lies in the deep waters they have entered.

The difficulty, the necessity, and sometimes the impossibility of forgiveness—forgiving others or forgiving yourself—are all confronted in Tolstoy's story of pride, violence, self-pity, and despair, themes familiar to troubled men in all times and circumstances. For the probationers, the final rung in this downward descent has been judgment and punishment, accompanied by shame and humiliation. Only a few of them have succeeded in loosening this terrible knot, pulled so tight as to choke out everything else. Even when they have discovered a provisional solution, in religion or in a woman, or in some other source, they cannot always find a name for it. "Love" and "God" are little more than familiar labels for what can be hard to think about in the patterns of rational discourse.

Tolstoy's emphasis on forgiveness shifts the perspective dramatically. He offers a new way to think about hitting bottom, one that encourages readers in similar circumstances to relinquish obsessive explanations along with anodynes like drugs, alcohol, and street life. Opening their hearts to other probationers in the same boat seems to allow them to imagine, in their writings, the possibility of positive gestures of reconciliation, instead of remaining clenched in anger and pain. One by one the men I have been quoting take a deep breath and reveal themselves to us all, not merely in the personal stories they tell but also through the enlarged ethical and spiritual perspective they find in literature, revealing how much they share with their classmates as well as with wider humanity.

In cases like those of Luis and Randy, reading may serve as a vicarious means to new awareness and inner peace. Others, like Albert and Dave and Trevor, find their way in conversations where they share their stories and discover they are not alone. And here in these writings collected over the years we see how a third form of coming to terms with hitting bottom can also be transformative. When some men pick up a pencil, they are able to revisit the past and make new sense of horrific experience that, at the time, they may not have been ready to comprehend. Writing, especially when it's done impromptu in the classroom, combines three kinds of self-examination: the silent remembering and retelling occurs in the midst of others doing the same thing, and because it takes shape on the page, your own story becomes a different sort of testimony, a mirror to look at yourself in. Sometimes all of these forms of revelation come together, as in this final quotation from past semesters, an extraordinary amalgam that also echoes our readings in Douglass and Malcolm X:

> It was my first time in jail. And it was a week before Christmas, and this C.O. locked me in my cell for no reason at all, just because he wanted to and could, I guess. Anyways, I started acting crazy, yelling and screaming and cussing the officer out.
>
> The next day this older guy says to me, "Excuse me, brother, but why do you young brothers get so mad when they lock you in your cells, don't you know you're only going from a rectangle to a square?" Still quite angry from the night before, I say, "Yeah, whatever."
>
> Don't you know, like three days later what the older man had said to me popped into my head. And I was immediately calm, like the wisdom of this man had eased my anger, like the sun jumping out behind the cloudy grey sky dissipating all gloom, with its powerful shine.
>
> What he was saying is, "No matter where we are, inside of the jail, we are still locked up." From that day on I never got angry when I was made to stay in my cell. I would read a book or the Good Book to keep my mind busy. Because you can incarcerate my body, but never my mind!
>
> . . . I have always been an outgoing, free-wheeling type of person. I couldn't stay in one place for long. I remember how I used to get up and out at like two a.m. on my bike and ride up River Street into Mattapan Square, then ride all the

> way up Blue Hill Avenue into Grove Hall, turn onto Washington Street, and ride down to Codman Square, turn down Norfolk Street, and follow it back to Mattapan Square. When I went in the house, I would be able to go to sleep. I would do this almost every night.
>
> Being locked up, I didn't have such a luxury to come and go as I pleased. I learned to be more patient. I had no choice. I was forced to sit down and take it slow, one day at a time. And with all this time I thought a lot about who I was and what I wanted to do. I also started reading—all kinds of books, the Bible, and I even started reading the dictionary. I would just jot down words that I didn't know—put them in a sentence and memorize them just to broaden my vocabulary.
>
> There I learned anyone can make a mistake and go to jail, or go to jail by a mistake of the system. It can happen to just about anyone. But it's really not about that, it's all about what you do to better yourself while you're there so that you don't make a mistake return trip!

I have been quoting here from several years of answers to our questions about hitting bottom, in order to provide a broader look at the men who come to Changing Lives from such crises, their new self-awareness surfacing unpredictably from the depths of despair. Are any of us ever really prepared for the moment when we feel ourselves changed, with genuine leverage on life for the first time?

It may be that the selective gathering together of so many testimonies, at once uplifting and unsettling, tends to distort the truth about these awakenings, perhaps making them seem more dramatic and intense than they actually were. It's a paradox, for self-discovery requires much grubbing in the dirt, often losing your bearings before you find them, and yet in a moment it can all become clear, an epiphany, when you suddenly look up and see where you are. The writing we invite in the course of the semester has some of this paradoxical quality—lots of just breaking rocks, sometimes coming up with a golden perception. Recently we've begun experimenting with another kind of writing that compresses all this into a tighter, more explosive compass. I want to end this chapter by quoting, without comment, some results from this latest experiment, not yet completely integrated into our still-changing life curriculum.

**On Top of the World**

I have everything I want,
even some things I don't want.
It comes to me even if I don't ask for it.
O, I got the world by its balls,
today the world is mine.
I was just told today
that I had no money, no car,
and no home to go to.

Tried to use my credit card
but it would not let me.
As I walked by a homeless man,
I looked at him. It was as if
I was looking at myself.
He asked me for a dollar or two,
I reached into my pocket
and all I came out with was dust.

**When Your Ass Is Out of Luck**

To me rock bottom is when
your ass is out of luck.
You can't get no help from no one,
not even family.
And it is very hard
to get on track
because if you get to
that stage in life,
you were doing something wrong
and people don't like being bothered
with someone who is doing wrong.
So try not to hit rock bottom.

**Waiting for Good Life**

Waiting for good life on the fast lane,
people being brought down
by unhappiness and unfaithfulness
which causes pain.
Kids running wild still scattered
while people in the streets
are starved and battered.
Before the day is done
another has just begun.

**Hitting Bottom**

Alone in this world.
No friends, family, no love.
Coming or Going, I'm alone.
Always feeling useless, no matter.
I am Hungry, Dirty, Lost
and I don't want to be found.

**As Low As It Gets**

Can't get lower than *rock bottom.*
  All support has now backed away,
wanting nothing to do with you or your problems.
  When relationships seem to add
to the stress level (if able to engage in one),
  you become a rebel rebelling without a cause,
so everything from then on done
  only emphasizes flaws.
Only thing that might help is
  to be a *bottom feeder.*

**In the Darkness**

I see the clearest
with no light to
show the no ones.
In the dark
I can't see
where I'm not.
In the dark
each step
is forward.
In the dark
everything is up
even your down.
In the light
I see my road
and I close my eyes.
Look at Life
Look at life,
see how short it is.
Tomorrow is
no promise
to nobody.

# Chapter 12

# *Neville*

Every man in our program is unique. There's no predicting what surprising individuals will turn up, confounding all expectations. But notwithstanding this unpredictability, each semester's class regularly brings together men on three main life courses, roughly equal in numbers though very different in character and prospects.

First of all, there are those who seem centered and confident, on an upward path that they have chosen for themselves—Harry, Luis, José, perhaps Dave.

Then there are the older men, whose troubled lives seem to have leveled out into holding patterns, sometimes in heavy fog but surviving. Men like Ross and Deighton, Charles and Randy, have faced the worst life has to offer and made a kind of peace with it—rarely a victory.

Finally, there are those who find themselves at a crossroads, who know they must do something to change, now. Life is giving them a second chance, unprepared or irresolute as they may be. Most often these are younger men like Willy, Trevor, Anthony, and Neville, though sometimes there will be a determined forty-year-old like Albert who wants to start over. They often describe their present situation as one of crisis. When asked to recall a past occasion that felt like a moment of crisis, they may recount some early trauma, but Anthony says simply, "I go through a crisis with my mother every day," and Neville writes, "I just pray that this crisis ends some day for me."

All of these men, young or old, want better lives—they want to stay out of prison, kick their bad habits, and find a place in society that has the respect of others and will restore their self-respect. No matter how many doors may seem permanently closed, they all come to the Changing Lives program with the hope that its name can be taken seriously. Nonetheless, not everyone is ready for the challenges that profound change entails. Perhaps especially in periods of crisis and desperation, when people have nothing left to lose, the requisite courage of faith may be lacking. Few who come to such a crossroads in life recognize it for what it is—an invitation to grow. When confronting the abyss, many are too frightened and confused, or too exhausted to start again on a new path. Like Anthony, they may turn back to what seems like safer ground, or they may pause and pray for new strength, like Neville.

Every person's life is open-ended, every morning a new morning. The crisis faced by Albert and Neville is a turning point that anyone in the program could experience, deciding which direction their lives will take from here, the steep upward climb or the whirlpool that spirals downward. In both symbolic and practical ways this crisis of self-determination is shared by the entire class. If one can make it, there's hope for all.

I have already tried to suggest what this challenge means to Albert, and how fervently he wants to rise to the occasion. Let us end with Neville, the probationer who embodies so literally the burden of hopelessness and defeat that weighs on many of these men. In previous chapters I have often relied on his example to stand for what others also undergo—early humiliations that undermined self-esteem, addiction to substitute gratifications that are a curse, stubborn resistance to any risk-taking that might lead to new failures and further shame. Neville's case stares us in the face because his bodily encumbrance leaves him no place to hide—not near the door like Charles, not in the back corner with Willy. Even so, we have seen only the surface of Neville's story so far. There is more to tell.

Some of Neville's past was revealed in what he wrote about his present crisis, but he was so painfully unsure of himself as a writer that he rarely handed in more than a sentence or two. He was much more forthcoming in the small groups, where a strong connection with Bert gave him the confidence to share his story in their circle each week.

Neville lives with his parents in what sounds like a large extended family, some of whose members also tend toward obesity. His mother is so alarmed by Neville's condition that she wants him hospitalized, though he's already attending an "obesity program." In general he reports his family as supportive, and when we asked the class what children need to grow up healthy and happy, his answer—"to feel loved, and wanted, and protected"—suggested a normal childhood where such needs were met. But in a conversation with Bert following a class exercise on punishment, a darker story emerged: "Coming for someone like me," he said, "punishment would cause you to hate. And I say that because of the type of punishment I went through as a kid!"

Nonetheless, Neville seems to believe that a firm hand is sometimes necessary in child-rearing. He imagines himself dealing sternly with disobedient children of his own: "I would try and try my best to let her or him know the road their father went down! And if that didn't work, I would tell them to get out of my home!" In his own childhood, the result of the firm hand was learning "to respect my adults." Spelling it out, Neville's voice moves into a deeper register:

> For me, my childhood was to respect my adults and to know my education was important to me and my future. I learned in my childhood responsibility and right from wrong. I learned to respect myself and others. And I also learned to take my future seriously. That life is not a joke.

I remember how that final sentence took me aback when I read it halfway through the semester, the night we asked the question, "How did you learn what you needed to know in your childhood?" I kept thinking how the open spirit of a young child might be closed down by the premature discovery that life is not a joke.

Neville's punishments continued long into adolescence. When we read Langston Hughes's "Last Whipping," a fanciful episode in his "Simple" stories, Neville offered a grittier real-life anecdote:

> My last whipping was when I was in school, when my mother got word I was driving a car to school that didn't belong to me. I knew it was wrong, but I was just trying to fit in with the rest of the boys.

By this time, when Neville was fifteen, his family had moved to Dorchester, and he told Bert that the move coincided with his initiation into street life—drugs and other teenage delinquencies like car theft that "the rest of the boys" in his new neighborhood were already practicing. Like others in the class, Neville began to look to peers rather than family members for his code of behavior. As Luis, José, Dave, and Anthony all agreed, this transition begins in middle school and is complete by fifteen or sixteen.

During his adolescent slide into delinquency Neville had new friends to impress. Though he has now begun to call them "the wrong crowd," as Anthony does, Neville still feels a sense of loyalty to them—no matter how troubled and self-destructive some of these friends may have been. I will have more to say about this important fact in a moment. But much earlier in life there was a prior rupture that was probably more damaging to his character. When this fateful first encounter with the social order and its enforcement occurred, he had no peers to identify with, no means of reassuring himself that his failure didn't cut him off from everyone else.

I have already quoted and discussed Neville's story of being humiliated on report-card day in third grade, but it was momentous enough to bear repeating in full:

> One of the biggest crises of my life was not being able to go through school, and keep on going like I really wanted to. And I say that because I loved school, but I just felt like I couldn't learn for some reason! And this trouble started at First Grade.
>
> I had so many dreams as a little boy. I will never forget once when school was just about to let out, they passed out report cards in the Third Grade. And all the kids, my friends, were so happy about what they had gotten. And I couldn't wait to get home to show the family! When I opened to see what I had, which were all Fs, my teachers saw me just cover my face and say NAW! They let the class out and came to me, and gave me a long talk about trying a little harder next time if it meant so much.

Neville's moment of crisis dramatizes in a single tableau what happened to many of his classmates more gradually over years. When his teachers convinced him that his failure was his own fault, the result was not that Neville tried harder, but that he gave up trying altogether, as he explained later in the semester:

> I would say I'm a weak person, and only because I really never learned how to read or write like others, which has kept my self-esteem down for many of years! And I really don't know how to spell. I believe if I was strong like others that really don't do anything with the smarts they have. . . .
>
> Me, I feel like I was let out somewhere along the line.

Between the original crisis, which must have happened when he was eight, and his self-assessment today, there must have been similar failures and chastisement chilling his love of school, but I cannot report the particulars that eventually brought him to our classroom. I do not know when he left school or what he did to be arrested and imprisoned, though it's likely that "street smarts" and drugs had something to do with it. The next glimpse we have of him is in jail, where two very important things happened, two responses to incarceration that seem powerfully at odds with each other yet deeply connected as well. On the one hand,

> I got a taste of being in jail and believe me that is a place I'd never want to go back to in my life! . . . The time I was there I seen people in and out, in and out! Like they loved it.

On the other hand,

> For me, my crisis started when I went to jail. Putting on all this extra weight that I cannot get rid of has caused me to have a very bad sleeping disorder. I tell you! you talk about punishment! . . . It's like I am a walking zombie with no life.

Neville believes that jail time taught him a lesson, and he is determined not to go back. "I would say having a last chance made me want to change my life." Shocked by seeing how other men cycle through prison over and over, he realized that he doesn't want to be like them. "Today I know if I do wrong I would have to pay for any action, and I'm doing everything right today. . . . Yes, I would just have to say I'm a lot stronger than I was."

His horror of incarceration has helped sustain a resolve to change his life. Yet at the same time Neville brought something else home with him from prison, so that he is not only on probation but continues to be locked up. While doing his time he palliated panic and boredom with junk food and television—his usual anodynes, drugs and friends, being hard to come by. He's been out on probation for a year but has not been able to kick these new habits—whether or not he's quit the old ones.

He tries. Firm with himself all day, he can't sleep at night, and then he binges on junk food and television as if he were still in lock-up. Of course, the obesity and the insomnia go hand in hand and have combined with his long-standing addiction to cigarettes, so that now he also has chronic asthma to contend with, making it all the harder to sleep. "You talk about punishment!" His jail time was nothing compared to the living death he now experiences.

In these circumstances how can he say that "I'm a lot stronger than I was"? I do not have an answer to this question, but I think Neville was trying to deal with it himself at the end of his account of "hitting rock bottom" near the end of the semester:

> But me, I never will give up on God, no matter what happens in my life. There will always be hope for me! And yes, I've hit rock bottom before, when I was in jail. All I did was pray every time I thought about God. . . . I feel I've hit rock bottom right now, with this weight problem I have. But like I said, I will never give up on God. I will keep on asking for his help!

Perhaps Neville *is* stronger now than he was before hitting bottom. Perhaps not. It remains to be seen.

I said a few pages back that I would pause to speak of the complicated loyalty Neville feels toward his friends, including those who are also in trouble with the law, and whose influence he recognizes as negative. Although he asserts that "doing everything right today" includes "not hanging with negative people and being around positive people," it's obvious that many of his former friends remain in his world, still offering support as friends do, but also unwittingly strengthening his determination to change, as he watches some of them hit bottom without even being aware of it—treating life as a joke.

When he speaks of people who cycle in and out of prison "like they loved it," he is thinking of these friends. Some of them "can do real bad, by using drugs and doing this and that." One young man has "taken his father's life, only cause his father wanted him to get a job to take on his responsibility instead of running the streets doing wrong." Others hit bottom when they lost their car, their job, their home. One friend hit bottom when he contracted a sexually transmitted disease.

> Now they have something that they can't get rid of, all hope is gone. "Fuck it! I'm just going to give it to whoever!" They don't say that, but that's what I see happening. And that's not right.

With this friend's case Neville found himself in a moral dilemma. What was his obligation to warn others of this fact?

> I be wanting to say something so bad, but really it's not my place to. But if it is someone I know, then I would be like, "Yo! Either you do it or I will."

Neville has not given up his friends, but he is learning from them in a new way. His old need to be just like the rest of the boys has changed, and this in turn is changing him. Consider the fact, mentioned in an earlier chapter, that on the night he joined our class he brought one of his friends with him, a young man on probation from the neighboring Roxbury court, whom Neville had talked into coming to Changing Lives with him. This impulse seems a clear sign of his own determination to change his ways, not by letting go of what is most important to him—his friends—but by trying to change their character too. Maybe this strategy will pay off in the long run. I hope so.

I began the semester concerned about Trevor and Neville, both of whom seem stuck in the mud of their lives, spinning their wheels. Trevor: handsome as the devil, full of charm and a taste for life's pleasures. Neville: at least 100 pounds overweight, asthmatic, insomniac. Trevor had been making good money dealing drugs, but now he's working "a lousy job" stocking shelves in a little grocery, not getting along with his new girlfriend, not seeing much of his toddler daughter, and feeling tempted by the streets again. From Trevor's perspective Neville almost seems to have "a good thing going"—on disability, living amicably with his family, doing what he wants, no job, and not really looking for one.

In both cases their self-esteem seems tied in knots. Trevor boasts unabashedly of his selfishness, but there's so little left in his life to support his adolescent narcissism that even he is beginning to harbor doubts about himself. We gathered this from conversations, but in his writing Trevor stays cool, steering clear of topics or tone that might suggest he cares about anything. Neville, on the other hand, describes himself as a man without self-esteem, yet he takes pride in having learned a lesson Trevor hasn't yet confronted—using his "smarts" to avoid another stretch in jail. Neville is right to be proud of his resolve, and it's significant that he is able to put it in writing, no matter how ashamed he is of his spelling. In the end, writing was to be how he regained his self-respect in Changing Lives.

Neville was probably the most unlikely member of our class to achieve anything at all as a writer. From the start he approached all writing assignments with puzzling ambivalence. Even on his first night in class—a week late—after dutifully answering all of the questions regarding what children need to grow up, he failed to place his contribution on the pile on his way out, and we didn't see it till three weeks later, when he finally brought it in after some nagging from me. Another night, he gave us a few sentences written in class but forgot to hand in his homework on the same topic until two weeks later.

This was to be the pattern with Neville—late arrivals, little or no homework, class exercises scribbled out but rarely handed in. What was going on?

Pressuring him to give us those classroom exercises finally turned out to have important consequences. During the fifth week, answering a question about how the weak can defend themselves against the strong, Neville wrote the following sentences, a series of false starts and passionate exclamations, like an engine revving up and shorting out, his pencil barely keeping pace with his racing thoughts. I've already quoted some of these sentences, but I want to reproduce them once more, spaced out on the page as they seem to have come to him, in gusts:

> I would say I'm a weak person, and only because I really never learned how to read or write like others, which has kept my self-esteem down for many of years! And I really don't know how to spell.

I believe if I was strong like others that really really don't do anything with the smarts they have! . . .

Me, I feel like I was let out somewhere along the line.

If I had it I wouldn't even be here right now!

As with the law! I got a taste of being in jail, and believe me that is a place I'd never want to go back to in my life!

So I would say having a last chance made me want to change my life.

The time I was there I seen people in and out, in and out! Like they loved it.

Yes, I would just have to say I'm a lot stronger than I was.

Neville is wrestling here with his true subject matter. He has taken the question about weakness very personally, and so his answers reflect his sense of defeat, his fear of further punishment, and his uncertainty about whether he has the strength to change. Of course, these are the obvious concerns in a program like ours: how punishment works on a boy over the years, from failures in school to incarceration as an adult, wearing down self-esteem and habituating him to feeling weak and incompetent. Not an uncommon story. What is unusual here is Neville's effort to take a hard look at his past and see what can be salvaged—which is why he starts out saying others are stronger and ends up realizing that he is stronger than he thought. He for one knows that he wants to change, while others seem to have accepted their lot, content with life at the bottom.

Subsequent assignments, revolving around issues of manliness and violence, gave a new spin to Neville's writing, but he kept returning to these themes of failure, wrongdoing, and punishment, in which the retribution seems always in excess of its provocation. Sporadic though it was, Neville's writing seemed to have settled into a strong pattern of self-criticism and new resolve, twisting tighter and tighter as he surveyed his own bumpy road to manhood. At the same time, we had him talking valiantly about his eating disorder with Bert and Randy in their small groups.

In his overall engagement with the course's trajectory he was connecting to a far deeper and more important theme than any of our assignments explicitly raised. Paradoxically, this deeper note was being sounded most loudly in Neville's strange reluctance to hand in the writing he was producing, whether in class or at home. The puzzle was finally solved halfway through the semester, when he wrote about his traumatic memory of report-card day in third grade. His resistance was not to the effort of writing but to the risk of having it judged.

What seems most significant in Neville's history of early humiliation and subsequent self-doubt is not so much its content—crucial as that may seem in all his later anecdotes of misdoings, punishments, and abject surrender to authority—but the fact that Neville has been able to find his way *back*, to the original schoolroom drama, by means of writing. He has put his finger on the turning point. Most poignant of all is the unspoken connection between Neville's early love of school, squelched so disastrously in third grade, and his current ambivalence about writing. On the one hand, he composes with increasing directness and passion, and on the other, he remains so certain his work is incompetent that he does everything in his power to avoid submitting it to the scrutiny of others.

Not only is he now confronting the key memory, but, even more important, the act of writing about it changes the meaning of the original event, proving that he really does have "the smarts" he was accused of lacking back when he was eight.

I told Neville something to this effect in my written comment the following week, and after class I went over to him—just as his teachers had done in third grade!—and elaborated my response, adding my own version of "try harder": "Why don't you hand in your work?" I urged. "I see you writing the exercises every week, but then you never give them to us." When Bert seconded my plea, Neville uneasily admitted that he had saved most of his writings and promised to bring them to class. Indeed, the following week he gave us a whole sheaf of torn and crumpled pages, each with a paragraph or two penciled on it. I have already quoted passages from each of the previous three classes, now handed in at last. In addition there were four new paragraphs, the most he had ever written, on our current assignment, "Hitting Bottom." He had apparently taken heart.

Rather than typing up these paragraphs as separate fragments, I saw a way of organizing them into a single long essay without changing more than a few words here and there to establish continuity:

> They say we as black men are a product of our society. But really, what is our society? It's full of criticisms, judgments, and relies totally on status. There is no room for any type of forgiveness, so what do we do as black men? We take it out on the one person we know best—ourselves (me!)—meaning mothers, sisters, brothers, fathers, etc., etc. I can't learn or practice forgiveness when it is not available to me—period!
>
> Every person should have the right to protect themselves, family, property against oppression and injustice. Personally, we as a people have been oppressed for so long, we no longer defend ourselves against it publicly. Privately, however, is another issue. We always talk in secret about how we as a people can come out of this oppression. I have come to the conclusion that in order to protect ourselves from it, we must not only talk about it but be about it.
>
> Hitting bottom—I've known so many other people that are like that. I have friends that can do real bad, by using drugs and this and that. They are okay until their car and their home is gone. Lost their job. And to me that's when you've hit rock bottom.
>
> But for some people rock bottom can be a sickness. I have a friend like that also. Now they have something that they can't get rid of, all hope is gone. "Fuck it! I'm just going to give it to whoever!" They don't say that, but that's what I see happening. And that's not right. I be wanting to say something so bad, but really it's not my place to. But if it is someone I know, then I would be like, "Yo! Either you do it or I will."
>
> But me, I never will give up on God, no matter what happens in my life. There will always be hope for me! And yes, I've hit rock bottom before, when I was in jail. All I did was pray every time I thought about God.

> For me, my crisis started when I went to jail. Putting on all this extra weight that I cannot get rid of has caused me to have a very bad sleeping disorder. I tell you! you talk about punishment! I just pray that this crisis ends some day for me. It's like I am a walking zombie with no life. It also tears my mother apart, just seeing me like this. She wants to put me in a hospital so that I can get some help. She really worries about me. I really pray to overcome this crisis that is in my life today, someday real soon.
>
> I feel I've hit rock bottom right now, with this weight problem I have. But like I said, I will never give up on God. I will keep on asking for his help!

I duplicated these paragraphs for the class. In its combination of social commentary, public testimony, and personal reflections, driven home with a loud *Amen*, Neville's essay was the most sustained and resounding pronouncement anyone had written all semester. A remarkable turnaround accomplished in eight short weeks.

As at the first session he attended, Neville brought a friend with him to our final class, the night I handed out copies of his work to everyone. Of course, they were late. Willy was also tardy, but he didn't head for his usual place in the back corner, instead sitting where Neville always sits—the only chair in the room without an attached desk. I noticed how much weight Willy himself has put on during the past ten weeks—an ex-football player's hazard. "Neville will need that seat," I loudly reminded him. But in his typical school-kid style, Willy pleaded exhaustion. "I'll move if he comes."

A grinning chorus came from the class: "He'll come!"

I passed out copies of exemplary homework from the previous week by three students—Albert, Willy, and Neville—for all to read while we waited to see if and when Neville would show up. The room was quiet; soon even the rustling of pages stopped, so I decided to distribute the opening exercise. I had begun giving out pencils when Neville and a friend came in. Willy hauled himself ostentatiously to his usual place at the back of the room, and I handed Neville and his friend copies of Neville's patched-together homework along with the pages by Albert and Willy. It came as no surprise that they read Neville's page first.

Everyone else was busy with the writing exercise, which asked for final comments on our class, but there was also a silent awareness of the drama unfolding at the front of the room.

Slowly Neville's friend raised his head from the paper and turned to Neville, speaking softly but audibly, with amazement in his voice: "You wrote *this?*"

Neville looked up, looked down at his page again, and muttered, "Yeah, I guess I did."

His friend kept on shaking his head in admiration and disbelief—as if he had seen an apparition, a dream come to life. I felt the same way. There were smiles on other faces in the room.

Neville's friend turned to me and quietly asked whether there were extra copies. What was he going to do with them? Give them to their friends? Neville's family? Did he guess that Neville was too shy to ask for them himself?

Meanwhile, people were finishing the opening exercise. After a bit I broke the silence to ask Willy, "How does it feel to be published?" For weeks Willy had been complaining that I never chose *his* homework for the exemplary handout, and last week in particular he was disappointed that I hadn't duplicated a paper he wrote about the death of his grandmother. Tonight he had seen Neville's name on one sheet and Albert's on the other, and never thought to turn them over to see his own production on the reverse. Now he was taken aback, and for once his banter failed him. Here at last was something he couldn't joke about. "The one on my grandmother was better," he finally said. Although I denied it, he was probably right.

Willy had already completed the opening exercise—or perhaps his concentration was broken—so he rose from his chair to get a soda from the vending machines in the hall. He was at the door when Neville called to him, "Bring me one too." "Sprite?" "Yeah." Neville fished for his dollar while we all watched. Both of them were celebrating.

By the time Willy returned, everyone, including Neville, had finished their lists of memorable events during our semester together, and I asked for volunteers to read their favorites aloud. As usual, Albert wanted to go first. He seemed quite altered to me now, much more confident. He even *looked* different. Standing up straighter. His had been a real transformation. Each week it has been easier for him to talk, and his eagerness to do so had been a model for others.

Amazingly enough, tonight even Neville is ready to give it a try. Although he has a hard time saying what he feels in front of us all, the pat on the back from his friend has allowed him a modest cry of victory:

> The most important thing that I've learned is that I really can learn. All these years I've been thinking that I could not read or write. Here, look at me now! Reading and writing and spelling. And I know some of the things are going to be misspelled, but what really matters is that I keep trying my best.

Listening with pride in him, I find myself remembering the first sentence Neville wrote this semester that drew my attention: "Life is not a joke."

# Part Six

## *What We Learned*

# Chapter 13
# *Graduation Day*

The Dorchester District Courthouse is a newly renovated building in Codman Square, a busy crossroads in the midst of one of Dorchester's very mixed neighborhoods, nineteenth-century mansions with two-hundred-year-old copper beech trees down one street, shabby apartment houses and hole-in-the-wall shops down another, a racial and ethnic congregation on the sidewalks that would take pages to describe.

We come singly, most of us, arriving at the security checkpoint not long after the doors open, along with all the courthouse workers and citizens having early business with the court. Our graduation ceremony will be held in the First Session, a big room airy and light, with many rows of pew-like seats; a few tables in front of them for attorneys and their clients, court clerks, and functionaries; and at the very front of the room on a platform raising it high as a pulpit, a massive desk behind which the judge will sit—the Bench. Ordinarily one judge presides over this "session," the busiest in Boston, with other judges assigned to the several other sessions of the Dorchester court. And here in this room will assemble all parties to today's proceedings—defendants to be arraigned, aggrieved parties, family and friends of both, attorneys, probation officers, court officers, and so on. But on this morning, when called to order, these persons will rise for the entrance of not one but four or even five judges, who will climb the stairs to the high bench and gaze solemnly upon a group of fifty to a hundred people.

"Be seated," says the court officer at the end of his Hear ye, but the row of black-robed judges remains standing. Dorchester's presiding justice, the Honorable Sidney Hanlon, is a diminutive woman of vigorous middle age, whose bright face and very curly red hair seem oddly incongruous in the black robes of a judge. But so too does Judge Thomas J. May's benign countenance look strange to those of us accustomed to Tom's sweaters and slacks on Tuesday nights. The fact is, we are all in formal attire this morning, wearing jackets and ties, Sunday dresses, colorful shirts, or freshly laundered work clothes for those on the way to their daily labor. We are dressed to signify respect, for one another and for the public dignity represented by the court.

I sense a fine-tuned symbolic statement in the probationers' choice of apparel on graduation day, especially the men. Like most males I am somewhat bemused by the subtle language of female costume, but whatever the cause, I remember only male attire from these occasions, even years later: Jorge, a middle-aged, obviously successful small businessman, who came prepared to make a speech, garbed as he might choose to be for a presentation to a client. Some of the African American probationers, brothers and dudes in their teens or their forties, having worn signature clothing to class all semester, must now outdo themselves. I recall vividly one gentleman who came to court in tux and tails, looking for all the world like band-leader personality Cab Calloway when I saw him on the stage of Omaha's Orpheum Theater back in 1949. Though James carried himself more like a deacon than a celebrity, his performance that day drew cheers as full-throated as Calloway's "Hidey hidey hidey ho!"

We never know whether any students at all will summon up the courage to make a speech on graduation day, yet if one probationer breaks the ice, others will usually plunge in. Though often eloquent, these are never rehearsed or scripted, nor are they delivered in the soapbox manner telling you how "once I was blind but now I see." No doubt there are people in the courtroom who could profit from such an exhortation to renounce their vices and get clean, but that's not what our students have to say. Indeed, the message is not in what probationers say so much as in the fact that they're saying it at all, here in the courtroom where most of them have been tried and sentenced, now transformed to the scene of a return to grace and respect.

Even if they decide the night before to risk a few words, many probationers get cold feet at the last minute. Just standing up and walking to the front when their names are called is daunting for many of them—and downright impossible for a few who contrive to be late or who never show up at all. When they do stand and come forward, you can see in their faces how flustered they are, shy and proud with embarrassed grins, and eager to get back to their seats. Even Mario, one of the most eloquent and voluble students over the years, was at a loss for words on this occasion. In his earnest yet unassuming way he said that he had made a lot of mistakes in his life and many times resolved to do better, but he had failed so often that most people had given up on him—except for his probation officer, and so he wanted to thank that gentleman for believing in him and recommending him for Changing Lives. And then Mario sat down.

There's no way to reproduce the live drama of such scenes, not even if we had them on tape or film. You have to be there to see all heads turn with Mario's as he thanks his probation officer standing at the side of the room; or to watch Tim, a fifty-year-old truck driver, unforgettably looking round at the judges standing behind him, pointing to himself and reminding them that each person coming before them, innocent or guilty, is "first and foremost" a human being; or to hear Shawn, a mother's son still in his teens, speak so poignantly of his loneliness that John Christopher chokes up and can't continue calling the roll. Even if I could quote such speeches verbatim, you'd miss all the echoes and undertones here in this courtroom, the original scene of their disgrace.

In any case, on their graduation day not one of the men I've been writing about in this book could bring himself to speak, despite the lists we all made at our final meeting, of what we'd remember from our weeks together. Since I can report no such speeches, the next best thing will be to rely on their written testimony from that last class exercise, recollections that might have welled up again in the courtroom. In fact, my own speech on graduation day is always a simple recital of passages from their farewells to "Our Class."

I have already quoted Albert and Neville proclaiming their epiphanies in chapters devoted to them, and I can now add similar valedictory statements by Dave and Anthony and others as well. But first, for a more panoramic sense of what we are memorializing at a graduation ceremony, I want to introduce similar reflections written by other men who graduated from Changing Lives during the same time period. Their testimony is representative of what many others have said for themselves in the courtroom:

> Reading accounts of other people's experience helped me put myself in their shoes and see what I might have done. I am not really sure if the readings were the secret. I think the discussions were. Hearing people's opinions on what they read helped me view things more clearly. Reading does change lives. It creates knowledge, and knowledge is power, even if it's just for yourself. I don't know if it's a turning point, but to read about Frederick Douglass and how a little thing like reading and writing can so profoundly change someone's life, and how I take it so much for granted, makes you wonder what else I'm taking for granted, things like freedom. It will make me think my decisions through before I act on them.

. . .

> When I read about other people's experience, my own personal problems don't seem so bad. If I am going through some sort of difficulty in my life, and I read about someone who has overcome such circumstances in their life, I would feel a sort of comfort, knowing this ordeal can be overcome and also knowing I'm not the only one who has to face such problems.

. . .

> This class opened my eyes a little more to the fact that some people are all right. I tend to look at most people as jerks, losers, etc. I think that my attitude towards people is starting to soften up, kinda lighten up. That makes me feel good. It shows me that there is hope. There's light at the end of the tunnel. To me, to feel good about people—it's real important that I got that out of this class. I don't know when or how, but I'm thankful for the spark that has been ignited. In the first couple of weeks we was talking about kids. And the next week I brought my kids

here from N.Y. And now they're here again. I haven't seen them since December of '98 because I was locked up. So to have them back in my life now is really good. Especially now, since they're getting older. The bottom line is that I'm happy with my life, and proud to be who I am. Cause it ain't easy being me.

. . .

I can truly say I've gotten to know an armful of great men. Too bad I had to be arrested to be blessed with the opportunity to do so! Reading changes lives because it opens our eyes to the struggle and hardships of others and assures us that things at home aren't that bad at all.

. . .

From the readings that we have read, I've been encouraged to be a stronger person, and not be afraid to take chances for positive reasons and things. Since taking this course, I have went out and gained part-time employment. My wife looks at me in a different manner because she likes the fact that I have accomplished something by finishing this program, and that also makes me feel good.

. . .

The last few months of my life I have been feeling depressed, alone, afraid, insecure of the path I need to follow to reach what I expect of my life. A chain reaction of unpleasant events has been taking place in my life, making my old-time dreams vanish. I have been feeling like falling down in a deep, scary, dark hole of uncertainties. Until I began reading and listening to real life stories of classmates. People who have been falling in the same hole, or sometimes an even deeper one. But today I see, read, and listen to their amazing comebacks, and that has motivated my thinking, my spirit, my emotions in the last few weeks, and I feel somehow reenergized, renewed, jovial. I feel like I have a second chance, a good life to live out there, just like the group of gentlemen in this class. If they have been in situations better, the same, and worse than mine, and they had the determination, the courage, to open their eyes widely and stop the "falling down syndrome," by realizing their wrong-doings and changing their ways for better, positive actions, I am as good as them, so I can do it! This class helped me look at things differently by making me realize my wrong thinking, by helping me open to changes and by motivating me to say, Enough! I can be the best of myself!

In quoting these passages, I have the advantage of picking and choosing among the most expressive from several years, not just one semester—I trust without exaggerating their claim to be representative. When these men are moved to share such thoughts on graduation day, their speeches seem lit from within.

Whether or not probationers themselves testify, there will be a number of other speeches to mark the occasion as solemn and significant. Judge Hanlon begins with a brief account of why the program was initiated more than fifteen years ago, emphasizing how her own perspective has been affected by sitting with the women's group each semester. As presiding justice, she is aware of the influence a program like Changing Lives can have on the ethos of her court. Also conscious of the crucial contributions of the probation department, she thanks Dorchester's Chief of Probation Bernard Fitzgerald for his support, as well as the numerous probation officers who recruit our students from their caseloads. This semester Judge Hanlon adds a special tribute to two former probation officers from Dorchester, John and Teresa Owens, who helped her launch the program in 1994, along with Dierdre Kennedy, Bobby Spencer, and John Christopher. Even though they no longer work in our jurisdiction, the Owenses have been attending our graduation ceremonies every semester since the beginning. Bobby Spencer has arranged a little surprise this morning, bringing back a former student to present John and Teresa with a token of appreciation for their pioneering work, in the name of the several hundred probationers they have served.

While all this is happening, the rest of us stand off to the side, scanning the faces of the audience for late arrivals, hoping the graduates will all be present before we begin handing out diplomas. Some, like Charles and Albert, take their seats as soon as the courthouse doors open, but others have waited till the last minute, like Trevor, who slips in just in time to hear his name called.

Neither José nor Willy could take the morning off from work, but everyone else is in the room before the speeches are over—all except Deighton, who doesn't show his face until the very end—on Jamaican time, we kidded him later.

Deighton misses more than applause and handshakes from the judges. One of the most memorable parts of the graduation ceremony each semester comes when Judge May is invited to address the assembly and reads aloud student writing that has especially impressed him. This time he has chosen the two humorous anecdotes of childhood "lessons" by Deighton and Randy discussed earlier in this book. Deighton is not present to hear the laughter his archetypal story of playing marbles "for keeps" evokes in the otherwise solemn courtroom. But Randy is here for his own comic story with a moral, and I have my eye on his impassive face as Tom reads its first sentences, describing the splendid, square, boy's lunch box, and the undesirable oval one, so obviously a girl's. As the story unfolds, it seems to me that Randy holds his head even more stiffly than usual on his bull neck, eyes forward, expressionless—not the face he was born with. I find myself imagining him on parade in his Marine's uniform two decades ago, but today, even from the reviewing stand, I can see a tiny, private smile creeping into the corners of Randy's mouth as he realizes that it is his story Tom is reading to us.

After the ceremony Randy and Deighton and all the other graduates will come together for a celebrative meal, but Tom May will return almost immediately to his own courtroom, where he will have as many as sixty accused persons passing before him today for judgment, so many that it is obviously impossible to find out more than the barest essentials of their cases, and almost nothing of their lives, certainly not the kind of deeper truths he has learned about these two men. As he tells us now from the bench,

> Because of the overwhelming number of cases, a premium is placed on efficiency, sometimes referred to as "case flow management." Further, in almost every instance, defense lawyers warn their clients not to say anything to the judge, for fear it will make matters worse. Consequently, the relationship between judge and defendant is very much "subject-to-object," and the judge knows almost nothing about the defendant's humanity, who that person really is.

Tom relies on our weekly classes to keep reminding him that the men and women who come before him are not simply guilty or innocent of crimes, but inevitably people with lives like the rest of us, full of hopes and fears, good luck and bad, generosity and folly and anguish—and therefore in need of patient attention and compassion as well as admonition or correction:

> After fourteen semesters of Changing Lives Through Literature, I can testify personally it has changed me as a judge. It is no longer subject-to-object, but subject-to-subject. It has made me aware of the humanity we all share and the scars that each of us carries. It reminds me always to be respectful, and it rekindles my hope that we can all change for the better.

As an ex-slave on the abolitionist lecture platform, Frederick Douglass used to turn his back to the audience at a certain point in his story, raising his shirt to show the stripes inflicted by repeated whippings from his masters. When Tom refers to scars we all carry, he is speaking metaphorically and does not mention Frederick Douglass, but he takes the occasion to recount a similar dramatic moment from our classroom this semester, without identifying the man who bared his scars. It is Randy he is speaking of here:

> "Is there a difference between depression and despair?" I'll never forget the answer. He had been a twenty-year heroin addict. He told us of his umpteen times trying to kick the habit, and finally he bottomed out by trying to kill himself with a homemade gun. I couldn't believe it until he pulled up his shirt and showed the horrific scar above his abdomen.

For the sake of conscience and humanity Tom May comes to our class in order to know the men and women who pass before him every day, to take account of their scars as well as their names on the docket. But he does not come as a mere observer. The open and attentive way he interacts with them gives students a palpable sense of having been recognized as persons instead of problems. When Tom makes room in his graduation speech for Randy and Deighton, there could be no stronger proof that he has listened, that real persons from the other side of the bar have been taken seriously for once. Even though they may be too shy to make speeches of their own on this occasion, he invites us to attend their voices with respect and delight.

Tom's words are followed by the awarding of diplomas. One at a time, some twenty men and women will rise from anonymity in the audience and walk down the central aisle amidst applause, past the tables where defendants and their attorneys ordinarily sit, and up to the place of witness and testimony, where we stand ready to congratulate them.

Professor Ann Murphy, alternating with Tam Lin Neville, has taught the women's group most semesters since its inception in 1994. She starts things off with a short speech honoring her class. Then one of the probation officers reads the roll and hands out diplomas. The first student called is weeping as she comes forward. So is the second. Yet all of the women, even those with tears in their eyes, are grinning broadly and standing tall—until they bend for a hug from Judge Hanlon, whose stature barely brings her to the shoulders of some of these ladies. Professor Murphy has a surprise for them, a typed and bound compilation of the writings each of them has painstakingly produced this semester. Another probation officer presents copies of Zora Neale Hurston's novels, as well as a little basket of "favors" she has brought for them. As they walk back to their seats with all of this in their arms, several probation officers in the audience rise to congratulate their charges with an enthusiastic embrace.

Then it is time for the men's group to step forward, and I have my chance to speak. There have been so many speeches already, it seems right to make mine brief, but like Tom May I want to get the voices of the students into the room. I explain how often they enter the program with trepidation, then finish as today with pride in their accomplishments. In fact, one man had felt so fulfilled at the end of the previous semester that he asked if he could come back for another session. He wanted to read and talk about the same texts one more time, even though his probation period had now been terminated—the carrot without the stick. So today he is graduating once again. I then read aloud Randy's final reflections on his life-changing experience:

> I used to never like to read because it was hard for me to read something and remember it. But now my mind is like glue—everything sticks. My memories go back to having gone through so many things. As you get older, the more you go through life and its experiences, the more you have, the more you remember. The same goes for reading. Literature broadens my mind and makes me think of all kinds of things I would like to do or even maybe do. But it does change lives, you start to intermingle with others and get to know them, your classmates, as a person, and some of the obstacles they have had to overcome. I've seen changes in this class, where others tried to help others.

After finishing I ask Randy to stand, and again there is applause, especially from his fellow students, who clap and clap. He has spoken for them in a way that satisfies their own sense of what was important, and they are proud of him as well as themselves.

Unless someone is moved to join his voice to Randy's, all the speeches are now over. John Christopher reads the class list and hands out diplomas with their ornate borders and flourish of official signatures. Some of these colorful documents will be packed away in a safe place, perhaps ultimately lost, but I think many of them will end up in frames. As the men make their way to the front, Tom May comes down from the bench to give each of them a handshake and hearty embrace. The first names on the roster are Albert, Dave, and Randy, the three men most likely to find the courage to say a few words, but they're too shy; no one is ready to take the lead.

As the others come up one by one, I see each of them afresh, a new person. Perhaps it's the care with which they've dressed—Charles has left his baseball cap at home and is in a jacket and tie, looking his age, and Neville is sporting a beautiful "islands" shirt that looks brand new. But it's the occasion itself that makes the striking difference: everything that's happened to them this semester is now complete and seems to be written on their faces, in the way they walk and in how they stand while accepting their diplomas from John and Bobby Spencer. Next in line is Bert, who surprises each of them with the gift of a compilation of slave narratives (including Douglass's 1845 classic), donated by the Library of America—one of those elegant clothbound editions with the silk ribbon sewn into the binding as a bookmark. And I have with me something even more splendid in their eyes, bound collections of each student's writing, with the author's name blazoned in huge letters across the front.

Like the diplomas, these gift books and personal anthologies are transitional objects, providing symbolic closure that we hope will establish the foundation for further self-affirmation. Someday a graduate may point to the substantial book on the shelf and tell his children about Frederick Douglass, a story he knows well from our eighty-page paperback version. He might open that ampler volume out of curiosity, or to refresh his memory of Douglass, and find himself caught up in another of these powerful tales, half adventure story and half documentary, so apt to grip the imagination that abolitionist Theodore Parker called them America's one and only contribution to world literature.

The personal writings of students themselves are even more charged with magnetic energy. For some of the men these pages may feel very private, to be hidden away like a diary and never opened, the past literally a closed book. But they are also something to be proud of, thoughts and feelings possibly to be shared with family as they have already been shared with classmates. Opened or closed, these pages constitute a reminder of themselves at their best, and among the items they take home from our graduation ceremony they are surely the most potent, like buried seeds waiting for spring. I remember how Neville's friend reacted to his breakthrough as a writer. It's not far-fetched to imagine similar moments for other students, even years later:

"Did you write this?"

"Well, yes I did, but that was a long time ago."

When a man leaves the courthouse today and finds a moment to be alone and reflect on what's just happened to him, I like to believe he will turn to the pages he himself wrote, fragmentary passages of memory and revelation now reconfigured as the unfolding story of both the past ten weeks and also his entire life. When he comes to the final section and reads his own summing-up, I hope the writer will experience the same sense of fulfillment that others less shy may achieve in speeches on graduation day.

Just as with standing up in public to speak, so too with this moment of silent self-awareness; its significance lies not in any guarantees regarding future conduct or accomplishments but in its immediate transforming power. Hereafter thoughts, feelings, and acts will have a different meaning. No doubt there will be practical results, beneficial we trust, but as with many important life changes—coming of age, parenthood, a close brush with death—the initiate emerges a different person, and that is the essential function of all such rites of passage, whatever else may ensue.

This transformation and some of its implications can be discerned in the attempts students make to assess the impact the course has had on them. The quality of illumination is particularly strong in people like Albert and Neville, who have lived through a crisis during the semester. I have already presented the insights those two changed men shared with us at our last session, but I want now to put their separate self-realizations side by side in order to consider some things they have in common:

> Since I have been in this class, Changing Lives Through Literature, it has changed my life. It made me see that I do have something to offer in life, outside of hanging out in the streets with so-called friends. This class made me want to go back to school and further my education. . . . Now that I see what I have been missing in life, I am going to try and change my life for the better. (*Albert*)

> The most important thing that I've learned is that I really can learn. All these years I've been thinking that I could not read or write. Here, look at me now! Reading and writing and spelling. And I know some of the things are going to be misspelled, but what really matters is that I keep trying my best. (*Neville*)

Although Albert was the only student who imagined himself formally addressing his classmates in this final exercise, both his words and Neville's are valedictory exclamations of renewal and hope. "Here, look at me now!"

In their special cases the transformative event has come in the form of disavowing a label, "disability case," a long-accepted perspective that seems to have reversed itself as a result of telling their stories to others and finding themselves taken seriously in their efforts of self-definition.

Albert and Neville are not unusual in having discovered something important during their ten weeks, but their obvious elation was not matched by anyone else in the program. I don't think this difference is simply a matter of degree, these two at the high end of some spectrum of successful rededication. Rather, it's an effect of their sudden breakthrough in the face of what had seemed an absolute impasse. Because Albert and Neville are physically impaired in ways that others in the class are not—with the possible exception of Randy, at risk and ecstatic in his own world—more seems to be at stake for them. For most of the men a realization that their problems aren't insurmountable, and that other people "have it worse," seems to be enough to brighten their outlook. But Albert and Neville are teetering in an either/or situation: if not the depths of despair, then euphoria. As onlookers and celebrants we naturally feel a rush of delight in their newfound confidence—but on reflection, equally great dread for them. These paradoxical feelings come to their fullest tension at graduation time.

That's how I felt, anyway.

Most of the men do take heart from the shared classroom experience of reading, writing, and conversation—perhaps also from observing Albert and Neville work through their challenges. But the typical probationer's cautious optimism is more in tune with his true plight, rarely felt as so desperate and therefore not so spiked with highs and lows. However grim it may sometimes seem, life does not present itself as an all-or-nothing crisis. Or, if some students do begin to see themselves as potentially faced with ultimate choices of the sort Neville and Albert are confronting, they are likely to come to this apprehension vicariously, in reading the story of Frederick Douglass, the heroic figure they all accept as their model of manliness and self-determination:

> All the voices and ideas have helped me look at things in a different way, or a way that my mind wouldn't have thought of doing. I'll say that the first couple of chapters in the Frederick Douglass biography made me think of myself, to take advantage of the abilities we are now eligible of using. Off this program, I have begun to gradually read for no purpose, so I guess reading is what I'm going to get and take from this program with me. My family has told me I have made out good, and that I needed this to put me on track. And I have noticed I'm not on the street as much, and also have real legal goals that I am going to accomplish. Reading literature does change lives, especially if you're reading books of the slavery era. You commonly compare yourself to the characters being read, and you can see most of the time your advantages, things you might want to switch up. (*Luis*)

> By me, reading accounts of other people's experience gives me a new light on other people's lifestyle, like the old slave days, and what it was like growing up. In some ways I think it's the secret of our course, because you read, then you write. This course is mostly writing and getting the understanding of the past. When you're in the groups, it opens you up and it gives you a second chance at life. (*Willy*)

> This class has taught me that lots of people have it hard. And some got it not so hard. But people who do have a hard life should always keep on battling. Instead of going back, try your best to get there, because eventually you will. That's what I've learned out of reading accounts of other people's experience—the way it has affected my classmates. The best memory from this class was when we sit in groups and talk about what we wrote about. (*José*)

> I don't think reading literature changes lives, but I think it could change the way you use to think about something or somebody. Like, for instance, reading this book helped me understand what Frederick Douglass had to go through being a slave. There was things like the goals that Frederick Douglass wanted to accomplish that I didn't know about. That's what made him become a stronger man. (*Anthony*)

For students like Luis the life stories told by Frederick Douglass, Malcolm X, and Richard Wright seem to blend right in with the fictions by Gorky and Tolstoy, no less true to experience; but when Luis says that "you commonly compare yourself to the characters being read," he is not suggesting that he expects or would welcome any enormous changes in his life. Similarly, Anthony may be ready to change the way he thinks about some things, but he's not really aiming at self-discovery, certainly not at the cost of major crisis or hitting bottom. Lessons that come from other people's experience are not necessarily transformative, however clarifying or uplifting. "Lots of people have it hard," says José, "that's what I've learned." But neither he nor Willy is tempted to live in the eye of the hurricane like Neville and Albert. The four men I've just been quoting were the youngest in our class, and their concerns are those of the young, barely out of the house, still testing themselves in the streets and looking for exemplary characters in stories or in life to emulate.

Older men like Charles and Deighton have been through all that and are licking their wounds, just trying to survive with the whole weight of the past on them. If these veterans feel they have learned anything this semester, it's not so much through the heroic example of figures like Douglass as it is from conversations with classmates facing persistent hardship and long-standing problems. Their own troubles are winding down and are not likely at this point in life to come to a crisis or to resolve themselves in a flash of revelation. These older men belong to a kind of fraternity of suffering and mutual compassion, and they respond more powerfully to stories like Tolstoy's "Korney Vasiliev" than to Douglass's triumphs of self-definition. In the classroom they give advice to baffled young men like Anthony or Trevor, but they feel deeper comradeship with Dave, whose real-life saga of makeshifts and set-backs is very familiar to them.

Turnabout, in those same classroom conversations Dave could take comfort in the fact that he was not alone, and that even in his own seemingly endless muddle he might be an encouraging example for others:

> After starting this class, I got frustrated because I was going through some shit in my life. Things weren't going too good for me. I was in a messed-up situation, trying to work, and a new baby, and my living situation. I wanted to *quit* the program! But that would've been too easy, so I decided that I was gonna finish this program for the benefit of myself. And hopefully I could use what I got from this class and apply it to my own life and start making some changes, so that I could be a better person to myself as well as others. This has been a wild and crazy ten weeks for me, but I believe it was well worth it. Changing Lives Through Literature has opened my

> eyes and ears to knowledge that literature speaks, and once eaten and digested with some use of the brain and the heart and mind, it can be used as a tool or guideline in your problems and situations. In the last ten weeks I've read and actually been going through all of the problems of those older dudes (slaves and so on), to this day! I am not alone in my madness. So the search goes on for more power, the empowerment that gives me the right to make the best choices, the right choices in my life. I take with me the knowledge that I, through some way, maybe touched someone's life with my story. And that I can make a difference. Sometimes I just need to be given a chance, or a "second chance."

Dave falls somewhere in between the younger and the older men. What will he see when he re-reads the story of his "wild and crazy ten weeks" in Changing Lives? His was the thickest of all the booklets of homework and classroom exercises I gave out at graduation. I don't think he missed a single class or assignment, and writing seemed important in coping with his ongoing emergency, a means of venting and taking stock that gave him some respite and insight. In Dave's case there was a sense of crisis as with Neville or Albert, but it had a very different character, highlighted by its coming at the beginning of the semester, not the end of it. Dave almost quit the program in its early weeks—just as he was on the verge of quitting his family, is tempted every day to quit his lousy job, and wishes he could call it quits with the hospitable aunt who keeps reminding him of his responsibilities. His decision to stick it out is ironically similar to the opposite choice of Ross and Harry. The first few sessions seem to have helped those two men understand what work they need to do at this point in their lives, and they left to do it, whereas Dave realized that his own predicament required him to hold his ground, stay with his crisis in all its manifestations, and see what would happen.

Like the younger men, Dave admires "those older dudes (slaves and so on)" who persisted and made something of themselves. Dave will "keep on battling," as José puts it. But Dave's summing up of the semester's lessons is more somber than theirs, less confident that things are going to improve, and farther yet from Albert's fervid faith in some imminent reversal of character and fortune. As with the older men, Dave's soul-searching is modest and practical, not expecting much from the world and aware of his own fallibility. Charles reports laconically, "I have cut back on drinking alcohol almost to the point to stop," and Deighton reminds himself that "It's easy to tell someone that you forgive them, but it is hard to forget the things you forgive them for." Dave also knows what it's like to inch forward like this. He has forgiven his girlfriend, curbed his anger, and doesn't seem to be relying on drugs or alcohol as an escape from frustration and hardship.

Dave has not yet begun to see his life as irrevocably fated, but neither does he believe he's got it under control. He speaks of both "rights" and "chances"—"the right to make the best choices" and being "given a chance, or a 'second chance.'" For younger men that second chance can be quite palpable: "My family has told me I have made out good" (Luis); "When you're in the groups, it opens you up and it gives you a second chance at life" (Anthony). But Charles and Deighton have seen their possibilities dwindle to bare survival, just making the best of your fate.

I think Dave views these classmates as representing his own options at the crossroads, and so graduation day may be more problematic for him than for those who regard it as something definitive, whether back "on track" like Luis or keeping an eye on the nearest exit like Charles, who didn't stick around after putting in a brief appearance at the celebratory brunch. Dave has come today in his work clothes but will eat a donut with us upstairs and chat a bit before he plunges back into his wild and crazy world, grateful to find that he's "not alone in my madness," and that his story has "maybe touched someone's life . . . that I can make a difference."

Dave, Luis and Charles, Albert and Neville, Trevor and Anthony, Deighton and Randy—after the ceremony we all do go up to the second floor where coffee and donuts, bagels, and orange juice await us in the staff lounge. This scene is like no other all semester—twenty male and female probationers, some meeting one another for the first time, many of them newly discharged, and mingling with their teachers and probation officers, along with family members. The judges, still in their robes, poke their heads in before going off to their separate sessions where they must catch up after a late start.

It's too hectic for me. All the new faces are distracting, and everyone's talking at once. I find it difficult to absorb the profound events of the day and would much prefer to be sitting by myself somewhere, letting it all sink in. But that will have to come later, and gradually I begin to take in the one big fact: it's over, our ten-week retreat during which we've gotten to know one another in such extraordinary ways—on one level hardly at all, on another plane intensely and intimately. We're no longer talking about crisis or hitting bottom or defending yourself against unrelenting force. Today lots of practical business gets transacted instead. We have come back to everyday life, and it's inevitably a letdown, despite good spirits and the congratulatory atmosphere. There's always someone who finally decides to explore the possibility of getting his or her GED. This semester one of the women is interested. Probation Officer Dierdre Kennedy is our authority on such matters, and she also has advice for Randy about a Veterans Upward Bound program he might attend as a step toward professional training he'd like to pursue. Maybe this time the ceiling will not fall in just as he is about to be licensed for his archetypal rescue vocation—not firefighter, not EMT, but drug counselor. While Randy and Dee are talking, Albert asks me for names of people to contact at the university, to discuss his desire to study child development. Several other students head straight for Bobby or John, to find out the precise procedure for terminating their probation now that they've earned their six months' credit. And we must arrange for diplomas and books to be passed on to José and Willy by their probation officers. The room is buzzing with such negotiations in addition to the hubbub of rejoicing, handshakes, and farewells—like a locker room after winning the championship.

If I'm feeling at a loss in this welter of genial talk, so anticlimactic after this morning's grave formalities, I wonder how the probationers are feeling. Most of them have come alone today and end up chatting with one another, but there's Trevor sitting in a corner next to his girlfriend, a dazzling young woman in a white dress. He seems withdrawn and has not introduced his companion to anyone or joined in the general conversation, except for a brief exchange Bert later reported to me as sounding strangely flat: "I've learned something about communication." But he said the same thing, much more earnestly, on the last night of class:

> Through the course of this program I've learned how to communicate with people a little better. It seems like before I came to this program I was going numb. I can't remember the last time I picked up a book to read it or even skim through it. I also have a better relationship with my girlfriend. I try to think about other people's feelings now. It just isn't about me anymore.

When I look again in their direction a moment later, Trevor and his girlfriend are gone.

Having finished his business with Dee Kennedy, Randy stands in the center of the small room, apparently lost in thought while people mill around him. Although only a few of his classmates may have noticed, Randy was the star of the show today, his jolly lunchbox anecdote followed immediately by the description of the scar next to his heart, and then his account of what literature means to him now that everything he reads "sticks like glue." When he stood up to be applauded, perhaps only Tom and I, quoting him anonymously, could have imagined how he might have felt. As usual, his face is still a blank, but behind those unfocused eyes I know the wheels are spinning. I wonder if a new fantasy of sangfroid in emergency is already in the making.

At one point Albert brings his elderly mother over to meet me. As he approaches, I realize that Albert is dressed from head to toe in black velvet! With an earring in his ear! At the beginning of the semester I couldn't have guessed he would turn out to be such a dandy, or be bringing his long-suffering mother to the courthouse to witness his triumph. She too is all dressed up. With their smiling faces next to each other, I see a family resemblance—a curious diagonal to their faces, in her case as if her glasses had slipped awry. Later Bert tells me that when Albert introduced him to her, she said, "You peoples surely made a different person out of Albert." And he is a different person than the one we met on opening night.

There's a small patio-balcony just off the staff lounge, with tables and chairs. Gradually most of us gravitate into the fresh air—some to smoke, others to lean against the railing and talk quietly. At one point Bobby herds everyone out into the sunlight for the class photo he always takes. After that, people begin to disperse, though half a dozen stick around, then three, two, one. Dave and Deighton are standing at the railing, talking amiably, and near them, resting his bulk on a chair, Neville sits, smoking a cigarette, not quite close enough to join in, but not so far away as to seem alone. He's been sitting out here most of the time—away from the pastries and bagels. Too bad he didn't bring his friend along to help him celebrate.

Bert and I end up standing with Deighton after Dave leaves, and he tells us a little more about his life. He came to Boston to join his mother when he was sixteen—the same age Dave was when his grandmother died and he went into the streets. Bert asks him if he can still speak the Jamaican patois he grew up with. "Oh yes," he says, though not offering us a sample. Deighton's life has obviously been full, and sometimes painful, but unlike Dave he has no urge to tell anyone his troubles. While Dave is a worried man up against a hard world, Deighton is one of those easygoing people who make you feel immediately comfortable, as if life had no worries. Unhurried, utterly at home in the physical world and his own body, Deighton can laugh at himself—and was delighted to hear what a hit his "marbles" story had been when Tom read it in court.

How does he manage to be so relaxed and unperturbed, given the turns he's faced recently? His answer is characteristically Aesopian: Stay away from women. That's what gets you in trouble.

Bert asks him, "Are you married?"

"No!" is his emphatic answer. A grin passes over his usually solemn face. Then he too takes his leave.

Except for a few people tidying up inside, everyone else is gone but Neville, still sitting in the chair near us, smoking, with a look on his brow that says graduation day is over.

# *Epilogue*

Changing Lives Through Literature is full of reawakened dreams and hopes for a fresh start. Are such hopes justified in the long run? What has been the result for the men whose stories I have been telling? Has Changing Lives raised false hopes for Albert? Will these hopes vanish if he doesn't try to attain them by applying to a college? How lasting are his rediscovered self-respect and his sense of having been "listened to" as he unburdened himself in the Changing Lives classroom? Is his a "success story" whether or not he realizes his fantasy of college and a career?

There are two ways of addressing such questions. The one favored by our dominant social order, with its statistics and cost/benefit analyses, calculates the recidivism rates of "study groups" and "control groups"—de-identified human beings whose plights are assessed as variables and outcomes. Within the "at risk" period after their participation in a rehabilitation program, were they accused and convicted of new offenses? Important information we want to know—and so we do: a recent study of 700 men and women who have completed the Changing Lives Through Literature program shows that their recidivism rates are significantly below those of a control group with similar demographics, jurisdictions, and time frames. This is welcome news, and we hope that such evidence might influence the criminal justice system in positive ways, but it is not the kind of truth that this book has tried to present about the lives of real persons like Neville and Albert.

The highly respected Norwegian criminologist Nils Christie writes in his books about two contrasting and mutually exclusive approaches to the assessment of such lives. One approach, often dismissed as "merely anecdotal," considers "people in relation to each other. It has to do with social life, interdependence, communes, societies. It also often has to do with shades rather than contrasts, changes rather than stability, and with ambiguity and doubt." The other approach

> consists of categories rather than groups, and with clarity and accountability as major virtues. . . . But statistics are not only a counting system. They are also a thought system. They presuppose a certain way of thinking and also influence thinking. Statistical activities do not only describe what already exists, but contribute actively to the creating of new phenomena. (*Beyond Loneliness and Institutions*, p. 25)

Both approaches influence our attitudes and subsequent actions, and that has been a primary concern in the writing of this book, which does not focus on probabilities so much as possibilities, not on statistics but on specific life changes—how they come to be, and with what implications for future development and self-realization. In offering an "epilogue" to the stories presented here, I will retain this hopeful, living perspective, avoiding labels and the actuarial apparatus of foregone conclusions.

Although Neville, Luis, and Randy had no ambitions for more education, all three considered their past schooling as formative, and their self-images seem to have shifted as a result of reliving good and bad encounters there. In reflecting on these earlier impressions, they too have reclaimed for themselves a measure of self-esteem—which especially in Neville's case had long been denied him. One great virtue of the Changing Lives program is that it gives its students a genuine experience of "one step at a time" over a period long enough to look back from a new place and trace the path followed, perhaps glimpsing the "old self" hurrying along to catch up. Is this firm ground from which to move forward in life more confidently?

These are questions that only time can answer, but some of the possibilities may be examined in the light of a few other stories of men in the program, whose further experiments with education suggest what might be in store for Albert and his classmates.

Hughes was in our program in its early stages, when we sometimes thought of it as a stepping stone to college, at least for students who felt ready for the uphill climb. Several probation officers knew Hughes well, starting from the time he was twelve, just beginning to get in trouble, but he came to us in his mid-twenties after five years in prison. Born and raised in Dorchester, his family background was Haitian, and he identified strongly with the black diaspora. He liked to speak of "my Black African forefathers and mothers."

Hughes had attended the most underfunded high school in all of Boston. One of his cousins, bused to a well-supported suburban school, told Hughes he was being cheated of his education, and indeed he failed to graduate. He used his intelligence to master the streets instead. By the time he joined us he had been out of jail for over a year, had become a father, and was back in high school several nights a week. Probation officers and others tried to convince him to go for his GED, but Hughes refused: "Why go half of the way when I could go the whole distance and come out right and exact?" He was getting As and Bs and feeling good about himself.

Hughes loved history, and he read eagerly through Frederick Douglass's *Narrative,* alive to its bearing on his own world. He also reveled in argument and was often the one to frame issues in our class discussions—impetuously and contentiously. I remember him wrangling with a young man from the Dominican Republic over the relations between their often embattled homelands on Hispaniola, each of them asserting his version of the truth louder and louder. Finally Hughes bowed out of the debate, unwilling to dispute what boiled down to a matter of fact. The following week he was already in his chair when his blusterous opponent walked in, and before he could sit down, Hughes reasserted his claim, now citing an encyclopedia article. "Okay! Okay!" his opponent sighed, "You're right! You're right!"

Hughes relished this moment, his budding school smarts triumphing over street rhetoric, but he was no worshipper of encyclopedias or any textual authority. He loved to read, but he also had great respect for the experience and wisdom of others, especially the older generation:

> I read some what alot [he wrote in his shaky phonetic spelling] and I due alot of talking to older people. I look a lot of movies as well, true documents of the real thing. So all I see and talk about is factual and can not be disputed by anyone. Plus alot of pictures can make it real good and sometimes it could make it sad but either way your getting a good insite on what it is your reading.
>
> Since I due a lot of talk with the exspirenced people of the South back in those days it's mind twisting and exciting to me because I was not there and they were. That's alot of knowledge, wisdom, understanding. For me it is anyway.

After a few weeks we all began to hope that Hughes, with his alert intelligence and delight in knowing things, might want to go on to college for further validation of the sort he was enjoying with us—but first he needed to get his high school diploma.

Not long after the Changing Lives graduation ceremony in December, Hughes's mother died. She had been a strong supporter of his new enthusiasm for school, and though he took her death hard, he finished out his night classes in high school and in May he got his diploma—"with the biggest smile a child could ever have on his face." He told us proudly that there was a statue of Frederick Douglass in Faneuil Hall, the famous Boston venue where his graduation ceremony took place. Hughes did indeed have a beautiful, childlike smile.

Soon after that he got in touch to explore the possibility of entering the university. I suggested that he audit a course I would be teaching in the fall, to get the feel of the workload and to strengthen his writing skills. The course was titled "The Black Presence in American Literature," and the first assignment would be Frederick Douglass's *Narrative.* So it came to pass.

But college work proved too much for Hughes, especially given his other responsibilities. After the first week with Frederick Douglass, he rarely finished a book on time and was at a constant disadvantage in the daily quizzes and discussions. A master of dodges, he would come to class late in order to avoid the quiz, and then busy himself with his homework while his discussion group grappled with issues raised by the quiz question. His writing was exclamatory and superficial because he was bluffing, relying on his street smarts. This routine, no doubt perfected in high school, was systematically undermining his chance to learn the "mind-twisting" things he had most enjoyed in Changing Lives. But he had to find his own way.

Hughes was aware of his ploys and not really ashamed of them. He felt his own hard life had endowed him with skills and knowledge that more conventionally literate students lacked:

> A black writer expresses himself a whole lot different than a white person. It's from the heart, experience, stress, oppression and everything else you could think

> of that the black man had pass down to him from slavery. That's alot to have on your shoulders to deal with when your black. Now a white person or man don't have that kind of life to even think about. Everything he knows is from someone else's account and not his own. He's more like a reporter interviewing a person to get the story just to report it.

Hughes knew that in order to succeed in college he would have to learn to write like "a white person"—that is, he would have to master the practice he was denigrating here, the habit of looking dispassionately into matters and writing them up as a reporter might. What would it cost him to do this? As things now stood with him, he knew what he knew, and he could count on his firsthand experience as rock bottom truth. But if he were to write about things he had not experienced for himself, he would have to borrow "someone else's account," as he did in an essay he brought one day on "The Statue of Liberty"—a plaster cast from the encyclopedia, and exactly what he complained about in "white" writing.

At the end of the semester I shared my misgivings with Hughes. He had the intelligence and drive necessary to succeed in college, but he certainly could not be late day after day, neglect assignments, or write them during class time. And with his family responsibilities, a full course load (required for financial aid) might prove too demanding. In the end Hughes decided not to continue. What determined his choice I do not know, but the crucial factor may well have been his unwillingness to give up so much of who he was in order to become a person he was not sure he really wanted to be.

In this decision he differed from several other men in Changing Lives who did go to college and received degrees. Ernest, for example, began preparing himself for college on his very first night in Changing Lives, when he asked me if he might bring self-assigned writings to class for feedback and revision—something no other student has ever done. He went directly from this regimen to a community college, making the Dean's List every semester.

One night we invited Ernest back to address a new Changing Lives class, where he proudly reported that he now owned his own house, a truck, and was in business for himself—a success story that might have had more weight with his auditors if he had mentioned having been before the judge again as a result of an altercation with his wife. Just because you have a degree doesn't mean you are no longer bound to your wheel. Ernest was still struggling with his temper.

We learned later that Ernest's domestic problems had been resolved without the need for court action, and indeed it was evident that he owed much of his success to family support, especially from his mother, who encouraged his further education just as Hughes's mother had done. Time would tell how far the impetus would carry him, but Ernest seemed to be on a roll.

A quite different story was that of Lionel, who came to the program after a decade of incarceration for serious offenses. Early in life Lionel had been caught in the crossfire between school smarts and street smarts. Although he "grew in school" as a child, once he hit adolescence he "also absorbed the negative teaching which the streets offer." Survival lessons came at a very high price. By seventeen he was running from "a hail of bullets," in which his best friend was killed. Lionel spent his twenties in prison, where "sponging up knowledge saved my sanity" and brought him, like Malcolm X, to a new form of self-discipline forged in a fusion of race and religion:

> It was at this time I started to devour books by the hundreds, in my thirst for knowledge. I ran smack into the teachings of Elijah Muhammad. I had already made my mark in the prison, so fear was not my reason for acknowledging Islam. It was the truth which captivated me, to the point I dissected every book of Elijah's. I quit pork and other negative behavior. Although I never fully converted, I bear witness this was the only religion for the Black man.

By the time of his release Lionel had prepared himself spiritually and intellectually for a different life. Too much his own man to join the Black Muslims, he chose to follow a path more like Ernest's, betterment through education. He entered college and earned a bachelor's degree in business; he became a father; and yet his transformation was not complete. Prison "polished all my rough edges, only to have them surface upon my re-entering society." His street smarts took over once again, and he had been incarcerated for another year before coming to the Changing Lives program. As with Ernest, a degree was no guarantee against backsliding.

In jail again, Lionel took a close look at himself: "I discovered as a man, as a person, and most of all as a father, that I was a failure." He knew he must change, but books were not the answer. A chance encounter in prison gave him the push he needed:

> Two weeks before I was released I was still weak mentally. Because of my lack of finances, in my mind there was no way I could remain legit. One evening, in deep contemplation, I was approached by this young man who noticed the troubling look I gave off.
>
> So he questioned it, and I explained my dilemma. He stated to me, Lionel, you must do the things that LAST. The fast cars don't last, the faster women don't last, the drugs don't last. But the way your daughter runs to you on visit day with a big hug and an even bigger smile, that LASTS.
>
> It was at this time I vowed to do the things that last.

With this resolve Lionel had come to the Changing Lives program, and inspired by men like Frederick Douglass and Malcolm X, he began to take seriously his own gifts as a writer and as a man. This time his goal was not a degree but a new attitude toward himself and his responsibilities. Perhaps the difference was in his sense of no longer having to go it alone, a long habit that neither streets nor prison nor college had ever questioned. At the end of the semester he formulated the following challenge to himself:

> I had been making excuses and not picking up the pen or reading for that matter in about a year. Yet once I sat in the class, the desire again re-surfaced. The only way one can become good at a craft is to practice, and this I ignored long enough. Many times as men we do not challenge ourselves mentally, since we talk sports, women, somewhat current events. Yet we do not continually keep educating each other. Due to my past lifestyle, I am and was secluded from society for the most part. My only interaction was at work, and that is limited to seeing I work hard. At any rate, I feel this class has re-opened the desire to write, and write I will!

Hughes and Ernest might well have said much the same thing. However differently it played out, all three men were marginalized loners who accepted society's decree that a college diploma shall be the passport to respectability and upward mobility. Their careers show how difficult it is to ride the seesaw of street smarts and school smarts; favoring one over the other leads to a fragile victory. The former lands you in prison sooner or later, but the straight-and-narrow path is also filled with pitfalls, especially carrying a criminal record on your back. And however helpful in credentialing, ultimately it is not formal education that opens the door to self-realization but rather the resolve to confront honestly who you are and what you want from yourself. Moreover—and this is crucial—self-realization is not a transformation that can take place outside community, without the support and mutual encouragement of others you trust and respect. To find out who you are, you must give yourself to others.

Just as Hughes and Ernest surfaced again after completing Changing Lives, so too did Lionel. One night Bobby Spencer brought us good news in our perennial quest for alternatives that might serve the reawakened ambitions of people like Lionel or Hughes once they have no classes or assignments, no diploma to work for. One of our recent graduates had formed his own reading group with four or five other men, including one or two from Changing Lives. The group met at the local library and lasted about a year, after which we heard no more about it, but the model seemed so promising that we decided to set up a little pilot program, meeting Saturday mornings in a local community center. Bobby talked it up with men like Lionel who might be interested, and on the first day three of them showed up, along with Bobby and two volunteer facilitators from the university. We had high hopes that Lionel's appetite for books would prove contagious, and indeed, the facilitators reported a lively discussion at their first meeting, choosing what they might read and talk about. But the following week only Lionel reappeared, and after that, nobody, though the staff kept coming for another two Saturdays.

Why didn't it work? There were many contributing factors—the size of the initial group and its chemistry, the auspices, even the meeting time, Saturday mornings when other people would be taking it easy—but I think the experiment failed for more substantial reasons. It had no base in personal commitment or group solidarity. The attempt might have succeeded if it had been initiated by the men themselves rather than our staff. Their hearts weren't in it because they didn't own it, and the enterprise didn't last long enough to cut loose from its origin as somebody else's idea of "their own good." This exercise of authentic choosing is the key to the transformation that occurs somewhere in the middle of every semester of Changing Lives, when the men become aware of themselves as a self-created community.

The stories of Hughes, Ernest, and Lionel reveal a single fundamental dynamic. All three believed in schooling as a means of self-improvement: Ernest saw it as the stairway to economic success, Hughes as a boost to his ego and perhaps a reality check as well, and Lionel as all of these at different points in his story, but ultimately as a way to take responsibility for his life, using writing for self-scrutiny and avowal. Bolstered by their participation in Changing Lives, to some extent each of them succeeded in his aims, but it was not further schooling that lifted them up, however much it might have served as the place where they tried their wings. The crunch came in the moment of choice, when the weight of awareness exploded into action. If we try to put our finger on turning points, they would be found at very different junctures: for Ernest it was on his first night when he initiated his writing project; for Hughes when he went back to high school, then when he decided to risk his ego in a college classroom, and finally when he chose not to continue there; for Lionel it came when he vowed to do the things that last, and then when he exclaimed *And write I will!* The issue is not whether further schooling might benefit men whose previous education has been warped or truncated, but under what conditions self-discovery and personal growth can occur at all. The Changing Lives program can provide the challenge and support to awaken some men to new faith in themselves, but not everyone is ready for the vulnerability of self-examination or the anxiety that comes with giving up old ways of life. Ten weeks is a very short time even to begin such daunting soul work. But a first step in the right direction may then lead to another, and another.

The actual results of new ambitions and determination can be frustrating. As we have seen in Dave's testimony, he went to every job interview aware that it would end with the same fatal question, and Lionel discovered that even a college degree is far from an infallible key to success. With plenty of material as well as emotional support, the prudent course might be to imitate Ernest, to start a business of one's own where the prospective employer is not going to run a CORI check. I recall one well-educated man telling of attempts to land white-collar work after his prison term for armed robbery. Tim was qualified for many such jobs but never even got to the interview stage. Finally he saw an ad for a position in an insurance company, and he decided to answer "no" to the question on the job application concerning felony convictions. He got the interview and the job. Tim's first four days were great: he liked the job and his new colleagues liked him. Then the termination slip arrived—not for having a CORI but for having lied on the application. They get you one way or the other, he said bitterly: "Maybe I should pick up the gun again."

Tim graduated from Changing Lives without having conquered his bitterness, and it is not hard to understand why. I don't think he was likely to follow through on his threat, at least not soon, but his experience in the program could not be called a "success story," even though he obviously enjoyed the small and large group conversations, where he blew off a lot of steam. He got his six months off probation, and he found a job washing dishes, but he may well have felt more anger and self-defeat when he left us than when he started.

Such "failures" in Changing Lives are infrequent, but of course they do occur. Some men violate their probation or commit new crimes even while attending classes. Although Dave graduated, we saw him again in a later semester, back on probation after some new infraction. His determination to provide for his family was strong, but he simply could not find work that paid enough to move out of his aunt's apartment and give them some breathing space. Others from his class also reappeared. It turned out that Ross had left us early because of a probation violation, and he came back to earn his six months the following year. Even Randy might also be counted among the "failures," though he was not arrested again so far as I know. His mother died a year or so after his final voluntary semester in the program, and one night I got a call from him saying he was back on heroin. Was this a cry for help? It's not for me to say, but when I called back a few days later, his new girlfriend told me he wasn't able to come to the phone. Then, a year after that, he called again to say his girlfriend had died and he was living alone in a single room; but he was apparently off heroin and back on methadone. I'm sure the story doesn't end there.

Which of these are success stories, and which are failures? The answer depends on your criteria, but in any case these lives are open-ended; as Grace Paley wrote in one of her short stories, "Everyone, real or invented, deserves the open destiny of life."

In general, men like Tim who have had some college experience report less "benefit" from the program than those who never finished high school. This does not mean they are unaffected, only that their relations with the social order are usually more crisscrossed with double-binds. Sometimes a man falls somewhere in the middle, like Greg, an imposing figure, big and self-assured in his tight do-rag bandanna, but without a chip on his shoulder. He was an exceptionally intelligent and genial fellow who was the catalyst for many of the best conversations during his semester. "I really like this class," he said one day. "It's the best thing the court has ever done."

Although raised in Boston, during a year of family crisis Greg had lived with relatives in Chicago and had been the only black student at a suburban high school. He told us how, after a long uphill struggle with the prevailing racism there, his patience and cheerful forays in light banter had finally won him the respect of his teammates on the basketball team, and then the rest of the student body. This testimony was particularly fruitful during a Changing Lives semester when the black-to-white ratio was three-to-two rather than the usual nine-to-one. Members of the small group to which he told his story were soon trading anecdotes of their own testings of the color line. In the midst of this lively conversation Greg suddenly stood up in the middle of his circle and announced that he needed to pee—that he had needed to pee for quite a while, but didn't want to miss anything. They laughed when he enjoined them "not to talk about anything without him"—and in fact he was back in two minutes. At the end of the evening this group didn't want to break up. They kept at it long after all the others had handed in their writing and vanished.

This was Changing Lives at its best, men in each circle establishing their own agenda, mutual trust, and conversational decorum—much of it due to Greg this semester, whose delight in these exchanges was so evident and infectious. He'd made a big difference in the group feeling, all the more impressive since he had actually attended only four classes by this, the eighth meeting of the semester, and had been warned that he was in danger of failing. I had already begun to prepare a makeup assignment that might allow him to scrape by—if he missed no more meetings—but he didn't show up for the ninth class, and on the final night the probation officers told him he could not graduate. Greg argued vehemently: He had missed opening night because he had not yet been informed he could join the program, and on one occasion he had stayed away because his child was being born. Was he to miss the chance to see his son born? The probation officers were uncomfortable, but rules were rules. Even counting this last evening, he had attended only half the classes. Greg stormed out of the room in a fury. As he left, I called to him, "You could come back in the fall. . . ."

"I'll never come back!" he shouted, and was gone.

No doubt the probation officers were right, but so was Greg. As I see it, the real question has less to do with rules and their interpretation than with what Greg took with him when he stamped out the door. There had been so many occasions when he energized this class that recognized him as its sparkplug, and he himself was obviously heartened by the exchanges he inspired. Did this experience in the program help solidify his self-respect and good intentions? I hope so. But his angry exit may have cancelled out such gains, just as his absences nullified his six months' reward upon graduation.

There is no way of knowing the answer, but Greg's case throws new light on the problem of assessing success and failure. How a student like Tim or Greg regards his performance is surely crucial in determining its meaning. Although graduates often say that simply completing the program feels like a great accomplishment in lives full of blind alleys, it seems mechanical to call exactly ten weeks of obligation, validated by six months off probation, a success story. Aside from graduation day, there is no definitive point at which a student could be said to have reaped his harvest, and a man in Greg's situation will surely see his experience as positive or negative depending on when and how he surveys it. Official measures—completing ten weeks, getting off probation, going back to school for a degree, or reoffending, carrying a CORI wherever you go—all of these count decisively in the realm of institutional regulation and statistics, but they do not touch the wellsprings of self-knowledge or self-renewal, which may bubble up at any time. Among the dozen men I've described in this book Harry and Ross dropped out early, after what seemed like remarkable bursts of self-realization, whereas Neville and Albert had their epiphanies at the end of the semester. We do not know the final story for any of them. Some, like Ross and Dave, were destined to return to Changing Lives and complete a second round for their reward, while Greg, true to his word, was never seen again. Can an aborted semester be *both* a success and a failure? Such absolute terms are simply not applicable when assessing how lives change.

Regardless of immediate outcomes for graduates of the program, the question of ongoing support and mutual aid remains. Further schooling has not proved a viable option for most of these men, and our attempt at fostering a follow-up reading group led nowhere. Other possibilities have been explored. Local action groups have come to invite probationers to join community efforts toward self-help in areas like CORI reform, or prevention of what newspapers call "youth violence." Over the years Changing Lives students themselves have suggested the possibility of volunteering as youth workers—after all, who understands the despair of the streets better?—but the hope of instituting such a follow-up program begins to fade when we consider official reaction. A man with a CORI cannot legally hold a job in *any* human services under state auspices in Massachusetts. Even supposing that we could find a way of circumventing this statute, what would be the public response to some ugly incident—that might well occur no matter how carefully such an experiment were undertaken and monitored? The scandal would bring Changing Lives down along with its spinoff venture.

For a long time we did not recognize that we had a solution to this dilemma right in front of us, not focused on young people in the streets but on men who have already entered the revolving doors of the criminal justice system. Why not invite graduates from the program to return as staff members?

Both LaVerne and Rob were quiet, self-possessed men, though in very different ways. Rob was a man in his early fifties with a drinking problem that could flare up in times of stress, so that he was not quite sure of himself. Thoughtful and compassionate, he had a sense of humor that graced his truce with adversity. LaVerne was equally soft-spoken though neither shy nor self-doubting. He had stuttered as a child and had adopted silence as a means of defense, which ultimately became a lifelong practice of self-discipline. His mild demeanor was that of a veritable bodhisattva, who apparently did not need to prove anything to the world.

I still remember the night I first imagined them as comrades, which was the germ of my notion that they might join our staff after they graduated. A vigorous class discussion had grown out of an opening exercise on "Street Smarts." Rob and LaVerne were the only students who did not wholeheartedly endorse street-corner ideology. They had already crossed one significant boundary line that usually separates students and staff in our classroom.

### Street Smarts

> "Street Smarts" is the Philosophy of the Fool. People learn them when their time is idly spent—hanging intimately with worthless people. "Street Smarts" are useful only when you're busy trying to devise a plan to "Get by" or "Get over" on something or someone; it carries with it an air of "Sheisty-ness" or conniving. People who have "Street Smarts" are proud by them, but it is really their way of justifying the things they felt they had to do while living thin—through hard times. "We all work with the tools that God gave us." So, maybe growing up in a city—living in

the streets—you have to learn to adapt to situations quickly, so learning "Street Smarts" is a natural consequence—maybe. But to cultivate good character and have peace of mind, the "Street Smarts" is not needed. A smart person is smart not because they learned how to get by in the "city life"—but because they are smart enough to adapt to *any* or most lifestyles—that's my opinion. (*LaVerne*)

**South East D.C. Street Academy of Alley Economics**

A proper thug. Someone who has been exposed to street life, knows how to use it and yet has learned to contain it and perform well in today's society. At some point around the year 2000, after being incarcerated for 2½ years, I came to the conclusion that street smarts in some situations can be beneficial, and if used in the wrong environment can be detrimental. I came to a conclusion that most of our politicians would not stand a chance on a project corner. The proper thug has learned from his street life, and has street smarts. Has risen above his street life and is striving to become a productive part of society. It is not easy but it can be done. Containing a knowledge that all have not acquired. Be proud of all knowledge, and use it properly. (*The Proper Thug* [aka *Rob*])

The ensuing discussion soon raised the question of what a person might have to give up or forego in the acquisition of street smarts—what is it like to live so warily, always expecting the worst from everyone? Wouldn't it be better to take the risk of trusting strangers, for the sake of a heart more open to surprise and opportunity?

Aware of the price paid for his own urban savvy, Rob was not entirely comfortable with his view that survival in the streets requires being constantly on the lookout, though in the real world he saw no other choice and thought the solution was to use street smarts to transcend the streets. "Maybe," LaVerne would say, but it was not how he wanted to live: "At every moment of your life the choice is yours to make. You can be who you want to be." Or, as he put it in a poem,

Expansion is abundance
and is man's true inheritance.

Many other voices were raised as we debated the issue, but these two antagonists provided the framing perspective that kept us on track. And later that night, as other students were pulling on their coats and hats, I saw Rob and LaVerne making their way through the empty chairs to meet in the center of the room and shake hands. That was when I had the idea of inviting them to join our staff next semester. After due consultation, I took them aside on graduation day to ask if they were interested, making clear we could offer them no recompense other than the experience itself.

They became excellent facilitators, partly because they knew how to be silent and listen to what others had to say, and partly because they knew the plight of the probationer inside out. New participants immediately trusted them. Looking back now, I'd add that LaVerne and Rob taught the rest of us, students and staff, something invaluable about where we stood with each other. Their presence was a bridge constantly under construction during their two years with us.

The possibility of trusting others is inseparable from being trustworthy oneself. Sooner or later the one entails the other, and the Changing Lives classroom is founded on this truth. When we invited LaVerne and Rob to cross—or *dissolve*—the boundary between students and staff, we were reaffirming the underlying potential in every student to relax his distrust and make himself similarly vulnerable in the "safe emergency situation" he has entered. As LaVerne kept repeating, choice is always available to us no matter what our lives have been before. If fully accepted, the choice to trust others can be transformative for those whom society has deemed untrustworthy. Once allowed to return from prison and probation to his interrupted life, it will be each man's personal choice whether or not to go back to the streets where trust is dangerous and distrust can be death to the spirit.

It may be that further education can be of some advantage to the freed prisoner, and it may also be that the challenge of renouncing old vices and weaknesses can be met in part, as Rob says, by utilizing inner-city know-how as a means of "rising above street life." But neither street smarts nor school smarts is enough. Whatever the future may hold for Changing Lives graduates, or for any of us for that matter, the ability to pay attention to our opportunities and to choose wisely depends on what we should call "life smarts"—rising above self-absorption and obliviousness, distrust and cynicism, to take charge of our lives more deliberately, with fuller consciousness and compassion. Rob and LaVerne said it very well:

> Collect my surroundings is what I learned to do at an early age, bringing it all inside for examination. Sometimes too late and after the fact, and sometimes growing stronger not having to look back. Pushing forward is sometimes such a hard thing to do. But it seems for me it's the only way to get through. Challenges in my life, they come and they go. But when I went through them, pushing forward made me stronger, and I did grow. For me it seems to be that no matter where we are in life, if we go inside ourselves to the quietness of our minds and search for answers, they will come, sometimes fast, oftentimes slow. And often I needed someone to push me into the know. . . . The earth is quite consistent in giving us another day. (*Rob*)

> When a man begins to realize that his state of mind is his only real enemy and *no other* force outside him, things then begin to change. When he cleans up his mind, his vitality increases, attracting good health, fortune, friends, and as he elevates his mind-set like this, after a few consistent months, he notices that his life is improving and connections getting stronger, from a conscious change in the way he thinks about life in general—coming closer to the truth does set you free. This is my personal take with "weak" and "strong" as I experienced my own change. All challenges to me are a blessing and I give thanks for them. I know who I am now, and that is for me Eternal freedom. I don't complain. (*LaVerne*)

These two men were remarkable, no doubt about it, but I am convinced that almost any graduate of Changing Lives could serve equally well as a facilitator for our next group, or for a similar class in some other courthouse. In my opinion, this would be the ideal follow-up for every student, and for our program as well.

In recent years, with a growing class size (an average over twenty, and once nearly fifty men) we have instituted a number of changes, including a larger staff (ten counting Rob and LaVerne) and an added meeting at the end of the semester, to which we invite various dignitaries to honor our graduates with their praise, as well as agency representatives in a position to offer their services in applying to the university, looking for work, joining local community groups, and deciphering and perhaps ultimately sealing their CORI records. At the end of their semester students are ready for such an event, less formal than the courthouse ceremony that follows in a few days, but a meaningful gesture from prominent figures like the chancellor and provost of the university, members of the Boston City Council and the Sheriff's Office, public advocates for CORI reform, admission counselors from the university, and so on. Their enthusiastic congratulations and invitations are greeted with a mixture of pride and hopefulness. But the most eloquent speeches of the evening do not come from these emissaries. Before our visitors are even introduced, the class offers its own assessment of Changing Lives Through Literature, each man rising to share his feelings about the community we've created together. There is always someone eager to go first, thus setting a positive tone, but sooner or later everyone finds his tongue, and even the most recalcitrant person in the room has something he wants to say. One's own truth has a way of coming out at such times, regardless of how others may see things.

Although staff members listen quietly until the students are well launched and momentum strongly established, we too have been touched and changed by our time together, and so we also stand up and take our turns saying how we feel. This is our opportunity to express our gratitude for what we have learned here, this semester, from these men.

Probation officers and judges often do their work in a single dimension determined by the gridlock of the criminal justice system, in which a judge adjudicates as many as sixty cases a day, and where a probation officer with an equivalent caseload may have less than ten minutes to devote to the client who waits—and pays—as if the hard benches in the lobby were a dentist's office. Changing Lives judges and probation officers agree that spending an evening every week in earnest and free-ranging conversation goes far to humanize "cases" and "clients" and can transform how everyone is treated at the courthouse. A judge may hear little else but excuses and defiance all day long, but the Changing Lives judge typically finds himself listening with sharper ears to the person standing in front of him. The docket is full, and court officials try to hurry things along, but he waits patiently for the accused to grow calm and say what he can for himself. Similarly, a probation officer may come to regard a sullen or evasive individual as an intractable problem to be dealt with by the book. But unless moved by some deeper awareness of the probationer's plight and human potential, interactions between them are likely to be merely mechanical, and opportunities for breaking through the street armor will be missed. He too learns how to listen more patiently and compassionately in our classroom.

This same weekly encounter with people who have laid aside their masks overturns preconceptions that other staff members may bring to Changing Lives, no matter what good intentions may have led us here. The program has been blessed with university students, attorneys, youth workers, pastors, reentry instructors in correctional facilities, and teachers both active and retired from high school, college, and law school—all of us leading middle-class lives. But behind these roles many of us have ourselves been at risk in our younger days—coming close to the abyss through substance abuse, or at the mercy of bipolar disorder, or marginalized and tempted by the streets, or raised in grim dysfunctional families, a prey to anger and despair. The same may be said of judge and probation officers. We all need to be reminded of who we really are and who we might have been. And we take such lessons back with us, wherever we work and live.

In almost every semester, fateful decisions must be made in our classroom. Should a student who is disruptive or nonattentive be allowed to stay in the program? What about the recovering alcoholic who shows up drunk? Or the man who never seems to have done his homework? The final call is the probation officer's in most cases, but other staff members frequently take part in the deliberation. Every situation is different, and often there is no obvious solution. Even when the course is clear, intervention is not automatic or unfeeling; other students see that and absorb the complex lesson. But more often—and this is a dramatic manifestation of the lesson we learn in Changing Lives—the class as a community can be trusted to discipline itself, in a spontaneous mix of forbearance and confrontation that accords each man the respect of attention and honest response. Sometimes the result is electrifying. I'll never forget the night when one bold participant in a vociferous argument with four or five other students suddenly raised his hand like a traffic cop and said, "Why are we yelling at each other like this? It's part of our problem, it's why we have so much trouble in our lives. We don't know how to listen!"

Such insights into group dynamics are among the most liberating revelations as each new class finds its own equilibrium. In feeling our way to this delicate balance, students and staff from whatever conditions of life find their roles and self-images dissolving, aware that everyone has his demons to deal with and his good angel whispering within. We all have the potential to enter the unconditioned space that Rob and LaVerne inhabited so naturally, standing on their own feet and not toeing any line. Letting go of one's official status can be tremendously freeing for a judge or a professor as well as for a man who has long been defined by his CORI. Heartfelt exchanges about the deepest and most problematic issues of life transfigure these men who have been stereotyped in our culture as felons and jailbirds—revealing them as living souls instead of mug shots—but this transformation works both ways, for in recognizing their shared humanity, staff members are also humanized, relaxing our own postures of authority and self-righteousness. Close contact makes better human beings of us all, not because we are "doing good" or "being compassionate" but because we are facing the facts of life together; their facts are our facts, we are all one body and spirit. As my friend Bert puts it, "To open hearts, one's own heart must be open, and being part of the class has helped teach us how to open our hearts."